PENGUIN BOOKS

THE WATER IN BETWEEN

Kevin Patterson is a practising doctor who put himself through medical school by enlisting in the army. His short fiction and journalism have been published in numerous magazines. Now moored on Salt Spring Island, the *Sea Mouse* is his permanent home.

The Water In Between

A Journey at Sea

Kevin Patterson

PENGUIN BOOKS

PENGUIN BOOKS

Published by the Penguin Group
Penguin Books Ltd, 27 Wrights Lane, London W8 5TZ, England
Penguin Putnam Inc., 375 Hudson Street, New York, New York 10014, USA
Penguin Books Australia Ltd, Ringwood, Victoria, Australia
Penguin Books Canada Ltd, 10 Alcorn Avenue, Toronto, Ontario, Canada M4V 3B2
Penguin Books India (P) Ltd, 11 Community Centre, Panchsheel Park,
New Delhi – 110 017, India
Penguin Books (NZ) Ltd, Cnr Rosedale and Airborne Roads,
Albany, Auckland, New Zealand
Penguin Books (South Africa) (Pty) Ltd, 5 Watkins Street, Denver Ext 4,
Johannesburg 2094, South Africa

Penguin Books Ltd, Registered Offices: Harmondsworth, Middlesex, England

First published in Canada by Random House Canada Ltd 1999
First published in Great Britain by Viking 2000
Published in Penguin Books 2001
1

Copyright © Kevin Patterson, 1999
Maps copyright © Jonathan Howells, 1999
All rights reserved

The moral right of the author has been asserted

Pages 293–4 constitute an extension of this copyright page

Printed in England by Clays Ltd, St Ives plc

Except in the United States of America, this book is sold subject
to the condition that it shall not, by way of trade or otherwise, be lent,
re-sold, hired out, or otherwise circulated without the publisher's
prior consent in any form of binding or cover other than that in
which it is published and without a similar condition including this
condition being imposed on the subsequent purchaser

This book is for Shauna

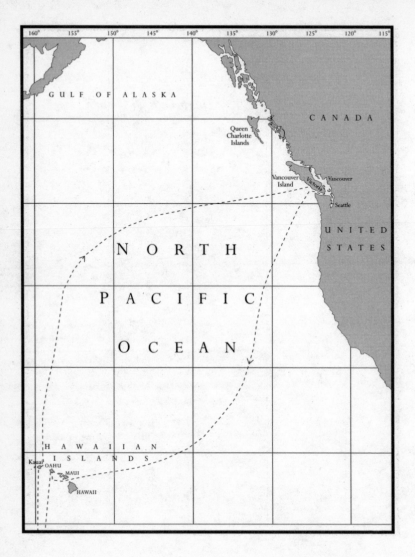

NORTH MAP

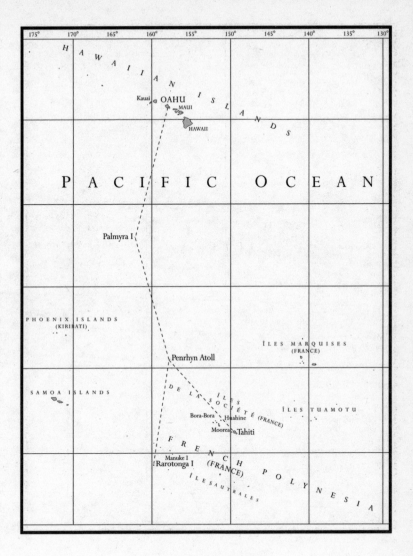

| 175° | 170° | 165° | 160° | 155° | 150° | 145° | 140° | 135° | 130° |

H A W A I I A N   I S L A N D S

Kauai OAHU
       MAUI
       HAWAII

P A C I F I C   O C E A N

Palmyra I.

PHOENIX ISLANDS
(KIRIBATI)

ÎLES MARQUISES
(FRANCE)

Penrhyn Atoll

SAMOA ISLANDS

DE LA
ÎLES
SOCIÉTÉ (FRANCE)   ÎLES TUAMOTU

Bora-Bora Huahine
Moorea Tahiti

F R E N C H
Manuke I.
Rarotonga I.   (FRANCE)   P O L Y N E S I A
ÎLES AUTRALES

SOUTH   MAP

People who live on continents get into the habit of regarding the ocean as journey's end, the full stop at the end of the trek. When North Americans reached the Pacific, there was nothing to do except build the end-of-the-world state of California. For people who live on islands, especially on small islands, the sea is always the beginning. It's the ferry to the mainland, the escape route from the boredom and narrowness of home. It's what you have to cross, even if you do it by plane, whenever you want to strike out and make a break for it. Islanders also know how the sea goes on and on, in a continuous loop of shoreline and life, without a terminus. Knocking about from port to port, you keep on going past the port you originally started out from.

JONATHAN RABAN, *Coasting*

CHAPTER ONE

I N AUGUST OF 1994, I bought a twenty-year-old ferro-cement ketch on the coast of British Columbia. I did this in an effort to distract myself — at the time I was so absorbed in self-pity my eyes were crossed. I had been wandering around marinas sorrowfully leaning my head against dock pilings and losing my train of thought; I had the demeanour of an aging milk cow with the scours. People who met me thought I was either drunk or deranged. The most immediate cause of all this was a woman half a continent away who had been headed further for months. My sadness at our parting was histrionically out of proportion to anything that could have been justified by events.

I spent weeks chain-smoking and staring at the ground. At the time I was working as a doctor at a summer camp for Canadian army cadets in the B.C. Interior. It was an absurd job and I made an absurd picture, shuffling around the dusty parade grounds, hands in pockets, sighing grandly and ignoring the columns of pubescent boys and girls marching stiffly past me. I was twenty-nine and had been out of the army myself for only a year.

That summer, many Canadian medical officers were being sent to Rwanda and Bosnia. The army had always provided a doctor for the camp, but now they were short-staffed, which is how I had come to be there. When they called to ask me to fill in, I was working up in the Arctic, on the coast of Hudson Bay. It was late June, and so cold that even the river ice hadn't broken yet. The sea pack was solid to the horizon. I said yes without even thinking.

At the time I was drifting and had been since the previous summer — ever since leaving the army. I had been in Winnipeg, on my way to the job in the Arctic, when I met her. There was a week of slow suppers and long, delicious conversation. This was earlier in the winter and she was gentle, very beautiful and a little melancholic, and I was entranced by her. When it came time for me to fly north, we made imprecise plans about how we would meet. We agreed to call and write often. I started work at a small hospital on the shore of Hudson Bay. My second day there, an old man became very sick and needed to be transferred to the intensive care unit in Winnipeg. I volunteered to accompany him. I called her from the airport. After leaving the hospital I took a cab straight to her house.

During the time I was up in the Arctic, we telephoned one another almost daily but avoided the question of whether I should move to the city or she should move up there. It was an obvious but awkward issue. Part of the delight we took in seeing one another was the intermittency of our contact. It is a banal and familiar circumstance. Among soldiers, or the nurses in the Arctic, it is a cliché.

Then the army phoned, with this job in British Columbia. I would be just as far from Winnipeg, working there. Off I went.

About a month after I arrived at the summer camp she came out to visit me. We stayed together in a resort near the army base with the memorable name of Teddy Bear Lodge. There were small cabins with televisions and a swing set for children. The mountains rose up all around, and across the highway from our cabin was a long, deep lake. We tried to swim there but it wasn't possible. It was much too cold.

Before this we had only had the hurried, lip-biting kiss-filled visits in Winnipeg when I had come down on the air ambulance. The Teddy Bear Lodge got our hopes up, but in the sustained company of the other, we each forgot two-thirds of the words we knew. After two weeks she went home. Saying goodbye at the bus terminal, we didn't confront the issue.

A month later, she telephoned me at work to tell me about the man she had met. She told me his name and apologized. She subsequently married him and they now have a baby daughter. Our mutual friends tell me that she is happier than they've ever seen her. Her graciousness and kindness in our limited intimacy only made my anguish more potent and my feeling of victimhood more laughable. To feel unentitled to your self-pity about triples it.

My roommate at the summer camp became alarmed and embarrassed as he watched me involute into a black and anguished puddle of self-obsessed sorrow. It felt ridiculous even at the time. I was tearing my clothes over one of the most abbreviated love affairs I'd ever had; it made no sense. If I went back to the city she lived in, which I had lived in before the army, I thought that I would drown. In the army, desperate for distraction, I had daydreamed about sailing on the ocean. I was from Manitoba; I knew nothing about sailing and had never been on the ocean in a little boat of any sort.

I found myself standing on a dock in Genoa Bay, on the southern tip of Vancouver Island, in the company of a sixty-year-old man with a whiskey nose the size and colour of a bruised and overripe beet. His name was Peter Ericson and he owned a sailboat brokerage, but his consuming passion seemed to be the promulgation of his theory that the Pacific Islands and most of the New World had been colonized by an ancient Scandinavian seafaring culture that revered magnetic fields. And maybe herring.

Before Ericson would even let me see his boats he had showed me his publications in the local *Boat Journal*. These were supposed to be advertisements for his business, but in fact they were long rants on the forgotten nobility of the Great White Gods, the Vikings, who journeyed forth in the ancient mists to show the less savvy races just how it was done. But the ghosts of the Norse sailor-folk could rest easy now, for Ericson had figured it out. And was bound to inform the world. Or, at any rate, me.

Even after I had steered him out onto the dock, he harangued me with evidence of blue-eyed Indians and tales of white-skinned gods in the Polynesian mythos. I wondered how he managed to make a living selling boats. I tried to get him to tell me about the boat we were standing in front of but he seemed obsessed with this idea of forgotten exploration. He told me that proof of contact between the Vikings and other civilizations was everywhere. For instance, the alignment of the Mayan temples in Meso-America corresponded precisely with lines of constant magnetic variation (whatever that was) and only a seafaring culture could understand magnetism so thoroughly. The great heads of Easter Island represent you-know-who, staring out to sea, of course. And could there be any doubt how the Polynesians came to possess the sweet potato of South American origin? Could there be?

In an attempt to forestall his quoting *Chariots of the Gods* to me, I quickly glanced around. The boat nearest us looked very beautiful. The sign on it said the hull was made of ferro cement. "How does it float?" I asked.

The inanity of the question stalled him. His face twitched and twisted and he forced it into a more benign and patient gaze. "Steel doesn't float but steel boats do, right?"

"Oh, yeah," I said. It turned out that Ericson had been instrumental in popularizing the technique of ferro-cement boat construction twenty years previously, and he launched into another great enthusiasm. He assured me that such boats were immune to rot and rust, stable and sea-kindly in heavy weather. I wondered if the man had any ambivalent opinions about anything.

Ericson asked me what sort of price range I was thinking about. I told him how much money I had to spend. Remarkably, that was just the amount this boat was going for. I grew up in Manitoba. Farm country, basically. Mostly we played a lot of kick-the-can. "Shrewd" was a name you called someone smarter than you that you didn't like.

The boat was named the *Sea Mouse*. She looked lovely to me.

Ericson unlocked the companionway. He winked at me and said that he would let me putter about by myself, to have a look at the bilges or whatever. He'd be back in an hour or so. I sat below at the teak salon table and looked around her. The polished wood shined like a memory of grade-school wooden floors. I lifted up the hatch over the engine and peered into the mass of machinery. I had no idea what I was looking at. Satisfied that there seemed to be a proper number of belts and hoses and things, I closed the hatch. I stood up and looked out the forward hatches at the mast and pulpit. I thought about Ericson's idea of the Vikings, threading their way around the world in the first millennium. I could almost hear the waves surging over the deck. Me, clinging to the wheel and smiling wryly, my bronzed and newly muscular shoulders glinting in the sun. Lovely polished wood. Just lovely. I patted it. I wished I had a cheroot.

I poked through the lockers in the galley. There was a propane stove and oven, and a refrigerator. There was room for half a year's worth of rice and pasta and tomato sauce and dried mushrooms and apples and garlic and balsamic vinegar and bottles of wine and canned bacon and dried fish and sacks of onions and cabbages and potatoes and jars of marmalade. I imagined how that would feel, to have a boat, and all the food I would need for six months on her. Able to go anywhere I wanted. Enough stores to go halfway around the world.

Two hours later Peter found me there, grinning stupidly. The *Sea Mouse* was thirty-seven feet long, rigged as a ketch, and displaced twelve tons. Her lines seemed to me as graceful as a dancer's. She carried tanks for sixty gallons of fresh water and forty of diesel. She had two masts and booms of spruce, the stays and shrouds were of stainless-steel wire and she had a forty-five-horsepower diesel engine. There was a six-mile radar and a head. Later on, as Peter and I sat working out the details of the purchase, the kerosene lamps glowed as orange as whiskey against the varnished teak and made the boat feel like a small and warm mountain cabin. She had a diesel furnace for heat. As the sun set there was a sense of rightness, of safety, within her. That sense of safety seemed like it would be only more striking at sea, in heavy weather.

Suffused with optimism and rum, I told Peter I wanted to sail to Tahiti. He squeezed my arm and said I must have Viking blood in me. I allowed that my mother's parents were Danish. That set him off for another hour, explaining again how historians were blind to the obviousness of his theory. I had just bought a boat. It wasn't hard to indulge him.

Peter's face softened as he recounted his fantasy. Once a sailor gets into the tropical trade winds, he told me, even the slowest boats make a hundred miles a day, three weeks to go two thousand miles. And the wind is so constant and warm, you could travel on a raft with a bedsheet for a sail — look at Thor Heyerdahl's *Kon-Tiki*. Compare that to the North Atlantic, scoured by contrary winds and storms like tantrums. Imagine a Viking crew, accustomed to sleet and steep frigid seas, driven south by a gale and finding themselves surrounded by water as warm as urine, pale blue and languid instead of green and frothed. Imagine that.

Pallid skin darkening as the filthy tunics and soiled sheepskins are shrugged off and accumulate in the stern of the boat — can you imagine what they felt then, as they pulled ashore in Huahine, in the South Pacific, and found mangos and coconuts, and water-falls pouring down green mountains?

I found myself hoping that it had happened as he believed. I ignored the part about the Vikings teaching everyone else how to sail. (How exactly would the Polynesians have *gotten* there, if they couldn't navigate?) Peter had grown up in Manitoba himself, on a farm near the northern margin of arable land, and I pictured him in the 1940s, huddling in a draughty farmhouse as some January blizzard roared through. Longing to escape.

I asked him how long it would take me to get to Tahiti. He said five or six weeks. I told him I knew nothing about sailing. He assured me it was in my blood. He had taught himself to sail, after all, on the Tasman Sea, the day after the Australian Excise Police visited him and the boat he had just bought in Sydney, asking about some matter of back taxes. I asked him what one did out there alone at night. When you went to sleep, did you put out a sea anchor or what? He took a moment, as if contemplating his response, and then asked when I could get the cheque to him.

We stayed up drinking on my new boat until we were both very drunk. He told me again how the Norse had left their mark on all the cultures of the New World; did I realize the temples of the Mayans were oriented along lines of magnetic variation? I looked up from a chart of the South Pacific and finally asked what magnetic variation was. He said I would want to learn that. I agreed. He asked me again how much sailing I had done. I said none. He slapped me on the shoulder and congratulated me on my pluck. I asked him if he would show me what I needed to know. "Oh sure," he answered.

It was the first night I had ever slept on a boat. At some point, from real or perceived boat motion, I had fallen out of my berth. My back hurt. There were overflowing ashtrays and puddles of spilt rum and coke. Someone knocked on the hull. Peter Ericson was standing there in the morning sun, looking puffy. "I've been thinking about this singlehanding business," he said. I had been thinking about it, too.

"There's someone I know who I think you should meet."

The notion of sailing off into the sea alone and heartbroken retreated before me. So I wasn't quite as brave as I imagined. I pictured the navy helicopters pulling my swollen and bloated corpse from the water, the solemn commentary on the evening news.

"Who?" I asked.

I called the number he gave me. The next evening I met Don Lang on Peter's boat *Stormstrutter*, which was moored near my new boat. He was sitting at the galley table when I walked below. He and Peter and Peter's wife Pat were drinking rum. I had imagined Captain High Liner. Don was deferential to the point of timidity. He looked liked Andre Agassi, but shorter and sadder. I said hello and he stood to shake my hand softly. We smiled at each other. Peter pounded all our backs and poured some rum, then started talking about the pyramidal prayer platforms of French Polynesia and their similarity to Mayan temples and how there was only one explanation. Don was polite but unpersuaded. I liked how gentle he was with Ericson. I asked him if he wanted to see the *Sea Mouse*. He said yes.

We walked down the dock in the dark. I told him I was going to leave in the next month and that I didn't know anything about sailing. He said that Peter had explained that to him. We stepped aboard the *Sea Mouse* and I showed him around her. He checked out the mast and all the rigging fittings, worked the halyard winches and sounded the wooden cabin top with his knuckles. He said he had already had a look at her on his way down and he thought she was a fine boat. He told me I had paid too much money for her, though, and I told him I had suspected as much. "But it's not like you've got a bad boat here, either," he said.

"Thanks," I said.

"So how come you want to go to Tahiti?"

"I've always been interested in the place."

"What do you know about it?"

"It's a long way away," I said. "You?"

"It's supposed to be pretty expensive."

"Want to go?"

"Yeah."

Don was a sheet-metal worker; he installed ductwork for furnaces for a living. He had also been a baker, a cook, a welder and a commercial diver. He was thirty-two, three years older than I, and five-nine, maybe a hundred and eighty-five pounds. His hair was long and permed and thinning; his friendliness was forward and unrestrained and unaffected. He had an air of puzzlement about him. He looked carefully wherever he stepped, as if the dock, or the boat or anything at all might break through suddenly and send him tumbling.

We went below and as I followed him down the companionway, I watched him stand up and look around. I asked him if he wanted a drink. He asked me if I had some rum. I said I thought there was some left. I poured. We both drank. I asked him how much sailing he had done. It turned out that he had sailed to Hawaii and back twice, had owned his own boat until a few months ago, but had sold it, partly under the pressure of his common-law wife. Who had walked out shortly thereafter, leaving all the cards and letters he had ever sent her on their bed, tied with a ribbon. She took her kid, and was gone just like that. "Don't you want to keep them?" he had asked her later, when she had phoned from wherever it was she had gone. No, she said, that's why I left them. Long pause.

"But the boat," Don said to me, "does need some work. The wind vane needs to be installed and the mizzen-mast spreaders need to be replaced."

"Jeez," I said.

"It's not that much work. With two of us going at it, a week or two maybe."

"So, how long will it take us to get to Tahiti?" I asked, fingering a piece of the woodwork.

"Forty-five days, minimum."

It was late August already and the first of the winter storms were only a month away. I had a week and a half of work left in my contract with the army. Don had a house to move out of, a job to quit and fifty chickens to sell. We figured we could be gone before the equinoctial gales. We spent two days making a budget for the provisioning of the boat and lists of things I needed to buy in Vancouver. We were both silent for long stretches as we worked and maybe we both wished it were easier to be exuberant. Peter Ericson kept saying, when he visited, that it would all sink in once we were out at sea.

Don said to me once, after Peter had left, "It has sunk in already."

We agreed to meet again in three weeks, back at the dock. Don figured he would need until then to extricate himself from his life, or what remained of it.

"It seems kind of crazy," I said, "to think that in three or four weeks we'll be out at sea, leaving everything here behind."

"It seems kind of great." Don lifted his bag and walked to his car.

Squids Out of Ink

At the army base there was a letter waiting for me. I would have preferred to pretend that my most recent disappointing love affair was the only one. It felt like the only one. But these things always form a history.

I had only a brief bit of work left with the army. Part of the point of all this was the shedding of ties. I winced when I looked at the envelope. I hadn't heard from Catherine in two years.

July 22, 1994
*   … Where are you? I ask because I must live in or around*
the States for the next six months. You see, I am finally divorcing
Frank, and I must live here to have an American divorce.

Let me clarify. I am undergoing a divorce on two continents. Frank is divorcing me in France, and I am divorcing Frank in America and I am so divorced from America by this point that I can only think of living near relatives and friends ...

Catherine and her husband had been separated for many years, both of them living in startlingly expensive apartments in Paris. She looked after their son during the day and wrote short stories as finely crafted and as robust as Fabergé eggs. Frank, her husband, was a lawyer and had seemed deaf to her insistence that their love affair was over. When I knew her, he still pined for her, and agonized over her dalliances.

I remember her telling me how he had begun going to readings, in order to persuade her that he wasn't a work-obsessed bore. I ached a bit whenever I pictured him, standing in some smoky bookstore, blinking and trying to understand the musings of some mumbling drunken novelist in order to persuade his wife to love him again. Whenever they met, he had a book sticking conspicuously out of his pocket.

I am miserable ...
Can you see me? I am free in August —

She had a disposition to believe in saviours. Or, more charitably, she fell in love completely and still believed in mutual salvation. The ferocity of her unreasonable optimism had frightened me two years earlier and had driven me away. I had kept all her letters, however, and in the time since we had last seen one another, I had reread them at random and had not forgotten the intensity with which she went through her days, the clarity with which she saw what she wanted.

I had to leave Paris in a matter of days to countersue immediately. I left everything behind. Now my book is on hold. I am

*afraid for Frank to know where I am. There is so much I want to
tell you. I would have none of these problems if I was willing to
let Sam live with Frank, but I know that is not best for Sam ....
I feel like a squid out of ink here. So I am calling you ...*

The distress in her letter moved me, and her life, even with
these new difficulties, had a panache about it that would impress
a Manitoban. Let her come over, I thought, maybe she can show
me how to face these things with style. Or at least distract me from
my incessant, whining self-pity.

We met at the Vancouver airport. She seemed both taller and
thinner than she had the last time I had seen her. Her son clung
to her and seemed taller and thinner too. It was a Friday at the end
of August and a long weekend stretched before us. I asked her
what she wanted to do. I thought I would show her my new boat,
but we had missed the last ferry to the Island. That night we took
rooms in a noisy hotel in downtown Vancouver, right above a bar
where a live band played covers of Def Leppard. I sat up late,
watching television. Catherine and Sam stayed in the room beside
mine. Through the thin walls I could hear her trying to reassure
him. He was eight, and frightened. I went downstairs to the bar.
When I came back up their room was quiet. The next morning we
ate breakfast in silence and then climbed into my pick-up truck
and drove onto the ferry.

During the two-hour trip, Sam clung to her. We didn't discuss
her divorce. Our conversation suggested that we were on the same
sort of outing as all the other young families on the ferry. We gave
the view of the Gulf Islands our approval, and agreed that the food
in the dining room was overpriced and salty. Catherine and I were
awkward with one another and Sam would not look at me. Careful
observers might have guessed that I had recently returned to my
young family and was attempting a reconciliation; they might have
wondered how bad the departure had been. What had the blinking
and uncomfortable-looking man done that the little boy would not
even acknowledge him?

When we reached the boat I unlocked the companionway hatch and let them below. Catherine carried in her makeup bags and suitcases and piled them on the chart table. She turned around in the small, cramped interior. Sam asked her where he could sit. After a moment she said she thought the boat was beautiful. It was cluttered and untidy; the *Sea Mouse*'s beauty was clear enough to me, but mostly in memory.

I asked her if she was in trouble.

"No," she lied.

Peter Ericson saw the activity on the *Sea Mouse* and came over to visit. I introduced Catherine and her son. I had told him I wanted to sail solo to Tahiti and now there was this family showing up here. Peter sat down with us and noted Catherine's blond hair. He told her she looked Scandinavian.

"Czech, actually," she said. Which stopped him for about a heartbeat.

"Ever wonder how the Pacific was explored?" he asked.

"By Captain Cook?" she guessed.

"Oh no," he said.

I asked him if he would help me take the boat out for a sail. He said yes, barely pausing in his narrative on how the only abundant source of magnetite, of lodestone, in the ancient world was in Scandinavia and that this is what gave them their advantage — the ability to navigate. Navigation is the real religion of seafarers, he said. To anthropologists, Odin's one blind eye was the price he paid for wisdom, he said, but to anyone who's ever been at sea in fog it's another thing entirely. Fifty miles offshore in the low winter clouds of the North Atlantic and you've plucked out both your eyes. Lodestones point north. No miracle the apostles ever performed meant half as much. Catherine asked him to go on. He did.

Then we put life jackets on Catherine and her son and took the *Sea Mouse* out. Peter showed me how to raise and douse and trim the sails and how to coil halyards. He asked me if I thought it would be reasonable to try to learn all this alone at sea. Catherine and Sam watched carefully from the cockpit, bundled in their orange life preservers. Peter asked Catherine if she was a writer. He wrote poetry, he told her. Catherine asked if she could hear some. I remember the boat heeling over dramatically as the wind freshened, Peter bellowing out his Kiplingesque rhymes and Catherine and her son staring at Peter while I looked straight ahead at the bow of the boat as it leapt in the waves.

That night we ate with Peter and Pat in a restaurant overlooking the marina. Pat seemed ill at ease. From where we sat I could see both our boats bobbing at the dock. Catherine was enjoying herself, comparing notes on child-rearing with Pat and asking Peter how he accounted for the lack of clear archaeological evidence to back up his theory. Peter was up to the challenge. For Sam, however, there had been too much change, too many strangers in a very short while. He clung to his mother and whined at her. Every time she turned to ask Peter a question, he pulled on her sleeve. When the food arrived he declared he wasn't hungry. He steadily escalated the tone and insistence of his complaints and I wondered how the coming months were going to go for them. Peter was describing the encounters between the Phoenicians and the ancient Vikings when Sam pulled his mother away again. Peter scolded him, told him to sit up straight, take his elbows off the table and stop interrupting. Sam howled. We retreated to the boat, and I left Catherine and Sam alone for a long time while I looked at the stars.

When I finally went below, Sam was asleep. Catherine was sitting up reading. I asked her how she was.

"I've been thinking about how there are no coincidences," she said.

"What do you mean?"

"I need to lie low for a while, you've just bought a boat and you're headed out to sea. It's all coming together, don't you think?"

"What do you mean?"

"Well, we could go to sea with you."

"Don't you think that would be dangerous?"

"Don't you?"

"Well, I think I'll be okay, but it's a small boat, you know."

"There's six berths. I've read of families who have gone to sea in boats half this size."

"I'm going to Tahiti. *Polynésie Française*. You'd be subject to French law there."

"Isn't there any other place in the Pacific that you'd like to go to? Easter Island, Samoa, Tonga, Pitcairn, Fiji?"

"I've always wanted to go to Tahiti."

"I could use your help here."

"I know."

She looked at me for a while and then she said she was going to bed. "Good night," I said.

After the weekend we drove inland, to the army base where I was to work for the next couple of weeks. We rented a little cabin by a mountain lake. It was even nicer than the Teddy Bear Lodge. Every day Catherine phoned her lawyer in Paris and her family in the States. I began receiving telephone calls from her mother and her lawyer while I was at work, asking me to please have her call them as soon as possible. Back in the cabin Catherine told me that she had already spent a hundred thousand dollars on lawyers in the previous three months. I asked her if she knew how nice a boat that could have bought her. Steadily she became more haunted looking, and it became more difficult to be around her and not agree to help her.

I bought baseball gloves for the three of us and we played catch. We set up in an isosceles triangle, with Sam and Catherine along the base and me at the point, drawing further and further away.

Finally the two weeks were over and I told Catherine that I would be going to sea with Don. She bought two plane tickets and I drove her and the boy to the airport. Just before they boarded Catherine began crying and Sam began hitting me on the arm.

Their flight was called. I watched her take her son's hand and walk through security. She waved goodbye.

I took the ferry back to the Island, feeling ashamed. I met Don on the boat. I asked him how things had gone, quitting his job, the house.

"Fine."

"How'd that business with the chickens go?"

"These things are never as simple as you imagine them to be, starting out."

"No doubt about it," I said.

Self-steering

> An almost essential requirement for long-distance single-handing is the ability to make a boat steer herself. It is obvious that the lone sailor must be able to leave the helm to perform necessary chores and satisfy essential body demands, most especially to sleep.
>
> RICHARD HENDERSON, *Singlehanded Sailing*

Genoa Bay, where I had bought the *Sea Mouse*, is lined by tall hills on three sides and cedars that reach right down to the water's edge. It is tranquil and excessively beautiful. Don had a few more days of errands to run. I sat on my boat and felt languorously content.

I read for many hours down below, drinking tea and imagining being at sea. I started with books about short-handed and solo voyages: Richard Henderson's *Singlehanded Sailing*, Joshua Slocum's *Sailing Alone Around the World*, then *Chapman Piloting*, *British Admiralty's Nautical Tables*, the *1994 Nautical Almanac*. *The Long Way*, by Bernard Moitessier, *The Oxford Book of the Sea*, *The Clipper Way* by Francis Chichester.

I flipped through another pile of books I had bought, ones I'd always meant to read but couldn't tackle as long as I owned a television: *Ulysses*, *Gravity's Rainbow*, *The Marriage of Cadmus and*

Harmony, The Odyssey and three feet of Russians. My previous inability to persevere with them could only have been a matter of distraction. Just cancel *Baywatch* and *Hard Copy* and watch my hidden genius emerge. I liked the look of these books on my bookshelf. So thick and substantial. I stroked them, picked them up one by one and began reading *Ulysses*. After fifteen minutes I put it down and picked up a magazine.

It rained those days and I remained below, reading sailing manuals and memoirs steadily and finding myself already settling into a kind of ease that I thought probably represented the object of the enterprise. I threaded the Strait of Magellan with Slocum and continued north to the Juan Fernández Islands and the memorial to Alexander Selkirk; we then sailed west to the Marquesas and finally landed in Samoa. I wondered if I even needed to leave the dock, and began to sympathize with the armchair sailors of the world, men and women in libraries and kitchens flipping through pages and pausing to sigh and scratch their bellies. I stretched and scratched mine, looking through the rain-streaked portholes of the *Sea Mouse* at the other boats bobbing beside mine. I began making lists.

I started with food: of the stores I needed to lay in, this was the only matter I had any experience in. I got a quiet thrill from planning the provisioning of the boat.

Fifty pounds of rice, in one-pound bags
Fifty pounds of flour, in ten-pound bags
Fifteen pounds of coffee
Ten pounds of tea bags
Forty quart jars of spaghetti sauce
Fifty pounds of spaghetti
Forty cans of pears
Twenty cans of peaches
Twenty pounds of sugar

The problem was one that has concerned mariners for millennia: things go bad. I rediscovered the anachronisms of the refrigeration age — pickled, salted, smoked, canned and dried fruits,
vegetables and fish — whole classes of foods and tastes made available to me by my boat. I canvassed grocery stores for canned butter and bacon. Cases of dried milk, lentils, rice, pasta, fruit leather,
egg noodles, salt pork and smoked fish. I hung bags of onions in
the forepeak, alongside the sails, with boxes of potatoes and can-
taloupes too. I stacked the dried provisions in the galley and felt a
surge of satisfaction move through me — I had a boat, and a third
of a year's worth of food on her. That, and I had been eating lentils
for a week.

Don returned at last and we untied the boat and took the *Sea
Mouse* up the inside coast of Vancouver Island to Nanaimo, his
hometown. He knew people there, and knew where to get the best
prices on the equipment we still had to buy. En route, we made
more lists.

The books all emphasized the importance of a self-steering
apparatus for the shorthanded or singlehanded vessel. There have
been many approaches taken to the problem of keeping the vessel
on course while her crew sleeps or tends to the boat. Slocum's
famous yawl *Spray* was so stable and sea-kindly, he claimed, that
he once spent less than three hours at the helm over the course of
a 2,700-mile passage from Thursday Island off Australia to the
Cocos Islands in the Indian Ocean. He just lashed her helm in
place, then trimmed her sails so she was balanced out and would
go where he wanted. Think about the difference this would make:
either fighting the boat to port and starboard or just letting go of
her and have her go where you want. In such circumstances, how
could you not feel that you were living right?

There are many self-steering devices to be studied in the back
pages of sailing magazines. The most popular, for weekend and
coastal sailors, are electronic autohelms, which function much like
the autopilots in aircraft. They use an electronic compass; you set
your course, and an electrical motor driven by a microprocessor

adjusts the helm when she strays. They don't keep the boat in balance but serve as electronic underlings to wrestle the boat for you. They make an annoying whirring sound. Satisfyingly, these devices are not the best choices for open water work. They consume electricity, a fickle thing at sea, draining the batteries quickly and necessitating frequent running of the engine. There are solar panels and wind generators that can provide electricity in lieu of the engine, but we begin down a slippery slope in that direction — devices in order to make the devices work. Pretty soon, you've loaded on a Cuisinart.

The magic is in mechanical wind vanes. These creatures — and they all seem lively, obstinate, capricious and animated — fly a sail that is hooked through levers and pulleys and shafts to a rudder below. The sailor puts the boat on course and then adjusts the wind vane to maintain the boat on a constant angle relative to the wind. Should the boat shift off the prescribed course, the wind vane recognizes this from the change in the wind direction and presses on the linkage to the rudder, allowing the boat to wander back on course. There is no electricity involved, only steel and wood and canvas. And the vane keeps the boat constant to what is immediate and present, the wind. Both the wind direction and the compass heading matter, but the wind matters above all.

Sailors all seem to have had epic struggles with their self-steering gear and invariably anthropomorphize them into unreliable friends. The first man to sail around the world alone non-stop, Robin Knox-Johnston, called his "the Admiral." Francis Chichester called his Miranda, after God knows whom, but the history of his relationship with her may be guessed. Donald Crowhurst's diary of disintegrating reason has long pages of rant about his gear; it is reasonable to conclude that it played a developmental role in his madness. Contained within the beauty of balances, it seems, is the fact that they are sometimes impossible to achieve.

On the Vancouver waterfront there is a man who makes art out
of rocks perched precariously on top of one another. Sometimes he
disappears for months on end. I don't know, but I suspect that he
hits terrible times when the rocks will not cooperate. I imagine him
at the bar before lunch drinking with brokers who have lost their
sense of the market, architects who have forgotten how to make
concrete look light and pool hustlers who have broken their
English. "Leave the bottle, barkeep, the rocks won't stack."

After a week of settled ease, the boat begins turning great mad-
dening circles and the sailor looks at the wind vane accusingly. No
amount of adjusting of the sheets or helm helps — what betrayal
is this? It would need a name.

Wind vanes fall into several categories. There are the servo-
pendulum models, auxiliary rudder types and trim tab versions.
They vary in the design of the linkage between sail and rudder
beneath and also in the sort of rudder used. They have vigorous,
martial names: Aries, Monitor, Automate; the owners of any one
model express almost religious zeal in support of their own betray-
ers. The *Sea Mouse* came with a Riebrandt Vane Gear that was not
mounted. Don and I examined it as we sailed to Nanaimo. It was
missing some parts and Don was concerned because he had heard
they were no longer being made.

In Nanaimo we made some telephone calls and established
that, indeed, the RVG wind vane was out of production but that
Richard Riebrandt, its designer, had retired to the San Juan Islands.
I got his number through directory assistance and called him.

"Yes, hello."

"May I speak to Mr Riebrandt?"

"Yes, this is him."

He was German and formal and I found myself standing up
straight on the other end of the line.

"Sir, I have just bought a boat and it came with an RVG wind vane. It's missing a few parts and I wondered if you could help me get it fixed?"

"Yes, I could fix it for you."

"Shall I bring it to you?"

"Yes, you should do that."

"Where do you live, sir?"

The directions he gave me were convoluted and imprecise. I was to turn three or four roads after the lights, at whichever intersection it was that had the church just visible from the junction. There was a general store where we had to stop to ask for further directions. Eventually we found ourselves following a path through a forest that stopped abruptly at a small shed. A dog came barking ferociously out of the undergrowth. We locked our doors. A man appeared.

Riebrandt, a fit seventy-year-old wearing a tape measure on his belt, was pleased to have the company, though he had the manner of a rat-tail rasp. We unloaded the wind vane from Don's truck and handed it to him. He snorted derisively at the flaking paint on the trim tab. He asked if it had ever been used. I explained that I didn't know much about it. He rubbed his whiskered chin and directed us inside his shed. The rain forest rose up all around, and the dense carpet of ferns absorbed all sound from the road.

Don and I looked at one another. We glanced around for banjo players.

The shed was well lit and fastidiously clean. There were vises and drill presses and welding electrodes; wire brushes hung in rows on the wall.

"Now, boys," he said, "tell me about this trip you are undertaking."

"We're going to Tahiti," I said, leaning forward.

"And what is the type of vessel you are taking?"

"It's a thirty-seven-foot ferro-cement ketch."

"What does she displace?"

"Twelve tons."

"Ah yes," he said and rubbed his chin again. "That is a heavy thirty-seven-footer."

"Ferro cement," said Don.

"You are in grave danger, you know."

We blinked at him.

"This wind vane needs a great deal of attention; without it you will die."

Me: "So you, uh, can fix it?"

"Oh yes."

"Well, that's good."

"You must look after your wind vane, you know. It will be a better helmsman than either of you."

"Well, you want to take care of your equipment."

"I worry for you two."

"But you'll fix the wind vane?"

"You've done a lot of blue-water sailing yourself then?" Don asked.

"When I was younger, yes, some. But not in many years, now. I became preoccupied by my business — my wives did not appreciate this. There was no time to see my children, let alone go out on the ocean. My life is simpler now. I am building a large metal boat, a powerboat. They don't demand quite so much emotion as a sailboat. When you are older you will understand."

"Maybe, maybe not," said Don.

"This device has been scarcely used, I can tell from the wear of the bushings. Abused, yes, used, no."

"I just bought the boat," I reminded him.

"Why are you in such a hurry to leave?"

"It's autumn already."

"Why not go in the spring?"

"I think you have to grab at chances like this."

"I was married to a nurse for many years, in California, where my factory was. I used to watch the boats sailing on the bay. They would visit me before they would go for their big trips. I used to get letters and postcards from all over the world. All I did was work. My wife left because of that. I hope those sailors appreciated it."

We were all wondering how the conversation had become so loaded. Don tried some small talk about how much nicer a place the Pacific Northwest was than California. Riebrandt agreed.

I gave him two hundred American dollars and we left. I thought about him, living by himself in his little forest house like a figure from a Grimm tale, isolated behind a wall of severity. Don and I were quiet for a long time as we drove.

"You wouldn't want to end up like that," Don said.

"Nope."

"I wonder how you do."

"I can't imagine that anyone would aim for that."

"I guess you just keep making the same mistake over and over again until you're living alone in a cave some place deep in the woods."

As we headed north toward the border the sun emerged. We stopped at a gas station and Don bought a twelve-pack of beer. We rode with beer cans between our knees and sang along to a country station. We were the only ones on the road. John Cougar Mellencamp thundered over the radio and I opened two more cans of beer. We tossed the empties into the back seat. Really carelessly.

We were on our way.

Gear

Ships' chandleries are magnificent places to explore. There are coils of line and chain and tubs of pitch, bales of caulking oakum; you can smell kerosene everywhere and brass lamps hang from the walls alongside charts and sextants. Even as a neophyte, you walk through all this gear and it gives you a feeling of wherewithal, of capacity.

Sea anchors to put out in storms, sail needles and thread and fuel filters and life rafts and emergency radio beacons; ocean suits of rubber and nylon, built to keep you dry and warm in any weather; spare bilge pumps; antifouling paint to discourage the barnacles; brass hanks and shackles — everything gleams and speaks of purpose.

We spent days carting crates of gear down to the boat.

I devoted one whole morning to looking over the different sextants. The man behind the counter had come to know me from our steady traffic through his store. I was looking through a black enamelled brass beauty that felt like a jewel in my hands. He asked me where I was going. "Tahiti," I told him, chest thrust out.

"When?" he asked.

"Next week."

"Pretty late in the season. Do you know how to use these things?" he asked.

"I've got a book."

"Let me show you our GPS receivers."

GPS receivers calculate position from signals they pick up from satellites; they require no calculations and no skill from the user. Four hundred dollars and the size of a TV remote control, they give you your position anywhere on the planet to one hundred feet of accuracy any time you want. The man leaned forward. "You really should get one."

I did.

Good and beautiful gear is a kind of drug. An anxious stomach is settled and soothed even as the gear is studied. Solid half-inch Dacron line for the halyards, sails triple-stitched and so heavy it takes two just to lift the main out of the locker, solid stainless-steel turnbuckles and mast shrouds — it makes you imagine the boat and yourself equal to anything.

At sea, "anything" means storms. In 1805, Admiral Beaufort of the British Royal Navy devised this scale for estimating wind strengths, based on observation of sea conditions:

The Beaufort Scale

Beaufort Scale	Wind Speed (miles per hour)	World Meteorological Organization	Effects at Sea
0	Under 1	Calm	Flat calm; smooth mirror-like sea.
1	1–3	Light air	Ripples and scales on water surface; no crests or waves; sailing vessels make way in smooth water.
2	4–7	Light breeze	Small wavelets with glassy crests, no wind can be felt on face; sea surface has a benign look; sails stay filled on ocean swells.
3	8–12	Gentle breeze	Larger wavelets with occasional crests; light flags may be extended.
4	13–18	Moderate breeze	Moderate waves with less than half having whitecaps; waves become longer. Sailing vessels may have to begin to reduce sail, depending on apparent wind strength.
5	19–24	Fresh breeze	Building with pronounced long forms, waves may reach 7 feet; whitecaps on about half. Spray starts coming aboard.

6	25–31	Strong breeze	Larger waves may reach 11 feet. Whitecaps everywhere; more spray comes aboard; the beginnings of streaks on waves. Difficult to make progress upwind; noise first heard in rigging.
7	32–38	Near gale	Sea heaping up and may reach 13 feet or more. White foam from breaking waves blown into conspicuous streaks running with the wind. Sailing vessels carry dramatically reduced sail; rescue of man overboard unlikely.
8	39–46	Gale	Waves lengthening and building to 18 feet or more. Tops of wave crests often blown into spindrift; streaks are much more pronounced and can be seen everywhere. Loud moaning or shrieking noise in rigging. Many sailing vessels hove-to or bearing away under short-ened sail. Spectacles may be blown from face.
9	47–54	Strong gale	High waves, 20 feet or more. Crests of waves start to topple and roll over. Visibility reduced by blowing spray. Dense streaks of blown foam. Sailing vessels employ storm survival tactics.
10	55–63	Storm	Very high waves reaching 30–45 feet. Foam blown into dense white patches with the wind; sea surface takes on a white look;

			visibility impaired; seas have heavy tumbling appearance. Noise from rigging very loud. Spray hurts face.
11	64–72	Violent storm	Exceptionally high waves; medium-sized ships may be lost to view. The sea is completely covered with patches of foam; visibility affected.
12	73 and over	Hurricane	Air filled with foam; sea completely white with driving spray; visibility greatly reduced.

Air filled with foam. I didn't like the sound of that much. But my numerous instruction books said there are things that can be done when the wind blows hard — take down the sails, for one. I read that in Henderson's *Singlehanded Sailing.* It seemed like an important point and so I underlined it. Also: before the seas get too rough, make some sandwiches — it is frustrating not being able to take your hands off whatever it is you are clinging to long enough to spread some Cheez Whiz.

All of the books I'd bought made it clear to me that I had immersed myself in a pursuit where there was a great deal to know. I knew none of it. There were knots I had never heard of (the Turk's head with the monkey's fist inside the sheepshank: a confusion of bitter ends and twirling coils); sails I didn't have; and astronomical phenomena I couldn't recognize (taking a sight off of Arcturus is easy once you've found the kite-shaped Bootes ...). It astonished me that so much arcana could exist about anything worth knowing. I pictured cardigan-clad patrician men fingering ships in bottles and rubbing their chins and writing ever more involved treatises on the shapes of waves and the colour of rain.

Some advice was more useful. I learned that when the sails are all down and the wheel is left untended the boat will adopt an attitude parallel to the waves. This is called lying ahull. It's usually

easy on the boat but hard on the crew, as the side to side rolling
can become taxing.

In larger seas it would become necessary to attempt some of
the manoeuvres spelled out in the most-read chapters in my how-
to-sail books. There are two real concerns in storms. Firstly, breaking seas are catastrophic, especially if they catch you broadside. It
is much better to have the bow split the wave, up where everything
is oblique and robust. Lying ahull stops being a feasible storm
strategy when the seas begin to curl over themselves. Secondly,
there was this capsizing business. Something else I didn't like the
sound of. In very large seas, if one lay parallel to the waves, one
ran the risk of the boat rolling side over side down especially big
ones. Imagine it. At night, in cold driving rain, with no moon out.

Also, even if one tried to steer the boat perpendicular to the
waves, surfing down a steep wave can get everything going so fast
that steerage is lost and the boat veers sideways, adopting the
aforementioned parallel attitude and subsequent immersion. So,
two things: in a storm, face into or directly away from the weather
and don't get going so fast you can't steer.

If you have a sea anchor, it may be let out from the bow or
stern so that the boat rides perpendicular to the wave trains
(alarming phrase, that). Sea anchors look like heavy canvas para-
chutes that are opened in the water and do their work by slowing
the boat down nearly to the point of motionlessness and forcing it
to face into the wind and waves and not go anywhere.

Another approach to riding out a storm involves flying a tiny
storm jib and setting the rudder and the sail in such a manner that
the boat sort of stalls in the wind, taking the seas not quite head
on — this is called heaving-to.

Don and I talked about what we would do if the boat ever
started rolling to the point that we were concerned that she would
go right over on her beam ends. We thought that we would trail a
long warp or loop of line — perhaps the hundred-fathom anchor
line, with the anchor at the middle of the loop. This would keep

enough drag on the stern (we hoped) that the boat would stay per-pendicular to the seas. Then we would wedge ourselves some-where down below and wait it out. I tried not to think about how awkward that would be, dragging the anchor aft with six hundred feet of jumbled rope and securing the whole mess in a storm so wild the air was filled with foam.

We also had a long conversation in the chandlery about life rafts. Life rafts cost three thousand dollars. I had already bought so many crates of gear I couldn't afford to spend three grand on any-thing that wasn't going to keep me literally fastened to the dock. But there are some beautiful life rafts out there — water-ballasted self-inflating eight-person palaces that come with a water desali-nator, freeze-dried emergency rations, radio beacons, flares, every-thing. We looked at them. We both knew the status of my finances. I thought, "That would be a bad day, when you found yourself dig-ging one of these out of the locker. If the sea is overwhelming your boat, think about being in it in a five-foot-in-diameter rubber tub. Freeze-dried emergency rations notwithstanding."

"Better to spend your money on something that will stop us from needing one," Don said, walking on to the bilge pump section.

"Good point," I said, following him.

One night before we left, Don and I sat below in the stillness, drinking a bottle of Southern Comfort. We hadn't gotten the shore power hooked up and so we sat talking in the pungent weak light of the kerosene lamps. The thing is, he kept saying, he hadn't seen it coming. He would have worked on things. You just don't down tools like that. He wouldn't have. Southern Comfort tastes to me like alcoholic licorice syrup; every swallow is a struggle not to choke. They did have some arguments, and she found it tough living on Vancouver Island, away from her friends. He knew that.

Swallow, shudder.

CHAPTER TWO

WITH THE *Sea Mouse* stuffed with crates of equipment and rolls of line, we untied and left Nanaimo for Anacortes, in the San Juan Islands, where we planned to meet Richard and our wind vane. After this, we were heading back to Victoria to say goodbye to Don's parents and then setting out to open sea.

The sheer quantity of gear below was at odds with my notion of progressive simplification, but all the books, and Don, were adamant about the need for adequate ground tackle, for instance, and storm sails and tools and toilet paper. With the dry land dust of Manitoba still working its way out from under my fingernails, I was in a poor position to argue. I just signed more cheques and agreed that only a fool would set to sea without a case of Wet-Naps.

We anchored for the night in a small cove off Galiano Island. It was the first time I had slept on a boat not at dock. We drank some whiskey and then rolled to sleep slowly, competing for space with the piles of gear. As I lay there, wedged between crates redolent of kerosene and engine oil, I smiled so widely I thought my face might split.

In the morning I awoke to the rumble of the engine and the sound of water streaming past the hull. I dressed quickly and went up top. Don was looking into the dissipating morning mist. "Couldn't sleep very well," he said. "Thought it would be best if we got a move on." He handed me a cup of coffee. We threaded our way through the dozens of islands, American and Canadian that, on the chart, looked like spilled jam, until eventually we pulled alongside a wharf on Fidalgo Island as the sun was setting. It was already another country.

We walked up the pier to the main street. It felt like the town of Anacortes hadn't much changed in fifty years. This couldn't be true, of course, and the impression of changelessness could only be sustained by refusing to acknowledge the butt-crack-waving fat men in blue jeans and beards tinged with maple syrup in the yellow-neoned Denny's beside the 7-Eleven, which flickered and blazed beside the Blockbuster video store.

The ethos of nostalgic sentimentality appealed to Don and me so much we were briefly tempted to join the Republican Party and wear Ronald Reagan buttons. It seemed to us both that earlier times had been kinder. Where fibreglass was now, there had been wood. As much salmon as anyone could eat. At our age, all eight of our grandparents had been married for a decade or more. Sepia-tinted fantasies about less complicated times filled our heads and we found solace picturing ourselves in coarse woolen trousers with fly rods over one shoulder. And great hats too. And hip waders.

As we proceeded down mainstreet Anacortes, garish fluorescent lights and dismal and squalid love affairs fronted by insincerities and ambivalence were replaced by various chiselled-jaw versions of our idealized selves in thick wool sweaters, standing in authentic wooden taverns full of proud but modest old people and admired by intelligent and determined natural fabric-clad women. "We're going to sea," we would tell them. I wasn't sure what we would say after that, or what they would say back. But we certainly looked fine in our sweaters.

We needed to buy something that could serve as a reaching pole, to hold the jib out to the side when going downwind. The fancy metal ones are a thousand bucks. Don thought we could find something cheaper that would do as well. I stopped paying attention to the details, enjoying the conversations in my head. We were just in town provisionin' afore headin' out to sea. Yeah, the storms were near all right. Nope, wasn't gonna be a cakewalk. Ooh, I liked this.

We found an establishment that sold ash logging poles that had been milled forty years ago and had been gathering dust ever since. It was a miraculous place — field telephones from the Second World War, knee-high leather logging boots, winches and nets and crab pots and rifles. If there had ever been a piece of gear that had ever served some purpose, it was for sale in that store under a dust-caked sheet of canvas. The men who worked there had done so for decades. They wore stained and extravagant beards and plaid flannel shirts that barely contained their contents. These men took our amazement and delight in stride.

"Oh yeah, we're real famous," one of them told me, "we've been on the TV lots. Everyone says we're quaint. Now, you were thinking about something in the way of a reaching pole, were you?" He told me that sailors from Seattle came all the way out here just to buy the dusty tarnished gear that had sat on their shelves for so many years. He pulled out a pole and sighted along it. "This one looks straight," he declared, handing it to me. I asked him why he thought people went out of their way to buy old corroded gear. I wanted him to like me and my tone made it clear I shared the pragmatic opinion I expected him to have. I sighted along the pole. "'Cause there're enough shiny new things in the world already," he said.

I wished I had said that.

I paid for the pole, hefted it over my shoulder and walked out into the street. The store was closing and a stream of Nautica-clad men and women were shooshed out after me, carrying various dusty objects. I watched them disperse. Don touched me on the shoulder and said that he was going to go make a telephone call. He disappeared up a side street. The plaid and bearded man I had been talking with exited and walked up to a minivan. He climbed in, started it and backed out into the street.

I walked down to the boat. I left the pole on board and then went back downtown. It was dark now and quiet. The Hotel Majestic dominated the block. It was white- and black-painted wood, a hundred years old and as graceful as a Grand Banks schooner. I couldn't understand why I hadn't noticed it earlier.

I walked inside and sat down at the bar. I asked for an espresso and studied my reflection in the mirror. It was a disappointingly familiar picture, weedy and pointy-chinned. Such round shoulders. I tried holding my breath. Shoulders back. That was better.

An old man approached me and asked if I would be staying the night. I exhaled. I told him I had a boat. "Oh, that's much better," he said, and retreated. I drank from the little porcelain cup and ate the cookie that came with it. I watched the prosperous and contented-looking burghers eating in the dining room. There was a fire snapping in the fireplace and civility all around. In a matter of days I would be leaving this far behind. That thought made the little cookie taste even better.

Richard was scheduled to arrive the following day. Don and I were just putting away the breakfast dishes when he knocked on the hull. He had brought along one of these bearded and plaid North-westerners, a man named Jerome who had the shape of a brown bear and the disposition of a giraffe. Richard had repainted the wind vane, changed every bearing and adjusted every moving part.

"I found the serial number," he said. "I had wondered what had become of it. I remember now, the man who ordered it said it was for a vessel such as this. He was going to Hawaii."

"Well, he made it," I said.

"Why did he use the vane so little then?" Richard asked.

"I just bought the whole package."

"She's in beautiful shape, you know."

"Well, we really haven't taken her out for complete sea trials yet, but things look pretty good so far."

But Richard meant his — my — wind vane, and in his confused nodding our differing obsessions were evident.

"May we come on board?" he asked. He briefly inspected the boat. When he looked below and saw the piles down there, I saw him flinch. I told him we were still stowing gear before heading offshore. Of course we wouldn't go to sea with things looking like that.

"Looks like you already have," he replied. Then he and Jerome set to work installing the wind vane. Don and I hung around and watched while they bolted it onto the transom of the boat. It was getting dark when Richard made the last of his adjustments and pronounced the vane satisfactory. He looked at the sky and realized that he wouldn't be able to go out for a sail with us. Don and I looked at each other thinking the same thing. Richard's face froze for a moment, and then he said he would be on his way. He was very abrupt and for a moment I wanted to ask him to come with us. I don't know how he would have responded. "Please be careful," he said, and was gone.

In Victoria, Don's parents met us and we all went out for supper. One of Don's old friends, Marcus, had brought his boat, *Ladeo*, around from Nanaimo to see us off. He ate with us too. The evening was stilted and melancholic. The restaurant was overpriced and among these people who obviously had known each other for thirty years, I felt like an intruder. I drank too much wine. Don's parents walked us down to the boat. It seemed to me that his mother and father wanted to tell him that it wasn't so bad. But they didn't. They hugged both of us. I went below while Don made his goodbyes. The air was full of unsaids.

A few minutes later, Don came down and we pulled out our sleeping bags. I was so drunk I had to put one foot down on the cabin sole as I lay in my bunk. Don quickly fell asleep and began snoring. The cabin spun. I got up and dressed. In the parking lot there was no movement. I walked around, breathing deeply, still drunk. I made a phone call to my ex–girlfriend. She didn't answer, which was probably a good thing. I walked through the emptying late-night streets and listened to the revellers returning to their cars and their beds. I stepped into an alley for a time and leaned my head against a brick wall. When I walked back to the boat and crawled into my berth, Don was still asleep.

The next morning I woke to the sound of him dressing. I put on my clothes quickly and went up top. We untied the dock lines. We motored through the quiet inner harbour until we came to the fuel dock. A middle-aged man was just opening for the day. We filled our tank to the brim and then filled each of the jugs we had lashed to the lifeline stanchions. The man asked us where we were headed. Don answered.

"Good luck," he said, looking at the persistent disarray of the cockpit, the sailbags extruding themselves from beneath the dinghy, tied down on the foredeck, and the indescribable chaos that could be glimpsed through the cabin portholes. "How long do you think it will take you?" he asked.

"Fifty days or so," I said. As the last of the jugs were filled I went into the office, to look around for anything that might be useful. I came back with a dozen ice cream bars, a block of ice and thirty cans of Pepsi. Don looked at me oddly. I put them in the cooler. I went back up top and paid the man. As Don and I stood there, Marcus motored alongside in the *Ladeo* and waved to us. We untied the lines and went to sea.

Outside the harbour entrance, the gentle swell of the Juan de Fuca Strait came up quickly and there was a crashing from below as seemingly secured crockery sought better resting spots. I cleaned up. The boat was pitching and rolling in a manner that seemed calculated to compel my limbs and forehead to compete with the corners of the galley counters for occupancy of space-time. Lurching and staggering like a drunk with no hope, I shut my eyes for a long time and closed my mouth tightly. I looked up through the companionway to Don. He was steering the boat and looked completely implacable. I reached into the cooler and grabbed two ice cream bars. It was so cold we both wore sweaters, jackets and hats.

"Thanks," he said.

"No problem. I thought it might be nice to have some snacks over the next few days."

"I don't know if they'll last that long."

"Well, we'll just have to be disciplined."

"No, I think they'll melt."

"Oh, I bought ice."

"I think that will melt."

"I guess we'll have to see."

"It was a nice idea anyway."

"It's pretty rough today, isn't it?"

He looked at me with a little smile. "There's always something that shakes loose at first. You can never know for sure at dock what the right combination of pitches and rolls will do to your gear until you're out here. There's always something."

"What would you say this swell is, six feet?" I said, looking at the water. He looked down and then at me, kindly.

"Maybe two."

"Really?" I looked away and rolled my eyes. Don finished his ice cream bar. I took the wrappers below and inaugurated our garbage bag. I looked back up at him and wondered if I was really doing anything here at all. I had effectively hired a guide to take me out for a safe little romp around the ocean, after which I could return to my friends to brag about my derring-do. "Akmed, my inscrutable and faithful guide prepared our supper and then inscrutably poured me tea. In his strange and savage tongue he prayed to his God and then set up our tent. As he rubbed my aching back I thought of England and the greater glory I would bring her through my arduous adventure."

Marcus approached from behind. Don spoke into the transceiver. *Ladeo, Ladeo, Ladeo, this is the Sea Mouse, over.*

Sea Mouse, this is Ladeo. We could see him fifty feet away.

Ladeo, come on over for a treat. Don gave me the helm and dashed below. He emerged with a handful of ice cream bars just as Marcus was coming alongside. The swell was sloshing us about so much I foresaw our boats slamming into one another and ending the trip right there. "Hold her very steady," Don told me and leaned out over the life rail. The ice cream bars were handed off. I shut my eyes.

Ladeo remained alongside us for most of that morning. I could see Marcus eating ice cream bars and looking over at us and I wondered whether what he felt was envy or concern. As we progressed up the strait, drawing closer to the North Pacific, the swell increased steadily and markedly. I gripped the sides of the cockpit coaming and braced myself.

"Okay, it's maybe three feet now," Don said.

"Do you ever get seasick?" I asked.

"Never in my life," he said, squinting at the horizon. "You?"

"Nope, not once." As if I could have, in the half-dozen ferry crossings of my experience. I looked out at the sea. The strait was opening up now, as Vancouver Island drew away to the north. The swell was lengthening, the waves growing farther apart and the troughs deeper.

By late afternoon, a rhythm had formed between the two of us and the boat. We took turns at the helm. We ate a lunch of fruit leather and iced tea. *Ladeo* turned away with a wave from Marcus and we were finally alone. Don raised Marcus on the radio again and they exchanged goodbyes. As I listened I appreciated for the

first time that this trip was two journeys — Don's and mine —
and that he was just as desperate as I was.

An American nuclear submarine appeared off the Washington coast
and its tall black conning tower sliced its way through the water at
thirty knots. Just the tower itself was longer than the *Sea Mouse* and
from the vessel's bow wave to its stern wash it was gigantic, hundreds of feet long. We could see sailors' sunglasses glinting in the
bright sun. We waved at them. They didn't wave back. They pulled
ahead of us in minutes and then abruptly dove, disappearing in a
swirl of froth. Don told me he had once met submariners in Hawaii.
He asked them how fast they could go. "Fast," they replied, and
looked steely, chests prominent. He asked them how deep they
could dive. "Deep," they said. Lips like pinched suction cups.

I had read an essay in *Harper's* about what it was like to live on
those ships, to cruise around the world hundreds of feet deep,
without surfacing. I thought about how strange that life must be,
and wondered what sort of person would choose it. The sun was
just now setting low in the western sky and horizontal orange
streaks were stretching out across it like an astral piece of mille
feuille. The only light those men on the submarine knew was the
fluorescent glow of the electric bulbs; the only rhythm, the steady
throb of the nuclear-powered boiler and the steam turbine. I wondered why the essence of the sea — the sky, the wave swell —
would be rejected for that claustrophobic monotony. Then I wondered if those submariners didn't represent the final extreme of the
decisions everyone out on the ocean that day had made. We had
all turned our backs on some thing or another. The distinction
between a rejection and a selection can be a fine one. But this distinction is crucial.

We cleared Cape Flattery as the last of the sun disappeared below the horizon. Ahead stretched unbroken ocean all the way to Japan, four thousand miles to the west. The sea became darker and more viscous and the swell continued to lengthen and deepen. Don and I grew hungry. He volunteered to make supper and went below. There was a satisfying crash of pots but when Don stuck his head through the companionway to declare it too rough to cook, I looked skeptically over the side and agreed. There was a pause. In the cooler, he found a Mrs McBean's Pecan Pie that we had bought in the days before our departure. He emerged a few minutes later with a couple of cans of Pepsi and two forks. We sat there in the twilight and ate quickly. The pie was only half thawed. The stars began to show themselves and we could just make out the Pachena Point lighthouse beacon. Off the rough western coasts of Vancouver Island and the Olympic Peninsula I looked for car headlights but saw none. Mount Olympus was visible even in the dark as a rising blackness on the horizon. Don and I patted our contented bellies and stared all around. It was night, and we were not dashing for shore. The horizon was empty of ships' lights. We set Richard's wind vane and went below.

We lit the kerosene lamps and sat together at the table. It was warmer down here and the orange flame of the lamps shone in the polished woodwork. It felt so safe, so comforting, that for the first time so far, the trip felt like something other than posturing.

Every ten minutes or so one of us poked our head through the companionway to scan for ships and check our position. But on this night the ocean was like a small-town main street on a Sunday night. Everybody was home eating dinner.

We each began reading under the kerosene lamp. I picked *Anna Karenin* out from the shelf of books. We were quiet for a long time. It was now very dark. A tapping began to sound on the cabin top and I went up to investigate. It was raining, and much colder than it had been. We continued to motor. We wanted to put as much sea room between us and the shore before we started messing around with sailing. The swell grew deeper yet and the bow of the *Sea Mouse* began plunging and rearing with the steady and alarming gait of a shopping mall Bucking Bronco ride. I went back down below. Don had one foot held out to grip the side of the boat. We each posted as best we could, pitch up, down, side, side, up, down. It seemed a little inconceivable to me that this was a normal amount of sea action but Don would not waver. I was both reassured and alarmed by his insistence that these seas were nothing out of the ordinary.

As we sat there — me, gripping a bulkhead for dear life — I noticed that I had begun salivating like a St Bernard at a summer barbecue. I ignored it at first, but it worsened. I swallowed frequently and wondered what this was all about. I began yawning as well and then abruptly I began feeling more and more claustrophobic. All I could smell was diesel fuel. I blinked at Don, who was reading an aviation magazine. "I think I'll go sit up top for a minute," I said. The rain began beating harder against the cabin top. "I could use some fresh air." I rose, stretching and affecting languorous ease. "After all, I didn't go out to sea to sit inside."

"Sure," Don said, not looking up.

I burst through the companionway hatch and breathed in deeply. My mouth dried a bit and I continued to swallow repeatedly. I faced into the wind and cool rain and felt better. I sat down in the cockpit and held onto the coaming as the stern rose and fell like a gigantic teeter-totter, my playmate hidden in the darkness off the bow. I grinned at him. But as my lips parted, a paroxysm seized my belly and, showing some remarkably quick thinking, considering the circumstances, I thrust my head into the dark over the gunwale, out of sight of Don. "Hoo-waaah!" I hollered. Mrs McBean's best efforts were propelled out into the darkness, hung there for a moment and then came back with the wind, seeking warmth, perhaps. I blinked through my speckled spectacles.

"You okay?" I heard Don call from below, without urgency. There was a long pause.

"Oh yeah," I yelled, wiping my face and grimacing. "Just slipped on the deck out here."

"You should be wearing your harness," he said.

"Yep, I'll put it on."

"Okay."

I clipped a tether to my jacket harness and one of the mizzen-mast shrouds and then I closed the companionway hatch. "To keep the rain out," I explained, to Don's glance upward. He nodded. I leaned against the back of the cabin top, alongside the hatch, facing aft. The circular window in the hatch emitted a yellow beam that glowed against the glistening and dripping mizzen-mast. I breathed heavily. More pecan pie began clamouring for release and then it too joined the sea. Despite the cold, I was perspiring heavily in my new foul-weather gear, which was now streaked with the love of Mrs McBean's kitchen.

I hung my head over the rail and held tightly to the shrouds as my body convulsed and pecan pie shot out of me like I was a tanker cleaning her bilges.

After a long period of pious and panting reflection, I opened my eyes. I was growing cold, and my mouth was no longer running like a hydrophobic rat terrier's. I stood and opened the companionway hatch. I staggered down the ladder and stopped in the galley. I braced myself against the stove.

"You were up there a long time," I heard Don say. "See any ships?" There was a tightened quality to his voice but I did not think much about it, preoccupied as I was with the business of swallowing and breathing.

"No," I said. "I was just listening to the wind. Do you, uh, think we should hoist the sails sometime, save the fuel?"

"Yeah, maybe," Don gasped, "it feels like the wind is freshening. What would you say it is, fifteen knots now?" I looked over at him. He had laid his magazine down and was holding on to the table edge, his eyes shut, his face pallid, beads of perspiration shining on his upper lip.

"Something like that," I said, pausing to lurch with an especially pronounced roll.

"Maybe I'll have a look up there, too."

Don climbed past me, pawing for air. I sat down at the table. I turned on the radio. *Ideas* was playing. Lister Sinclair intoned. I heard a bellow from above. I turned up the radio. The program was almost over when Don opened the hatch and poked his wet head below. "Yeah, I'd say there is enough wind to sail all right. We've got enough sea room, too, to be safe."

"Coming right up," I said, leaping up the companionway.

We swung the bow into the wind and I held her there while Don hoisted the mainsail. He waved me forward and I clipped my tether onto the jackline that ran around the boat. I crawled on the pitching and rolling deck and together we went up to the pulpit on the foredeck to prepare the jib for hoisting. We began hanking the jib on the forestay, pulling it in big handfuls out of the sailbag. The bow is by far the most active spot on a boat and with each plunge into the oncoming waves, a sheet of water swept over us, knocking us off our feet. Just as we finished hanking the sail on Don called out, "You'd better move!" As he reached for the steel tubing of the pulpit, I looked up and around and then at him, seeing at first no cause for his concern. Then, recognizing the pursed lip and bulging-eyed intensity, I spread myself flat, as if I was back in the army, crawling in the Manitoban mud under barbed wire. Pecan pie arced out in a parabola over my shoulders. I glanced up at him and he looked ashamed of himself. I grinned.

"You okay?"

He nodded and then clipped on the jib halyard.

At his instruction I made my way back to the mast and began hauling the sail up. Under the dim moonlight the white sail glowed and flapped, snapping in the wind. We retreated to the helm and turned away from the wind, to the southwest. The sails filled and the *Sea Mouse* heeled abruptly. Under the stabilizing effect of the weight of wind in the sails the rolling stopped and for the first time it began to seem bearable to be at sea on a little boat in weather. I looked up at the sails as Don tightened the jib and main sheets. The sails flattened out and it felt as if the boat's speed had just doubled, although by the knotmeter it had scarcely changed. Don shut off the engine and then it was finally and gloriously quiet. It seemed astonishing that we had not done this hours earlier. There was just the wind, and the boat surging along. The odour of the diesel exhaust dissipated. The rain even let up. It was entirely different. We sat there for a long while and then Don said he was tired. I said I would take first watch and he nodded and went below. Our first night at sea.

As the cabin lights were extinguished, the boat seemed to disappear beneath me. We rose up with the swell and then down, and it was like a hand was underneath me, holding me just a few feet above the water. The vanished *Sea Mouse* heeled in the breeze and the waves collapsed behind me. It was cold and very dark. I shivered and held on. It hit me that we were headed further out into the ocean. I had never seen dark like that before. Periodically I switched on my flashlight and looked at the sea running beside me. I checked the compass and looked at the cone of boat parts lit up in the weak yellow light. I switched it off. I checked my watch.

When Don shook me awake it was long past dawn. He said I had looked so tired when we had changed places that he had let me sleep. I was grateful but not particularly well rested. Don was standing in the galley and had large purple rings under his eyes. He had made coffee. He had seen four ships during the night; none of them came close. I dressed and he watched me. He looked at the stove and lifted up a pan. "Do you want anything to eat, some eggs maybe?"

"How about some pecan pie?" He put the pan back down. We both stuck to coffee. As anti-seasickness strategies go, caffeine is ill-advised but nothing like the invitation to calamity that pecan pie had represented. Don went back to the sea berth and I went up top.

Outside it remained grey and cold and volatile; the weather off the coast of Oregon and Washington is famously ill-tempered.

With the sails hoisted, however, the *Sea Mouse* felt like a dog let out to run. The wind was still blowing hard out of the southeast. With the boat settled over on her starboard side, over the next few days I began learning how to sail. Squalls blew through frequently and the nights were tiring and often we had to dash up to the foredeck to douse the sails. We stayed in our foul-weather gear almost constantly and it was too cold to properly bathe in the rain. We agreed that we would only use our fresh water for drinking and brushing our teeth. A film of salt and perspiration coated our sweaters and our skin. After a week it felt like we had been out there for months. It was hard. Not awful, but hard.

Several nights later I was on watch when I saw a squall approaching us quickly from the southeast. Don was napping below and I thought I knew what to do. I doused the main and rolled in the genoa sail on the roller-furling system that was attached to the port forestay. I tied the line that secured the genoa and went below as the rain hit. I didn't wake up Don. I sat down on the galley floor and fell asleep myself.

I woke up to Don rushing past me. My first thought was that he was seasick again and I began to laugh. Then I realized that the whole boat was shaking — I could hear the mast vibrating with sickening force and I jumped up and followed him out. The genoa had come loose and was whipping in the sixty-knot gale. Don and I ran forward and tried to wrestle the roller furling in. The sail was shredded in a dozen places and as tight as we wound the forestay, eight-foot-long tendrils of ribbed Dacron still flagged in the wind. They wound around the starboard forestay and, although we had eliminated the immediate threat of dismasting, we now had no way of hoisting a headsail, without which it would not really be possible to sail. In the mounting storm we let the *Sea Mouse* lie ahull and went below. This was a disaster.

In the morning we contemplated our problem. It would be easy enough to fix if one of us could go up to the top of the mast and lower the whole forestay down but in the seas we were in that seemed absurd. We looked at the chart. We were seven hundred miles west-northwest of San Francisco. We turned east half-heart-edly: we didn't have enough fuel to motor the whole way and under mainsail alone we made hardly any headway. Jesus Christ. I settled into a pout, and spent that morning below, drinking tea.

Hours later, Don called me to come up. He was standing in the cockpit.

"I think I've figured out how to fix it," he said. He had a spool of light nylon line in one hand and a U-shaped steel shackle in the other. We went forward, to the forestays. He attached the shackle around the starboard forestay. "This is going to be our pulley," he said. Then he ran the free end of the line through the shackle and tied it tightly to the bottom of the shredded genoa on the port forestay. Finally, he attached the jib halyard and another loose line to the shackle, so that he could raise and lower it along the star-board forestay. He then had me wind in the port forestay as he hoisted and lowered the shackle, slowly working his way higher as the streams of ripped nylon were caught in the web of nylon line that we slowly wound around the port forestay and the sail. Eventually it looked like a giant worm that had been ensnared and wrapped by a similarly large spider. The whole process took about fifteen minutes. We had a free forestay now and could hoist a sail. It made all the difference in the world.

We turned south once again and made for Hiva Oa, in the Mar-quesas. We were going to be fine. Losing use of the port forestay was a nuisance but nothing more. The jib we hanked on the star-board forestay filled easily and we began covering a hundred and twenty miles a day. We followed our progress against the landmarks of the American coast: we passed Crescent City in California, and then San Francisco and L.A. — and then we were off the Mexican coast, although over a thousand miles offshore. The climate shifted abruptly. Our foul-weather gear came off and stayed off. Now the rain was so warm that it was pleasant to remain outside in it and let the salt streaks wash out of our hair and underwear. And the sun was so warm that we began to darken quickly and at night it was as comfortable to remain up top in the cockpit as it was to sleep below.

The winds were steadier now. The wind vane steered for us and we began cooking more ambitiously. Don baked bread and I made elaborate curries. We both pretended to prefer each other's dishes. We read and we watched the ocean roll past. Every day we seemed to make better speed and put more miles behind us. We listened to Radio Canada International and heard that the first of the winter blizzards were hitting the prairies and gales were starting to come ashore on the West Coast. Around us, the trade-wind skies were filled with high fluffy cumulus clouds and each night Polaris sunk lower astern. Two thousand miles behind us, winter storms were in full force.

Distance

When I was in the army I spent three years holding my breath in impatience as I waited for the end of my obligatory service. Every morning I woke up in my neat little army house on a small artillery base in southern Manitoba and I sat on the end of my bed and just stared at the wall. Beyond the wall stretched thousands of acres of arid Manitoban prairie, rutted and grooved by the tracked self-propelled howitzers that charged from coulee to cutline, pausing to lob a few high-explosive rounds off someplace. The maintenance of those howitzers lent whatever meaning there was to the soldiers' days there. The walls of my little house shook and the dishes rattled with every detonation, so deep as to be almost inaudible, felt rather in the spine and kidneys. I had chosen the army as a solution when I had run out of money in medical school and so I couldn't even summon up the conscript's indignation as

solace. I read many books in that house and I listened to the radio.
I drank whole bottles of sweet liqueurs secretly, slowly enough that
I could hide being drunk if anyone visited me.

The artillery regiment I belonged to made many attempts to
involve me in its social life — the colonel's Christmas party, the
Easter ball. There was even a lingerie party the base surgeon's wife
threw that I was compelled to attend. I sat among these benign
and good-natured people and grinned, longing to be anywhere
but there.

I conducted a running resistance of misanthropic withdrawal.
Unless summoned by the adjutant and instructed to attend, I didn't.
When forced to show, I arrived late and left early. I was remote,
rude and sullen. I hated that place and I could not give to it one
more bit of myself than was absolutely necessary. On off-duty
weekends I drove as fast as my pick-up truck would take me into
Winnipeg, where I had friends to whom I whined unceasingly. I
will concede that there were more effective and mature responses
available to me.

I spent two insanely cold Canadian winters there at Shilo. After
a time my regimental colleagues gave me up as a waste of effort,
unsociable and aloof, and stopped trying to pry me out of my little house. When the weather was too surly to drive to Winnipeg I
passed whole weekends without talking to anyone; cooped up in
my little keep, I read novels and sipped Frangelico and sometimes
went all day without getting out of my bathrobe. My room started
to smell and I never noticed.

I read *The Alexandria Quartet* and imagined the Mediterranean
in vivid azure and tan. *The Lover* propelled me into *Indochine Fran-
çais*, drinking sweet strong coffee and smoking opium. This is what
appealed to me: foreign and physical beauty, heat, exile, resilience.
Cortazar's *Hopscotch* had me imagining myself an Argentine in
Paris; Lowry, a drunken Brit in white linen and perspiration stains.

Around me, meanwhile: peeling clapboard shacks thrown up in a few weeks during the war, fifty years old now and looking older, like the people there, scoured by crystalline snow accelerating all the way from the mountains.

I imagined myself on a train, with a roll of American dollars in my shoe and a small leather suitcase between my knees. Outside: green mountains clacking past. Headed away.

I packed that leather suitcase and kept it under my bed in my little house. When I was especially depressed, I pulled it out, unpacked it and packed it again. This is what was in it:

Three white cotton shirts
Four pairs of boxer shorts
Three pairs of cotton socks, one of wool
A pair of wool trousers
A pair of walking shorts
A bottle of ink
A sheaf of heavy letter paper
Envelopes
Five hundred American dollars, in twenties
One thousand dollars in traveller's cheques
A blank journal
Homer's *Odyssey*
Musil's *The Man Without Qualities*
An English-Spanish-French dictionary
A jackknife
My passport

It made me happy, that little suitcase. I remember standing at attention during regimental inspections and opening it up in my mind, unpacking and re-folding the shirts. I imagined fitting my socks and books together in a tight and compact lattice that wasted no space at all. Along one side I squeezed in my razor and toothbrush and beside my trousers, my jackknife. I remember standing among my colleagues in olive drab with my eyes rolled back in my head smiling stupidly at nothing obvious. At the compulsory-attendance TGIF sessions in the officers' mess I withdrew to the mess library and read novels, only emerging long enough to buy glasses of whiskey and catch the eye of the adjutant, demonstrating my presence in body. The wives of the senior officers made attempts to engage me in dialogue and I answered in monosyllables. They did not persist any longer than their husbands had and reported back to them my ill-mannered behaviour. This further irritated these men and eventually I was called into the office of my battery commander.

The major was an intelligent and kind man whose own struggles with the colonel's tedious wife and her estimations of him were frequently a subject of regimental gossip. I think that he had hoped we would be friends, caught alike in that dusty squalid place. He insisted that it could only become bearable if I made the most of it and took the people with a sense of humour. Nobody was really asking that much from me, after all, he said. He was right. A little bit of politeness and professionalism should not have been too much to ask. He drew his chair closer to mine and looked straight at me, paternally. "So will you do as I ask?" I met his eyes briefly and returned to my shirts, my books and my perfect little suitcase. Through the window the mountains grew steadily larger. The major's scalp glistened pink in the tropical heat.

Calm

When the genoa on the roller furler was destroyed it became necessary to stop off in Hawaii for repairs and equipment. At first, we did not want to acknowledge this. Then in subsequent weeks I reefed the mainsail improperly and tore it and then managed to lose our *anchor* overboard. For reasons I was not fully able to explain, I had disconnected it from the chain and lashed it to the bow roller with line instead. Line that had chafed through after two thousand miles of rolling and pitching. The anchor made a loud plop as it hit the water. Don and I looked at one another open-mouthed like Abbott and Costello and agreed that we would not tell any boat people about this, ever. We had another very small anchor aboard but there are no docks to tie up at in French Polynesia; a boat needs a proper anchor. We would go to Hawaii.

A thousand miles west of Guadalajara and fifteen hundred miles northeast of Hawaii sits the centre of a weather system called the North Pacific High. So does any sailing vessel that finds itself in it. Sits — in water like a brushed aluminum sheet. The weather report on the short-wave transmission out of Honolulu told us that the North Pacific High was holding well to the north of us and we decided to set a direct course for the islands. For two days we made great speed and then the high moved south and fell on us like a lid.

We awoke one morning to find the sails hanging limply on the mast and the boat motionless. We pulled down the sails to spare them the chafe and began staring at the horizon and imagining that we could see signs of a disturbance moving in.

These are called the horse latitudes, in memory of the desiccated and bellowing creatures the Spaniards forced overboard when water ran low. Navigators learned to hold well east, where the winds are more reliable. Today, sailors who know what they are doing take instruction from the dead horses and follow the galleon routes, keeping the Mexican coast within smelling distance and only turning west when the trades are well established and the high far to the north.

When the wind stops completely out on the open ocean the light is like a magnesium flare. The slow swell sags and bulges silently and the water vapour rises into a heated humid shimmering all around. The horses, for all their protest, might not have been entirely disappointed to hit the water.

Don and I only really got to know each another then, in the motionlessness. At first, we took it as a matter of another day or two at most. After a week, it became hard not to struggle. There were long pregnant pauses and many melodramatic gazes out to the sea. We baked bread. I read Cormac McCarthy's *All the Pretty Horses*. When we could get Radio Canada International on the short-wave we listened to news of the hockey strike and agreed that we might as well be sitting out here. We took turns spitting and we exchanged knock-knock jokes. Sailors who knew what they were doing would have packed plenty of board games.

I stopped counting the days. Each morning we recorded our position on the chart, but as the calm grew more prolonged, we stopped calculating the daily distance logged. An ocean takes a long time to cross at one mile an hour, which was basically our rate of drift. After the second week passed with no sign of any other vessel or even aircraft, we abandoned our habit of keeping alternating deck watches — the day began whenever we woke up. In the mornings I stood on the stern and peed into the water and watched the bubbles from my stream remain alongside the boat long after the completion of the act.

At nights the sky was so bright it was nearly possible to read by the stars. Whoever uses the word "void" to describe space hasn't been to sea in an unlit boat. We lay out there counting satellites and marvelling that such tiny metal spheres, a few yards across, should be visible tens of thousands of miles away. This reassured us, made us feel like we might be similarly detectable on our tiny little boat; we grew adept at picking out movement against the starry backdrop. When it was overcast, the starless sky lay on the horizon like black silk on onyx, distinguishable only by the textures of the blackness. It was most lonely those nights and Don and I talked a great deal. We made plans, revised on a nightly basis, for what we would each do after we stopped sailing, for where we would like to live, you know, eventually. We avoided discussing the circumstances behind our presence out here on the ocean. We thought about that too much already.

October 26, 1994
You know, you could go crazy on this cloudless, windless, motionless ocean. Sitting here reading copies of Harper's *and*

The New Yorker for the thousandth time. Reliving with bored masochistic not even pain — more like displeasure — the last words of your last love affair. Unsatisfyingly familiar, like a used-up fantasy, grown dull with repetition …

And you pass the time eating and scribbling and steering though what steerage is possible at one and a half knots; your companion and you scarcely speak, having said all that could be of interest to the other weeks ago. The night before, you spent three hours describing the plots of each other's favourite Star Trek: The Next Generation *episodes.*

The short-wave radio offers some respite, and after you've listened to the news on BBC, *Radio Australia, New Zealand, Netherlands, Switzerland and* VOA, *you begin to wonder if in fact these are different entities at all, or just the same building broadcasting the same news from somewhere on the planet, the North Pole perhaps, for otherwise how could they sound so astonishingly familiar? But that supposition does sound a little paranoid, and one does want to keep hold of one's mental reins in circumstances such as these …*

The striking feature of the state of being becalmed is the absence of any real requirement to respond to it actively. A gale is frightening, but there are things it makes you do, and in doing them, you imagine that you exert some control over the situation. The sails are doused and lashed down and then they can no longer be blown out. Loose gear on deck is stowed, and the strategies of heaving-to and lying ahull or playing out a warp can also be considered at least as hypotheticals. (In gales to this point, the *Sea Mouse* sat so squat and stable in the troughs of the waves that it seemed to us impudent to try and bully her into any position other than that which she adopted on her own.) In a long calm, however, the only challenge before the sailor is to stop staring hopefully at the horizon, and to keep busy with the available tasks of whipping line ends and checking the running and standing rigging. These tasks are best husbanded. In the meantime, you simply have to wait for the calm to go away. Later Don told me that when he was alone on deck those nights he often thought about his wife and had several times considered stepping off the stern. When I didn't reply, he said, "But I couldn't just leave you out here on your own."

As we rocked and swayed and read and scratched, the water took on a quality of continuity and invitation; it was only the water between us and room to walk, between us and cheeseburgers. Without interruption it stretched all the way to ice cubes and company. When I peed in it in the morning those ripples stretched out and washed up underneath Fisherman's Wharf, to Waikiki and eventually even those iced-over rocks on the shore of Hudson Bay. At night the water glistened and looked as cool and supple as English beer.

On the chart the blue was interrupted only by depth soundings, five thousand feet deep here, forty-two hundred feet there. Viewed from the bottom, our little boat would look like a snowflake. From a mile below.

We stood on the deck naked and hugging ourselves, looking at the water.

"It was your idea," he said.

"I'm sure there are no sharks."

"What would they be eating all the way out here?"

"It's a pretty big ocean, what are the chances?"

"You don't have any open cuts, do you?"

"Sky looks pretty settled."

"I've given up worrying about abrupt windstorms."

"Just don't thrash."

"Yeah, stay calm."

Testicles retracted up to my kidneys, I leapt. He followed.

The boat just stayed there. We swam a little way away. It didn't go anywhere. We swam further, in opposite directions. The slow gentle swell lifted the little boat up and eased it beneath the water.

Don too. When I thought I was maybe a hundred yards out, I stopped swimming. For long seconds I had the illusion of being entirely alone. A thousand miles from anyone. It should have been more satisfying. I started to lose my breath. I imagined I'd lost sight of the boat and I panicked and swam as fast as I could in the direction I thought the boat was. The next thing I knew I was hammering my head on her hull. I pulled myself aboard and sat on the gunwale and shivered.

CHAPTER THREE

Loneliness and Time

> We had become, with the approach of night,
> once more aware of loneliness and time —
> those two companions without whom no journey
> can yield us anything.

LAWRENCE DURRELL, *Bitter Lemons*

THERE IS a long history of sadness propelling travellers out on their wanders; you could argue that the road selects for malcontents and wobbly psyches and you will find nothing to refute that argument in the bus-terminal snack bars of my experience. And why would you expect to? It is not the most content and socially evolved among us who cast themselves out of their homes. Think about Paul Theroux's melancholy travels in *The Happy Isles of Oceania*, through these same Pacific waters, placing anguished telephone calls to his estranging wife as he paddled his collapsible kayak through the lagoons of all the "nesias." Mega, Micro, Mela and Poly. Eluding only the still waters of "Am." Think about his wife, picking up the telephone and hearing that satellite pause and hum, wondering why he was calling at all if he couldn't even be around for his own *divorce*, for crying in the sink.

But it was probably no contest, the kayak or the divorce. I think Theroux was drawn to the easy sense of self-possession that comes from having absolute and daily control over destination and pace. He felt stronger and more self-sufficient going from island to island with his kayak in his luggage than he would have felt sitting in the attic of his house drinking or weeping or staring into space while his wife packed below. As if being away from home is the same as not having one. As if breaking a promise is the same as never having made it.

The idea of the road stands for the idea of how easy it is to live without dyspeptic supervisors, uninterested bed companions and the flat grey light of fluorescent bulbs and shadowless winter afternoons. We imagine today that our lives are more mobile, that we wander the world more readily than before, but in fact it is less possible to extricate oneself than in earlier times. No stranger is trusted who can't verify his history, and bad debt clings like flour.

To the extent that we allow ourselves to be constrained by our institutions, we are, but the escape clause in every social contract is the option of flight. In the weeks before I'd left I had telephoned my old friends and told them about my plan to run away to sea. Only the happiest of them didn't claim to envy me.

My father has a cousin named Lawrence, a welder in his fifties, grey and unassuming at family reunions. He was famous in our family folklore for abruptly disappearing on his way home from work. Usually he took his motorcycle up into the mountains someplace. He would stay for a few days or a few weeks and then he would return. Each time his wife was less surprised and less upset and less inclined to forgive him. In the course of the ten years it took for her to give up on him entirely, she never once called the police or made much of an obvious effort to figure out where he went. I remember each time my father mentioned that Lawrence had disappeared again, he wore an uncharacteristic expression of contempt. Here *he* was, after all, just as young, kids, wife, all that, and he was sticking it out. He didn't need to be reminded that it was possible to quit.

In the army it was only ever recruits who deserted — the eighteen-year-olds, mostly from Quebec and Newfoundland, who arrived and were astonished at the prairie winter winds. They thought that Manitoba was hell on earth. Most of them endured, but each year there were three or four who one day did not appear for morning parade. They would be arrested by the RCMP in some small town somewhere and returned to the base in handcuffs, hating it more than even I did. Before they began their jail time, I had to examine them in order to declare them fit for cells. I always asked the military policeman to leave us alone. As soon as the MP had left the room, I would ask the young man how he had found the decisiveness to just leave.

One boy told me he had spent two months just doing all the stuff — learning how to load the gun and what the different rounds were that you could fire through it, how much the different rounds weighed and how far they would fly, running in the morning and preparing for the bed inspections afterwards, drinking in the mess on the weekends until he couldn't see — and then one night he couldn't sleep and he lay awake trying to figure out how anyone could live like that. So he got up, dressed quietly and called a cab.

After he was caught and brought back to the artillery base his bootlaces were taken away, as was the custom, and he was dressed in baggy and unlikely looking green overalls. The process is an exercise in humiliation far more than in intimidation. After his jail sentence he was re-enrolled in the battle school. If quitting had been as simple as walking away, every one of us would have.

The preposition that fits most easily with escape is from rather than to. Escape is a rejection; a selection involves a different attitude altogether. It is the difference between walking with your eyes over your shoulder and looking straight ahead. The moment the thing being fled is not visible, the urgency fades.

The dreary truth is that most of the disenchanted artillerymen, and my father's cousin, lost their yearning for open sky shortly after they got a clear view of it. The gunners were usually found making their way back east to the little towns they had sought to escape by enlisting in the first place; and Lawrence never made a complete break of it until his wife made it for him. The gunners as often as not turned themselves back in and, upon completion of battle school, often elected to remain in the army. This redoubled the determination of the commanding officer to go after those who fled. In the officers' mess he declared he was doing them a favour. Give them a chance to stick something out for a change. The pansies.

There were soldiers who didn't return, however, who disappeared from the army and the artillery for good. I found it impossible not to wonder where they had gone. A week after a soldier's disappearance, the colonel would telephone the soldier's mother and explain how he would not be able to work, or have health insurance, or attend school or collect unemployment benefits until he had sorted out his affairs with the army. If the soldier had gone home this almost always worked. But once in a while the woman would insist that she hadn't heard from her son and that if the colonel did, would he have him call her?

Like the great dumb beast it was, the military forgot about these unresolved cases quickly. A few months after a successful desertion I would ask the soldier's troop commander — a lieutenant or junior captain usually not much out of the spotted-face phase himself — about the escapee and he would shrug his muscular shoulders and mutter that he was "glad to be done with the fuck" and that his file was Off to Ottawa. That night I would sit at home and imagine the man in some tropical and remote paradise — Ecuador, say — walking along a road and wondering about the artillery base and what he could have been thinking when he agreed to *that*.

I wondered what my imagined man might have found in Ecuador. How long could he stay there, for instance, before he drifted home; could he find a sense of ease and belonging there? Surely we aren't all fated to return to our own private Newfoundlands?

In the convenience store on the base, among pornography of every imaginable bent, there were sometimes sailing magazines. Drawn to a cover photo of South Pacific palm trees and water like pale blue ink, I picked one up and read of a man named Bernard Moitessier. Moitessier had been born and raised in French Indochina. He served in the French army during the war there and upon his release his only desire was to get away. He bought an old fishing junk, knowing nothing about the open sea, and set out for peace. He made it to Singapore. There, he learned more about boats and set out again, this time for Mauritius, in the Indian Ocean. He had no chronometer on board and so, in that pre-GPS era, he had no way of knowing his longitude. It is possible to figure out one's latitude without a chronometer by calculating the angle between Polaris and the horizon. Moitessier used the old trick of the Spaniards, of running down the latitude. That is, he sailed due west on a known latitude until he came to an identifiable landmark — the Chagos Archipelago in the middle of the Indian Ocean. He met the Diego Garcia reef in the middle of the night. He describes how suddenly he became "just a poor jerk sobbing as he watched his beautiful *Marie-Thérèse* being torn apart."

He lived in Mauritius for three years, building *Marie-Thérèse II*, and then in South Africa for another two. He was very poor and used "phone company wires" as shrouds; he worked like a "yoked water buffalo" to buy even those and, eventually, he made his way to the Caribbean, where he again met a reef and lost his second boat. He shipped back to France as a deckhand on a tanker. I found one of his books, *Tamata and the Alliance*, in a bookstore in Winnipeg on a weekend off call:

"Paris was a great desert: garrets, sandwiches, the *France-Soir* classified ads. The money I had saved from the tanker job was melting away, with no relief in sight. I was like a sewer rat skittering along the sidewalks, tracked by danger in a heartless, completely alien world. I would have given anything to find some nice warm hole where I could curl up and forget about it all.

But still he kept faith. He worked as a pharmaceutical salesman and began writing about his long sea voyage home from Vietnam. *Vagabond des mers du sud* sold well and soon he had a new steel boat, *Joshua.* An understanding of the sea had accumulated in him like sediment settling. He moored *Joshua* in Marseilles and got her ready to go again. He persuaded a woman to come with him. They sailed through the Caribbean to the Galapagos, the Marquesas and then Tahiti.

After three years there, he and his now-wife Francoise sailed back to France, but instead of going by the usual trade-wind equatorial route, they went south and then east, rounding Cape Horn and reaching Alicante, in Spain, in one shot, in four months. This was a world record, for the longest non-stop small sailing boat passage.

The kind of exuberant delight that fills Moitessier's passages describing the sea are nowhere to be found in his descriptions of his time ashore. Deprived perhaps of an opportunity to hold forth flamboyantly to nearby seabirds, soon after his arrival in Paris after that four-month passage home he sank into a deep depression:

> Wrapped in total silence, sucked down by a huge inner emptiness, I sank into the abyss. [...] I felt madness burrowing into my guts like some hideous beast. I found myself wondering what last thoughts come to someone who has swallowed a lethal dose of poison and is watching his being becoming lighter and dissolving, just before tipping into the void.

I raised my glass to that, there in my little house on the army base. Moitessier chose the inevitable answer: a return to sea. This time, a grander trip even than the last. Reading his account of his decision, the man's volatility becomes evident:

Drunk with joy, full of life, I was flying among the stars now. Together, my heart and hands held the only solution, and it was so luminous, so obvious, so enormous, too, that it became transcendent: a nonstop sail around the horn by the three capes!

(You wouldn't want him as a roommate, I think.)

So, in 1968 he set off to carry out his "only solution." At the same time, the *Sunday Times* was organizing a solo race featuring exactly this route, offering a prize of five thousand pounds for the fastest passage. Moitessier was tempted by this money, and no doubt the attendant publicity, and what that would mean for his book sales. He entered the race, and departed from Plymouth in June of that year.

Six months later, he had rounded all the great capes and was back in the Atlantic and headed north for England when he realized that he had lost any desire to win or even finish the race:

> To return now would amount to never having left at all, to tacitly accepting the old rules of a game imposed by others. It would be to betray myself. The sun, the sea, the wind, the Southern Cross so high in the sky, and the albatrosses that see all things alike, gliding at wave-top, brushing the troughs and the crests to show me the way … all were telling me this in the song of the great luminous silence where I had been sailing my soul for so long.

He realized that he had already found what he was looking for in the South Pacific. He altered course and rounded the Cape of Good Hope for the second time. He laid in a route for Tahiti. Off Cape Town, Moitessier pulled alongside a tanker sitting at anchor, and with his slingshot he catapulted a film canister onto its deck. In the canister was a message he asked to be relayed to the race organizers in London. It read, "I am continuing nonstop toward the Pacific islands because I am happy at sea, and perhaps also to save my soul."

He ended up going one and a half times around the planet, and without stopping, in his forty-foot sailboat. Ten months he spent alone on that boat.

After Moitessier quit, the prize went to the jingoistic and eccentric Robin Knox-Johnston, who had entered the race because he couldn't bear the thought of anyone other than an Englishman being the first man to solo circumnavigate the globe non-stop. But Moitessier, in quitting, won a place in the imagination of the world that Knox-Johnston may only envy. The combined effect of Moitessier's feat, his rejection of the prize money and his chosen failure struck a chord with me and millions of others. This is from *The Long Way*:

> The violent things rumbling within me vanished in the night. I look to the sea, and it answers that I escaped a great danger. I do not want to believe in miracles too much … Yet there are miracles in life. If the weather had stayed bad for a few days longer, with easterly winds, I would be far to the north by now; I would have continued north, sincerely believing it was my destiny, letting myself be carried by the trades like an easy current with no whirlpools or snares, believing it was true … and being wrong. The essential sometimes hangs by a thread. So maybe we should not judge those who give up and those who don't. For the same reason … the thread of the miracle. I nearly gave up. Yet I am the same, before as after.
>
> God created the sea and He painted it blue to make it nice for us. And here I am, at peace, the bow pointed toward the East, when I could be heading north with an unsuspected drama deep inside.

The whole world loves a maverick and the whole world wants the maverick to achieve something nobler than simple rebellion. This was what entranced me about Bernard Moitessier's story. He found redemption out on the road as well as an exit. It wasn't just a feat, it was a transformation.

The travel writing of the last thirty years has come to fill a place in the popular imagination of an era desperate for ritual cleansing. Tim Cahill and Redmond O'Hanlon sell thousands of copies of their accounts of extreme travel. O'Hanlon floats his log raft down a river in Borneo shrieking at the mosquitos; Cahill is malaria-plagued in the Congo and all around is threat and menace. We belly-scratchers sit in our La-Z-Boys and read on, eagerly. Two things compel us — one is the idea of danger but the more moving appeal is the reverberation of this old idea of pilgrimage. Insight through journeying. Transformation through suffering. There is a reason a priest would never prescribe the suffering of the suburbs as penance: alienation and loneliness, boredom, fear, bad marriages and hostile mall kids are not sufficient to scrub us clean. For redemption, what is needed are heat and cold, squalor, vermin and hunger. Off they go, these travellers, into the heart of trouble, and they take us with them, yearning for the film of ennui to be peeled away, preferably by the claws of a jungle cat.

One night on the artillery base I picked up a book that sat on a dusty shelf in the officers' mess. It was Wilfred Thesiger's *Desert, Marsh and Mountain,* in which he writes about the crossings he made of the Empty Quarter in the late forties and early fifties, his travels among the Marsh Arabs of the Euphrates delta and his journeys through Afghanistan. Thesiger is now in his late eighties, the last of the great Arabists, St John Philby, T.E. Lawrence, all long gone. He has spent his entire life walking through that part of the world, and argues for the superiority of such an existence. He holds that the sedentary live less rich lives, are lesser people, than the nomad and the traveller. I read his argument and found it uncomfortably persuasive:

For untold centuries the Bedu lived in the desert; they lived there from choice. The great nomad tribes of the north could have dis-possessed at any time the cultivators of Syria or Iraq; bin Kabina or bin Ghabaisha could have settled in the valley of the Hadhramaut. All of them would have scorned this easier life of lesser men. Valuing freedom above all else, they took a fierce pride in the very hardship of their lives, forcing unwilling recognition of their superiority on the townsmen and villagers who feared, hated and affected to despise them. Even today there is no Arab, however sophisticated, who would not proudly claim Bedu lineage.

I fled my olive-drab tedium through the pages and pages of walking across deserts and through jungles and smoky bazaars. I spent most of my last year on that base slapping imaginary mosquitos and listening to the distant wail of the *muezzin*.

I read Eric Newby's *A Short Walk in the Hindu Kush*, which details an unsuccessful attempt to climb a twenty-thousand-foot mountain by the author and a friend of his, neither of whom were experienced climbers, but who had audacity, determination and humour to spare. I was delighted by Newby's account of a chance meeting with Thesiger high in those mountains.

[Thesiger is] a remarkable throwback to the Victorian era, a fluent speaker of Arabic, a very brave man, who has twice crossed the Empty Quarter and, apart from a few weeks every year, has passed his entire life among primitive peoples. [...] A great, long-striding crag of a man, with an outcrop for a nose and bushy eyebrows, forty-five years old and hard as nails, in an old tweed jacket of the sort worn by Eton boys, a pair of thin grey cotton trousers, rope-soled Persian slippers and a woolen cap comforter.

"Turn round," he said, "you'll stay the night with us. We're going to kill some chickens."

This is Thesiger's version of the same meeting, in *Desert, Marsh and Mountain*:

I travelled up the Panjshir valley towards the Chamar pass leading at sixteen thousand six hundred feet into Nuristan. One evening I encountered two exhausted Englishmen: desiccated, wind-chapped, lame, with bandaged hands, they looked in thoroughly bad shape.

Eric Newby and Hugh Carless were returning from their valiant attempt to climb with inadequate equipment the twenty-thousand-foot Mir Samir, that loomed at the head of the valley. We camped together and Newby included an amusing description of our meeting in *A Short Walk in the Hindu Kush*.

The Great Works of Travel Literature became for me instructional texts. The questions about endurance, loneliness, self-reliance and alienation raised by Newby, Durrell, Thesiger and Robert Byron, among others, seemed to me to be more explicitly addressed than by any number of pep talks from my friends in bars on Sunday nights. The capacity to endure that windswept and desolate artillery base seemed trivial next to Apsley Cherry-Garrard's forbearance across turn-of-the-century Antarctica in *The Worst Journey in the World*.

The first thing that will strike you is that the sea, now frozen in the bays though still unfrozen in the open sound, flows in nearly to your feet. The second, that though the sea stretches back for nearly twenty miles, yet the horizon shows land or ice in every direction. For a ship this is a cul-de-sac, as Ross found seventy years ago. But as soon as you have grasped these two facts your whole attention will be riveted to the amazing sight on your left. Here are the southern slopes of Erebus; but how different from those which you have lately seen. Northwards they fell in broad calm lines to a beautiful stately cliff which edged the sea. But here — all the epithets and all the adjectives which denote chaotic immensity could not adequately tell of them. Visualize a torrent ten miles long and twenty miles broad; imagine it falling over mountainous rocks and tumbling over itself in giant waves; imagine it arrested in the twinkling of an eye, frozen and white. Countless blizzards have swept their drifts over it, but have failed to hide it. And it continues to move. As you stand in the still cold air you may sometimes hear the silence broken by the sharp reports as the cold contracts or its own weight splits it. Nature is tearing up that ice as human beings tear paper.

I could endure my little army house on the winter prairie a few months more.

At this point my ambition extended only as far as endurance. I had no immediate prospect of getting on the road myself and wanted only to know that the cold and the snow and the featurelessness of my present life just wasn't as bad as I thought. Following the promise of Colder and Bleaker even than Manitoba, I continued on after *The Worst Journey in the World* to Bruce Chatwin's *In Patagonia*. Here, the ideas of coldness and expansive emptiness are the subjects of the book as much as the South American setting they reside in. *In Patagonia* introduced me to Chatwin's ideas about the nobility and the redemptive power of open spaces and of movement. Then I read his *Songlines* and I was done for.

The songlines, or dreaming tracks, of the aboriginal Australians serve as a springboard for Chatwin to launch into his real topic, his contention that humans are most themselves and most at peace when they are walking steadily. Cities enervate and bore us. Hierarchies are the invention of builders rather than wanderers, as are materialism and greed. Covetousness is a losing game when one already has enough to carry.

> Natural Selection has designed us — from the structure of our brain-cells to the structure of our big toe — for a career of seasonal journeys *on foot* through a blistering land of thorn-scrub or desert.
>
> If this were so; if the desert were "home"; if our instincts were forged in the desert; to survive the rigours of the desert — then it is easier to understand why greener pastures pall on us; why possessions exhaust us ...

Travelling light as a prescription for modern-day malaise: the idea itself was not new, and had already been espoused by Thesiger and almost anyone else who has been moved to tell a story about a trip. Thesiger saw clearly the beauty of the Bedu, Moitessier loved the sea and his boat, and both were changed by their experiences, which each assumed to be particular to themselves. But Chatwin moved quickly from the specific to the general. Humanity's essential nature, he argued, lay in motion, in nomadism and transience. The further a people moves away from that original fact, the worse it is, the less it becomes. One quarter of adults in Western cities are diagnosed with major depressions in their lifetimes and a third of us live alone — does anyone doubt that things are seriously amiss?

Chatwin's favourite landscapes were the bleakest, because, for him, the less there was to distract one from the process of putting one foot in front of the other the better. The most important thing was the tranquilizing repetition of this act, and the ability to contemplate plainly one's independence from houses, from home. In this, Chatwin argued, we return to the essence of ourselves, and can understand our world and our place in it in a way forever denied a city-dweller. The difference between Chatwin and Moitessier, Thesiger and the others was that Chatwin saw transformation as lying within the act of motion itself, not exclusively in the physical power and force-of-will of the traveller. Reading Chatwin, redemption and transcendence seemed for the first time achievable. "I could go for a long walk," I thought to myself, "and the next day keep walking."

Looking back, I think that after reading Chatwin it became inevitable that I would set out for a blank horizon and an inhospitable environment. But a desire for withdrawal into desolate topography comes from some place other than a writer's evocative suggestion. And is fed by something other than optimism.

In the bright sun and the heat, we spent days at a stretch supine in the cockpit, sleeping under our hats as our bellies browned. We read and we listened to birds of every size and shape crying and dipping and soaring. Even two thousand miles from shore, there were tiny little sparrow-like things that flitted along the surface of the ocean and grabbed whatever it was that they ate out of the wave-tops.

A booby bird perched for three days on the mizzen-mast. I became aware of his presence when a three-inch white and aromatic splatter appeared abruptly in the pages of *A Passage to India*. Right in the Malabar Caves. That bird spent most of the time he was our guest shitting in the cockpit. Don and I leapt to the sides, out of the field of fire except when the boat rolled oddly or the wind swept his projectiles to one side. We began shouting at him. The bird had been flying since Mexico and I felt ungenerous to be troubling him, but the third or fourth splat of what had once been anchovies wore out my benevolence. It looked like a gallon jar of vanilla milkshake had been spilt in the cockpit. Finally we took to throwing potato peels at him and he moved to the bow. There he remained, the foredeck now streaked with white ooze. I thought the bird must be sick, to remain so long at perch, but then I thought that if I was this far from land and saw a place where I could rest, I would rest a long time.

CHAPTER FOUR

Paris, Manitoba

I REMEMBER LYING in the cockpit nearly naked and staring up at the night sky. Left unoccupied, my thoughts circled often around our loneliness. It didn't matter that it would have been impossible for either of us to have remained with the women we were missing (and progressively distorting in our memory until they existed only out there at sea, at night: souls so fine songbirds alighted on their outstretched hands). What did matter was that these were failures.

On a small unlit boat at sea at night, our minds turned inward to gnaw at those memories until the appreciation of the beauty and the ache involved was more acute than it ever had been before we left. A pair more evolved than us might have been grateful for the opportunity but Don and I became caricatures of disconsolate self-absorption. We staggered around the *Sea Mouse* from berth to cockpit seat sighing grandly and staring off into the middle distance. We rarely spoke explicitly of one another's recent history, but it was at all times clear what we were thinking about. We each lost weight and grew preposterous-looking beards.

In an attempt to rein in my self-pity, to think about anyone other than the woman I was missing, I thought about Catherine, about how disappointed she had been in me. I thought she had a much harder road in front of her than I had. "Catherine," I thought, "Catherine has it worse: lonely, hiding from her husband, abandoned by the people she thought were her friends."

> *She wanted something pretty in her hand to take away the memory of the room and the Arabs and the dreary cafés and the messy affairs [...] She paid for the violets and noticed as she did so that the little scene — accepting the flowers, paying for them — had the gentle nostalgic air of something past [...] She would forget the rain and her unshared confusion and loneliness, and remember instead the Paris of films, the street lamps with their tinsel icicles, the funny concert hall where the ceiling collapsed, and there would be, at last, a coherent picture, accurate but untrue [...] and, after a while, mercifully removed in time, she would remember it and describe it and finally believe it as it had never been at all.*
>
> MAVIS GALLANT, *The Other Paris*

The summer I'd arrived on the artillery base I'd been on call every other week. One slow afternoon early in the summer, I'd been home ironing my uniform shirt when my beeper went off. My telephone had not been hooked up yet and so I put on my shirt and drove to work. The hospital, which had attended to little more than broken knuckles and sexually transmitted diseases for twenty years, was twitching with collective panic. Among the mobile homes and trailers clustered around the camp gates — home to

ex–soldiers and civilian support staff who worked on the base —
a disliked and eccentric retired army cook had decided to use his
goose gun to show his neighbour a thing or two.

The military ambulance arrived at the scene fifteen or twenty
minutes later. The neighbour's leg was shot through. The medic,
who had spent twenty years in a peacetime army taking penile swabs
from initially boisterous and subsequently embarrassed young men,
had never seen anything like this. He covered the spurting knee
with a bandage and sent the wounded man into Brandon, the closest town. The ambulance was pulling out just as I arrived. When
the emergency nurses in Brandon removed the bandage, the puddle of blood extended to the walls of the ambulance. The neighbour was dead. He was fifty-four.

His daughter was lying where she had fallen with a fist-sized
hole between her breasts. Her little boy was being restrained by his
grandmother. I looked at them as I kneeled beside the young
woman. Tendrils of grey lung poked through the hole in her shirt.
The boy yelled when I felt her groin for a pulse. We started chest
compressions. I started an IV and put a tube down her throat to
pump oxygen in and out of her lungs. Red froth came up the clear
plastic tube. We loaded her into a second ambulance and radioed
ahead to Brandon for a thoracic surgeon. He was waiting for us
when we arrived. He stuck his hand in through the hole. "The
right atrium's gone," he said to me, shrugging. They were just in
the process of abandoning resuscitative efforts on her father.

I saw the child in town a couple of times later; he always
seemed fussy and clingy; his grandmother seemed not to notice
either of us.

When my beeper had gone off, while the medic had been trying to cope with that spurting artery, I was ironing my shirt. I
remember being pleased that I was finally getting the hang of doing
the sleeves, army guys were always going on about sleeves. I got in
my car and drove to the hospital. I'd had no idea what was going
on at the camp gates. It wouldn't have made any difference for the

daughter, of course. But what her father had needed was an IV and a tight bandage. I was twenty-five years old that year. When I bought suits I took my mother with me. I was a captain. My uniform hung on me like it was made of stretched Plasticine.

That first winter in Shilo after the shootings was when I began to yearn to see Paris. The Hemingway in the officers' mess library led me to the memoirs of Kay Boyle and Morley Callaghan. In those accounts of that city in the twenties there was exuberance not much in evidence on my artillery base. My day's work typically involved a half-dozen sprained ankles and penile discharges, in varying combinations. I usually finished by nine in the morning. Afterwards I dozed and daydreamed at my desk. The image of the young woman's shattered chest and her father, the colour of frozen bacon fat, appeared often before me. I just kept thinking about it.

Searching for something kinder to think about, I became preoccupied with reading expatriate descriptions of Paris. The city is inevitably described as a sanctuary, tolerant of libertines and sophisticated in its pleasures. Paris is itself a *bon vivant*, believing that pleasure is a pleasure and suffering to no worthwhile end is madness. To its expatriate Americans, its English, its Irish, Paris is the opposite of the dour and pious winter-cities that prod writer after writer to discover unashamed beauty in the City of Light.

It is a lovely idea. And to the extent that places in literature do exist, the creation of Paris is maybe one of the finest achievements of Anglo-Saxon literature and culture. I found it best to avoid descriptions of the similarly named city in French literature, as in de Maupassant's *The Necklace*. Or Flaubert. Better by far to stick with the memoirists of the twenties and thirties, writing in English their hazy and soft-focused tales of drinking and laughing shrilly until unconsciousness supervenes. I imagined myself smiling archly at the witticisms of my Argentine friend Julio as he regaled a crowd of similarly clever young men and women, all of us in rumpled cotton and airs of worldly sophistication. *Un autre vin chaud, s'il vous plaît, Michel? Oh, pas pire, toi? Ha ha ha!*

As I sat in my examination room that winter, still haunted by images of a dead woman on parched brown grass, my dream world grew increasingly vivid and detailed: Parc St-Cloud and Beaubourg and the Marais and the Bois de Boulogne.

Sitting in the one coffee shop in the one strip mall on the base I read magazines, drank thin coffee and listened to the cacophony of the video arcade and the soldiers' children and wives. The poor wives — overweight and bored, every limb weighed down by another child — saw sympathy in my eyes. I learned this in a succession of increasingly distressing encounters. I also learned to stop doing house calls. On Wednesdays at the gymnasium there was movie night and before introducing the next action hero the theatre played "God Save the Queen." The audience stood and sang along, the men in crewcuts and golf shirts, standing straight and muscular and holding their arms tightly against their track pants. The women stood similarly erect, their arms tight against their slacks. It seemed entirely conceivable that after twenty years here, a man could snap.

All romanticism aside, Paris is at least not that.

My second summer in Shilo I was granted a month-long leave. The regiment was scheduled to be posted to Cyprus the following summer and officers had been encouraged to take their annual leave prior to the preparations for the deployment to the Mediterranean. "As good an excuse as any," I thought, "to get out of this fly-blown and thudding expanse."

I flew to Paris. I took a room at the Hôtel du Palais on rue de Rivoli near pont St-Michel for a hundred and ten francs a night. So pleased with myself was I at having proved that you could stay cheaply in that city, I was blind to the stains on the floor and the stench in the toilet. I don't think I have ever been so much from the Canadian prairie as I was that night, taking delight from Paris mostly because of the price I was paying for my room.

It was August and so hot and damp that the street garbage smelled like rotted meat and the wallpaper glue in my room gave out, sending curls of sticky paper rolling down onto my bed. The heat elicited an odour from the mattress and sheets that spoke eloquently of their history.

There were windows giving out onto the Seine and a skylight that, by the grace of all that was holy, opened. I raised it and peered around: a dozen Scandinavians had pulled their sheets up to the roof to sweat the night away underneath a grey Parisian moon and a breeze smelling of raw cheese and motorcycles. Across the street from us, along quai de St-Michel, the prostitutes wandered up and down the *fleuve*; we listened to their business all night long. The couple next door were inspired by the Gallic exhortations — slippery-as-soap skin and head-on-bedframe thumping enthusiasm — and only in Manitoba do I remember being as lonely as I was that first night in Paris.

The citizens seemed to me aloof and faintly offended at the presence of me and all the other tastelessly dressed tourists in their city, but there were less critical Czechs and Croatians and Poles in the cafés I stumbled on, and Americans. I met a blues singer named Rene, from New Orleans. He had been in the American army in Germany until the year before. He was intensely nostalgic about his time in the army and when he learned of my circumstances he seized me like a comrade. I couldn't for the life of me fathom his affection for his time in olive drab, but when I pointed out the awfulness of it — the food, the stupidity, the homogeneity — he savoured every detail and smiled. There's nothing you can do with a guy like that.

We were eating at a café called Le Mazet, on rue St-André-des-Arts, near the river off boulevard St-Michel, when a woman approached our table. She was looking for one of Rene's fellow musicians. Rene said he hadn't seen him. Her name was Catherine.

"This is my friend Kelvin."

"Pleased to meet you."

"And you."

She sat.

"You're from Canada?"

"Yes, Manitoba, that's sort of the middle of it … just here for a few weeks … no, then home … yes, I like Paris a lot."

Her rapid and evidently unflattering assessment of me completed, she turned to talk with Rene. I thumbed the copy of *Bitter Lemons* I had bought at a used bookstore that afternoon. It was almost my last night in Paris. I listened to their conversation for another hour or so and then I paid for my drinks and went home.

The bookstore from which I'd purchased *Bitter Lemons* was the famous Shakespeare and Company, on quai aux Fleurs, on the Left Bank. I had wandered into that part of the city after my sleepless first night and found myself trading smiles with American college kids and flipping through yellowing copies of beatnik poetry. A man named George Whitman ran the store. He was in his seventies and even he didn't understand how the filing system applied to the dusty stacks — it was like a hedge maze with vertigo.

He had opened the bookstore in the fifties, modelling it after the original run by Sylvia Beach and her lover Adrienne Monier in the late twenties on place de l'Odéon. Beach's shop was an institution in the expatriate writing community. She was the first publisher of Joyce's *Ulysses* and was friends with Eliot, Pound, Gertrude Stein and many of the other writers who would later dominate the literature of the time. Hemingway devotes long affectionate passages to her in *A Moveable Feast*.

When Whitman opened his bookstore, Beach's had been closed for more than twenty years. Whitman, a young man then, wandered into Paris with this idea: he would resurrect Shakespeare and Company, but this time on the quai near the tourist hotels, rather than place de l'Odéon. And on the walls he would hang up some pictures of Pound and Hemingway and Joyce standing in the original store; it would be as if the old bookstore had never closed. The Paris of Anglo-Saxon literature would have a physical incarnation, and if the Idahoan dentists and Californian school teachers preferred, they could imagine that the city of literature was right there, had never been absent. La Coupole and the café La Rotonde were open again, and filled with awkward young men and women scratching in their journals.

Above the main bookstore is a large and darkened room called the Sylvia Beach Memorial Library and it was possible to sit up there for hours reading unsold and mostly unsalable tomes. Its windows looked out over the muddy waters of the Seine, whose plodding barges bellowed beneath the bright light and sculpted stone. It was so beautiful. The room was nearly always empty and it felt like I could stay there forever. Below, someone hollered in New York indignation:

"What do you mean you don't take Visa?"

I sunk deeper into the overstuffed and wheezing armchair and the account of traditional sub-Saharan metallurgy I was reading. Nobody seemed to know I was there. As far as the army was concerned, that month, I didn't exist.

When I had mentioned the bookstore to Catherine she had expressed skepticism about the place and its authenticity. At first I thought she was being snobby but after my pilgrimages to La Rotonde and Le Dôme, it became clear to me that there was a point in recognizing the places in the city that had been manufactured for tourists. Those places felt false. Their overpriced and cautious menus gave them away, as did the roomful of naïfs like me, gawking at the walls in wonder and expecting F. Scott Fitzgerald to stagger in at any moment with Zelda on his arm.

But the Sylvia Beach Memorial Library was comfortable and pleasant and what did it matter that it didn't really have all that much to do with the original? The authentic truth was that I was a soldier from Manitoba. Here's to the false, I thought, as I sat up there, slowly turning pages and breathing in book mould.

The Royal Canadian Horse Artillery hasn't used horses in sixty years yet its officers still wear spurs on their boots at formal dinners. Army officers believe that their existence is justified by the deeds of their forebears and they cling to that past with self-interested tenacity. In their scarlet uniforms with polished riding boots — watch the furniture now, remember the spurs — they look at one another approvingly and imagine their lives tinged with a vicarious glamour. The next day they don their olive drab and climb into their self-propelled howitzers and roar away in a black and sour cloud of diesel smoke. Locked inside their turrets, they study maps by the green glowing light and record firing instructions from the radio. They load their guns and blow chunks of sod high into the air. They imagine they are preparing for the assault at Amiens, or Ypres, or on the Falais Gap. They make up scenarios that are read to the entire regiment before these exercises: how they are defending themselves against the uncapitalized red army (we are blue, all of us) or — in the spirit of glasnost — the Phantasians. Three motor-rifle divisions are headed our way and only we can save all that is Good.

Every bit of colour and grandeur in the lives of these men is borrowed from eras that are either a hundred years past or have never been. They misrepresent their own lives to themselves for the sake of vanity and for the sake of having a sense of purpose. Every peacetime army is like this.

A week after my return from Paris I came home to find a message on my answering machine from the woman I had met with Rene. I hadn't expected her to even remember my name. I listened to the message standing in my study, still wearing my combat uniform. Then I sat down at my desk with the front pages of the telephone book, trying to figure out how to phone Paris. *Paris.* I pressed one number after another and soon I heard a distant and unfamiliar ring.

Her voice on the telephone had a slow sensuality that, in my snow-swept gulag, soon had me entranced. She told me she was married to an American lawyer, had studied at Harvard, had a six-year-old son, and had won a fellowship of some sort to work on a Lorca translation project. That's what had brought her to Paris in the first place.

Our calls soon became a regular ritual and it wasn't long before the details of our lives were sketched out for each other. Her husband lived in Paris, too, but not with her. And each day, while her son attended the little public school at the end of her street, she walked through the parks and wrote stories that she intended to start mailing off any day now. She said she felt like she was still an undergraduate, still had no idea what she would do that was important. Apart from her child, she meant. She ate at cafés every day and she wrote many letters. That winter, most of the letters were to me.

The letters were amazing things: four or ten or twenty pages long, they arrived weekly and then daily and then at times even three or four a day. Every detail about them and about Catherine delighted me; the envelopes were thick vanilla-coloured cotton and her script was flowing and smooth, written in fountain pen, in brown or green ink. She told me of the little bump on the middle finger of her right hand, where the pen sat, and I imagined it. She sent me dead leaves from the Luxembourg gardens. Drawings by her child. Photos of her and her child. (Taken by whom?) She out-wrote me by a margin of ten to one and when these piles of mail would reach me at the regimental medical section, my sergeant would raise his eyebrows as he dropped them on my desk. Another batch of letters from Paris, sir. I'd nod my head and he'd wait for me to say something but I never did.

That's how the winter progressed — my telephone bills ballooned and in the mornings I was almost always late for work, usually stuporous from the hours-long conversation in the middle of the previous night. The box in which I saved Catherine's letters was filled. And then another.

Later in the winter she told me that originally she had doubted my account of myself, and wondered if I wasn't in fact a patient at a psychiatric hospital with an elaborate fantasy life. Rural Manitoban doctor indeed.

How did she account for the fact that we had met in Paris? I asked. There is no shortage of travelling lunatics, she replied. And, anyway, why couldn't she call me at work, if my work days were as slow as I said?

"That brings up something I've been meaning to talk about."

"What?"

"Well, I practise medicine here in the country like I said …"

"Yes …"

"But the thing I didn't tell you was that I'm in the army." Crackling transatlantic transmission noise.

"Why haven't you mentioned this before now?"

"Because I wish it weren't true."

"Yes."

Then I told her about the regiment and the base and the clapboard shacks. And I told her about the shootings and how I couldn't forget them. She listened without saying much. What else wasn't I telling her? Nothing, I said. When she hung up it was not at all clear if I would hear from her again.

A week passed and then a letter, halting and brief. I replied. Another arrived. Anything can be overlooked, especially if you can't see it.

But the matter could be sustained through letters and telephone calls for only a limited time; by February there was weeping over the telephone and frustration dominated our conversations. I finagled another week of leave in March and flew to Paris. She asked me once on the phone if I remembered what she looked like. As real as Memorex, I said, praying she didn't ask for specifics. She said to meet her on the pont de l'Archevêché behind Notre-Dame at eight in the morning. Bring me a present, she said.

I was half an hour early and sat on the bridge with my suitcase at my feet. Parisians walked along the river, striking melancholic poses. What in Christ was I *doing* here? I wondered. What time did Paris get going in the morning? It was Sunday. Across the bridge, along the river, a fat woman was walking a dog, and another was strolling with a young girl. No, she didn't have a dog and only had the one son. Wasn't that right? I was certain it was.

And then a woman in a long skirt and man's blazer came walking across the bridge. She looked older and more beautiful than I recalled, tall and thin and frightened in the cold-for-Paris March morning. She had little oranges, which she called clementines, with her. I ate them. I gave her a bottle of maple syrup. She had reserved a hotel room for me. We went there in the shadow of Notre-Dame, Hôtel Henri Quatrième, tiny little rooms in tongue-like projections off a sloped and suspicious-looking winding wooden staircase. I followed her up the stairs.

Eventually we slept. Her husband and child were arriving at the Gare de l'Est that night, she had to get going. She'd be back later that night, just rest here. There's a good café nearby if you get hungry, called L'Ail Fourni, you can get supper there for forty francs, do you need French money?

I fell back to sleep, poleaxed. I had worked in the emergency room the night before leaving and I had not been able to sleep on the plane. Then she knocked on the door and it was dark and I croaked hello and she came in and I was stuporous, with purple smudges under each eye and my mouth tasting ugly. She looked at me briefly and strode to the opposite corner of the room to open the window. She lifted the shade and turned and tapped her toe. You haven't gotten up yet. It was ten p.m. No. She remembered me as slimmer. Oh, that's just because I'm slumping here. Maybe I should come back after you've dressed. No stay. All right, I'll run a bath for you. I rose and yawned. Excuse me. She averted her eyes and held her mouth tightly.

The next afternoon she took me to meet her son. We stood on rue de Buci watching him walking home from school. When he spotted us he squinted at me. I wondered if he needed spectacles.

When he was still fifty feet away Catherine whispered quickly, "We can't call you Kevin, Frank's heard me mention your name on the telephone and it'll get back to him. What do you want your name to be?" I gaped at her. "Stephano," she said. And then he was there. How was your day, sweetie? This is my friend Stephano, will you shake hands with him?

The child's name was Sam and he was smart and lively. The two of us got along well, so long as I walked on the other side of him from his mother. While Catherine cooked us supper that night Sam and I played toro with a three-hundred-dollar Hermès silk scarf as a cape.

I hadn't understood how wealthy she was. We'd avoided the topic because she was embarrassed by the privilege she enjoyed and also because she thought that I would disdain her ease of life. I should have guessed — who is able to live in the Left Bank, in the *sixième*, no less, and not work, after all? And what about the constant trips to Corsica and the Alps? As an abstraction, the fact of her wealth was less important and less obvious than it was in my face. And it was true, like some rigid-jawed Presbyterian, I was appalled by the idea that she didn't work yet had a maid who'd be in to wash our supper dishes.

That day the maid had been sick. The apartment was chaotic and mad: dishes were piled high in the kitchen and hampers of laundry were spread out in the living room. The place felt to me by turns vibrant and neglected. She really did see herself as a student, bringing up her son by herself in her crowded apartment filled with papers and books and toys. When I listened to her now I could see why. Her gaiety and easy laughter, and the way that she conceived of her life, the succession of lovers she had taken, hopelessly doomed affairs with alcoholic but charming-sounding poets — all these were the actions and thoughts of a woman not at all cynical or world-weary.

She had a resilient beauty that was more striking for her not being twenty-two. There were small wrinkles around her eyes and her neck was straight and she did not slouch even a little bit. Her hair was straight and hung to her shoulders. She spoke with an intelligence and precision that testified to rather than betrayed her age. Yet for all that, there was what I took to be a wilful naïveté about her ambitions and the patterns of her days. Her writing, for instance — she seemed to think that it would come to her without forcing it. She was used to that, in every other arena of her life. She was used to being helped, too — her parents, her husband, her trust fund — always there was one agency or another that promised to look after her. The rich all seem young because they are, I thought. Children.

We fought in the Café de la Palette, near rue de Buci. I had gone out that morning, telling her I'd be a few minutes; I wanted to stretch my legs and pick up a paper. At five in the afternoon I was still out. We were to have driven to Chartres that afternoon, to see the cathedral. I ended up at the Musée d'Orsay, looking at the pictures and feeling overwhelmed.

Eventually the guards began ushering me toward the door and I wandered back along the river to pont St-Michel. I grew hungry and I stopped in at the Café de la Palette, which she'd shown me the day before. I was just starting into my ham sandwich when she walked quickly up to me. She stood there as I swallowed my bite. I drank some beer to help it down. I looked up at her.

"You had me wondering about you all day."

I bit into my sandwich.

"This isn't what I expected."

"I think I still have jet lag. I'm not myself."

"I'll say."

We went back to her apartment and cooked supper together. Her husband had Sam for the evening. In the debris of her cramped Parisian kitchen, we cut the vegetables and prepared the fish. We spoke little at first, and then slowly we softened. Neither of us wanted to fight. I had acted appallingly. I apologized again. She asked me how I felt about sauces and fish. I said I liked them.

We overcooked the fish but ate it without saying so. Her husband phoned around ten and I began washing the dishes. I had time to dry them and put them away, then sweep the floor, before she said good night to him.

The next morning she saw me off at the métro station under pont St-Michel. She was frightened-looking again, but still affectionate. It was especially cold for Paris and she wore this purple parka-like thing that I said was nice. The hood was trimmed with a rim of purple fake fur.

Flying into Winnipeg fourteen hours later it was like I had been on the moon. I barely had time to get home and iron my uniform before dashing off to work. I was even later than usual. My sergeant was bristling with impatience. I called out the first name before he could say anything to me and readied my penile swab.

Forty-eight hours after eating coquilles St-Jacques in the Luxembourg gardens I was eating pork and beans out of a tinfoil bag in the back of the ambulance; the regiment was in the field. But I'd also received news that I would be posted to Ottawa that summer and I could have a week in April to find an apartment. In my tent I scratched out a letter to Catherine, proposing that I visit her. Her reply came back a few weeks later: "Drop by any time."

I met her in a café on boulevard St-Michel.

"You did come," she said, as I sat down. She was eating breakfast with her son.

"I did," I said.

"Did you bring me anything?" Sam asked.

I felt my pockets and his eyes lit up.

"No," I said.

His mother looked at me.

We walked Sam to his school then went to the Luxembourg gardens and ate in the café under the plane trees there. It was very cold and Catherine and I each pulled our coats tightly around ourselves. We huddled over a metal table as we drank our coffee and brandy and it was so windy we had to raise our voices to speak. At least it didn't rain.

We talked about the army and the books we were reading. There were frequent long pauses. In those transatlantic conversations we had both imagined that "if only she/he were here" and it wasn't that way at all. She was disappointed about the distance between us. We both thought it was mostly my fault.

We spent the whole week trying to reach across that distance. I didn't feel like I belonged in her world and I thought she had no conception of mine. I remember cutting onions in her kitchen. Socks and underwear were hanging on the frame of a lampshade. The small proportions of the clothes made the lamp seem huge and surreal. She told me that she would like to visit me on the army base; she would even consider moving there. I pretended she was joking. She looked away then and clenched her jaw.

The morning I was supposed to fly home I awoke and looked at Catherine's alarm clock. I wondered what the time difference was, what the real time was, because it couldn't be that late. I ruminated on the question of why they don't just set the clocks in Paris to *Parisian* time. The fog started to lift. They probably do. Oh my God. If I was late getting back to the army they would discover that I hadn't been on any flight to Ottawa.

I dashed as fast as I could to the métro, Catherine running behind me as I sprinted. We kissed hurriedly. I had a pithy goodbye memorized that I had been working on all week and she probably did too but there was no time. We exchanged looks of panic and then a subway car door was hissing open.

I fell into the train and watched as her perplexed face receded. I got to the airport a half hour after my flight had left. The grim woman at the Canadian Airlines desk suggested I go back into Paris and she would see if she could get me onto a flight sometime that week. The army was deploying to Southern Alberta the next day and they thought I was house-hunting in Ottawa. This would be a court martial. I told her I wanted to buy a full-price ticket but that was thousands more than the limit on my credit card. I bought a package of cigarettes, sat down on my little leather suitcase and chain-smoked. I approached the desk again, asking if there wasn't *any flight* that day going *anywhere* in Canada that she could put me on. She said no, firmly. I saw the reflection of myself — hurriedly dressed, unshaven and cigarette-smoking — in her eyes and I knew that I would not be flying out of Paris on Canadian Airlines that day. I returned to my perfect little suitcase and sat down. Then the woman at the Air France desk next to the stern-faced agent walked over to me and touched me on the shoulder, motioning for me to follow. I was led through security and down a hallway and the next thing I knew I was being pushed through a door on an Air France 747, first class to Montreal. I remember trying to thank her and she just smiled and withdrew. The door closed and a voice asked me to put on my seat belt. As the plane took off I drank a glass of champagne and tried to slow my breathing. The film of perspiration that had covered me evaporated. Among all these dourly smiling first-class passengers, I could not deny I had an odour about me. I kept my arms tight to my sides. I counted the hours until I would be on the ground in Canada and able to phone my sergeant to warn him that I was going to be a little late. There I was, leaving Paris and headed back to the army and a two-month field exercise, and all I felt was relief.

I got back just as the trucks were lining up. I saw my sergeant running toward me, fairly foaming at the mouth. I ran into the hospital and changed hurriedly into my combat clothes as the medical section trucks started their engines.

That night we stopped in Saskatchewan at an army base to spend the night. Falling out of the truck after spending eight hours drooling on the shoulder of the man beside me, I walked around in disoriented circles as the medics unloaded their gear. Little clouds of dust sprang up around my feet with each step.

I went for a beer in the officers' mess. I reached into my wallet to pay and pulled out a handful of French francs. I looked up to see the colonel standing there. I looked at my hand and he did too. I put the money in my pocket. I smiled at him. I found some Canadian bills and paid. He said nothing. I walked away, feeling his eyes on my back.

We spent the early summer on exercise in the badlands of Southern Alberta. There were wild horses and rattlesnakes and thousands of pronghorn antelope. I spent most of this time spread-eagled on the top of an ambulance, snoozing in the sun and waiting for nothing at all to happen. Mail came to the regiment irregularly and I was relieved at not being confronted with letters from Paris. Finally I wrote Catherine a letter that said that I was sorry things had been so difficult between us. There was no reply.

When the regiment finally returned to its barracks I telephoned her. I told her I had been in the desert. She asked me what that had been like.

"There were rattlesnakes there."

"So you dropped one in an envelope."

I did not go to Paris again.

We are not as strong or as beautiful or as interesting or as ambitious as we wish we were. George Whitman's bookstore does not publish James Joyce and it is not the crucible for the best writing of this age. And on the whole it is a much less interesting and beautiful place than Sylvia Beach's bookstore was. But an aspiration begins with the conceit that things could be better, and the first step of realizing that aspiration is to pretend that they are.

I was twenty-five and that woman had died from the hole in her chest and I was completely alone; Catherine was surrounded by suffocating ease, her trust fund, her husband and her torpor — both of us were desperate to escape. Escape is always a flight from one truth or another.

On the flat silver ocean Don and I took turns cooking. I became absorbed by porridge and prepared elaborate oatmeal stews, boiled in apple juice, with freshly ground nutmeg and cinnamon. For dinner I experimented with pasta and curried cream sauces made with evaporated milk. Don had once worked in a bakery, and he baked pans of cinnamon buns and loaves of fresh bread. It was pleasant to rise through the companionway and present each other with our creations. Whichever of us was sitting in the cockpit would dip our book and smile and accept the proffered plate.

One night I was on watch, studying the high darkened outlines of clouds retreating as a squall passed over us. The appearance of clouds at night seemed ominous to me, the stars winking out as they are obscured. When the full moon shines, the clouds are backlit, as if in a platinum print. That night the moon was full and bright. As the recent rain retreated and left the air cold and pungent, I watched the pattern of rained-on water progressing across my field of vision and I looked up to see an arc in the sky, a rainbow lit by the moon. A moonbow. It was extraordinarily beautiful and I called Don to come see it. We watched for half an hour before it disappeared.

Because the boat had been so motionless for so long, a whole bioniche of molluscs and anemonae had grown up on the hull and rudder, and little schools of fish darted among the shadows of the boat. At times a larger, darker shadow would slip through and abrupt flashes of silver would sparkle as the smaller fish snapped off in a thousand different directions. In the always-moving water, anything solid becomes a source of life, a reef. We hung over the gunwales for hours studying the creatures living beneath us.

We found ourselves talking like brothers in bunk beds at night, not looking at each other, staring up at the sky. The boat pitched and rolled gently and Don told me that his brother had bought a sailboat from a friend sight unseen and sailed from the Caribbean to the Galapagos and then to Hawaii. Don, in his early twenties, had joined the boat for the trip back to British Columbia. Then, with his earnings as a commercial diver, Don had bought a twenty-eight-foot plywood boat that he had sailed to Hawaii, learning celestial navigation as he went. It took him twenty-six days. He stayed in Hawaii for a year, working in a sailmaker's loft, and then sailed for home. He was at sea for forty-eight days, becalmed in the fog off the coast of Vancouver Island for two weeks. Forty-eight days. On a boat smaller than the *Sea Mouse*. His brother thought that the keel bolts had probably let go. Don had finally drifted into hailing distance of a fishboat and accepted a tow into shore. He laughed as he told me, then I laughed. "Style points are for skiers and yacht-club members," he said. I was grateful for that. At the time, the *Sea Mouse* was over a month at sea herself. Rust streaks ran down her sides in great swaths, jugs were lashed to every secure anchor point, and we looked nothing at all like I had imagined us, sailing the South Pacific strumming our ukuleles.

Going to sea with a stranger has the potential for disaster. I can only imagine what I must have seemed to Don: desperate to get away, ignorant about the sea, easily distracted and referring obliquely to a great heartbreak that, it emerged, was hardly anything at all. I wondered why he agreed to go and then, briefly, my self-absorption let up a bit and I started to imagine his own desperation.

At sea Don was confident and gentle and deeply wise. This was apparent from the beginning, from the first flake of pecan pie. I imagined him finding that confidence on the forty-eight-day passage between Hawaii and the West Coast. When he talked about the weather and about boats and about frailty, whether in hulls or flesh, there was a humility evident that I envied.

But then he'd moved ashore and in with the chickens and nobody else seemed to see that for Don living like that was worse than living on his boat. His wife saw the boat as a toy and a threat. He was astonished but, thinking that what he found beautiful about the sea was contained partly within himself — and wasn't contingent on owning a boat — he sold it.

It wasn't just that she couldn't see how fine he was. He wasn't as fine with her, or even when talking about her. His wisdom and humility disappeared for a while in the suburbs. Away from the margins, the light wasn't strong enough to show his strength. It kept getting absorbed by all that stucco.

It's a wonder everyone hasn't lit out for Montana. What we do to ourselves. The places we choose to live.

We had become blind to our slow progress. When a boat does two knots, you look at the water and wonder if you're moving at all. But it's still fifty miles a day. Not so much — but more than none.

One day we consulted the chart and realized we were only three hundred miles from Oahu. We looked at one another. "Just think," Don said, "if we were in any other boat we'd be three days from land."

"If we were in any other boat we would have been there two weeks ago," I said, not stirring from my horizontal posture, in the cockpit, neck deep in E.M. Forster and idly adjusting the wheel with my foot.

Three days later a thick white smudge appeared on the horizon, south-southwest. Even as the trade-wind cumulus clouds swept

over us in a steady procession, the smudge didn't move at all. The
next day we noticed birds sitting on the water that we'd not seen
before, terns and small songbird-looking things that would abruptly
rise as we approached and dart about the *Sea Mouse*, screeching at
us. We looked at the cloud that still sat steadfastly on the horizon.
It seemed clear that that was where the birds were coming from.
Two days later, a sharp green triangle pushed through the horizon
like a jade arrowhead. Don was the first to spot it. It seemed so
strange, but there it was — land.

That night we were able to pick out flickering street lights by
the surfing beaches and suddenly a thick and sweet scent reached
us, of smoke and food and fires and pollen and lawns. I remembered smelling the sea the first time my family drove to the ocean.
I remembered how fragrant and unfamiliarly sharp the salt water
smelled to me.

We were still fifteen miles away. We could smell land so clearly
it felt like we were in a kitchen where bread was baking. Against
the stars, the dark outline of the mountain rose further up, black
and improbably steep. Little flashes traced the path of cars driving
along the north shore.

"Will you look at that," Don said, crouched on the bow, staring straight ahead.

CHAPTER FIVE

THERE WAS A BAR near the harbour in Waikiki. There were many bars near the harbour in Waikiki. The one I went to first, the Lighthouse, occupied a ground-floor corner of a condo high-rise complex. Next to it was an expensive seafood restaurant; late at night the waiters and cooks stepped outside for air and looked at the tourists. The tourists, in Docksiders and shorts, smiled back. The cooks and waiters looked away. They were locals, and they disliked tourists, as the locals mostly dislike tourists everywhere. I watched the tourists sympathetically. They called to one another in long friendly Midwestern vowels and grouped together protectively. It was very warm and there were palm trees always visible. I looked at the young men and women in backward-facing ball caps and aprons, smoking and leaning against the wall. I waved. They looked away.

Inside the Lighthouse, decorative cotton nets are pinned to particle-board panelled walls. Hurricane lanterns hang from the ceiling and there is a wooden ship's wheel bolted to one wall. A chalkboard spells out, in lovely purple and peach, the purple-and-peach-coloured overpriced drinks they serve there. Behind the carved wooden bar are many small painted mirrors advertising brands of beer. On the tables a laminated card says "Try our cheese-cake!" To its regulars it is the only place like it — which is both the suffocating and heartwarming thing about home.

My new friend Roland showed me this place. A year ago he'd bought a fifty-year-old teak plank-strip cutter, which sat next to the *Sea Mouse* in the harbour. At the time, he was a waiter, he said, had lots of money and loved the idea of buying a boat. He had got her for a good price and thought that the year or two he spent fixing her up would be much of the pleasure she would give him.

It was only after taking possession that he learned just how pleasurable she would be. He had her hauled out to scrape the bottom and put on new antifouling paint. When the gooseneck barnacles had finally been scraped off and the wooden hull had been sanded clean he had just gaped. She was exquisite. Solid teak and richly textured, even bare and raw in the boatyard. Solid *teak*. He kept a photograph of her then, scraped and gleaming. He showed it to anyone who stopped to look upon the subsequent chaos of her decks and, it was true, it was not possible to be un-moved. Having taken possession of her she had taken possession of him, and it was now impossible for him to abandon her.

Which would have been the only way out. Teredos, or ship-worms, had gotten into the rudder and the keelson. These had to be replaced. Roland had had as much of this work done as possi-ble and then when he began running short of money he tried to temporize, cutting out areas of obvious rot and then painting on cans and cans of epoxy. The boat was back in the water now, and he didn't have enough money to do another haul-out. He didn't have enough money to pay rent, which is why he was now living on his boat, among the piles of sawdust and cans of paint. Which is why he had lost his waitering job, which is why we'd ended up at the Lighthouse eating nachos and drinking beer that night in mid-November. Me paying.

Roland was in his late thirties and had an air of ongoing calamity about him. It wasn't possible to suggest to him that he wouldn't succeed with his boat, that it was destroying him. His identity was wrapped up in this rotting boat now. It was all that he was, all that he thought about. The other people on the dock called him "that poor guy with the wooden boat."

A week before I had met him, he had discovered rot almost all the way through the transom. This hadn't changed any of his plans.

The *Sea Mouse* was tied up at the work dock, immediately behind Roland's boat. On the other side of us was a charter deep-sea boat. Beside it, a middle-aged woman lived on a twenty-five foot-wooden sloop with her teenaged sons. Surfboards crammed her cluttered foredeck. She had come over after we had tied up and were waiting for the customs people and asked how the boat had gotten so banged up. We rubbed the toes of our shoes on the dock, still wobbly from the sea, and looked down. "Gale off Oregon," we grumbled, with manly vigour.

She said she wanted to sail up to Alaska some time herself. Her name was Alice and she had an easy manner about her. She lit up a cigarette and offered to show me around Honolulu sometime, if I wanted. "Thanks," I said. She nodded and fanned herself with a copy of *People* magazine.

"Want a smoke?" she added, holding out her pack.

Above the dock sat the Hawaii Prince Hotel. East of it was the Hilton Hawaiian Village, and beyond it a succession of giant hotels lining the beaches of Waikiki like grey dominoes. A sign at the top of the dock declared that the toilet was out of order but that the restrooms of the Hawaii Prince were available if necessary. The Hawaii Prince's lobby was a celebration of pink sandstone and post-modernist lines. I blinked at it. I expected to be escorted out brusquely, but the doorman smiled and pointed out the wash-rooms, which were very clean and cool. I sat on that completely still toilet for far longer than was strictly necessary. I leaned my head against the stone partition and breathed deeply. Lavender. That smell was lavender. I shaved in the sink and dabbed at my filmy grey body with paper towels until I was covered with fuzz.

There were tables in the centre of the lobby and at one of them I saw a copy of *The New York Times*. I began flipping through it. A sleek and immaculately clad Japanese woman approached me. I lay the paper down and was preparing to apologize but she only wanted to know if I would like some coffee, espresso, juice per-haps? Understand: I *stank*. My hair was matted like rotted hay and my shirt and trousers were crisp with sea and body salt. I asked her for a cappuccino. The morning light glowed all through the lobby and huge trains of tourists met their buses out in front, pale skinny-legged Texans in hats and shorts and Iowans in Lands' End everywhere: all around was traffic and noise. But I read the lovely newspaper and savoured that coffee.

Then I walked inshore. Waikiki shrank and dulled very quickly. There were two or three streets of souvenir shops, and then there were fast-food places and convenience stores, and soon after that there were vacant lots and paint-peeling apartment buildings. Ten blocks inshore the buildings were familiarly drab, possessed none of the jittery precision of the beach hotels, and on the steps of the houses and apartments fat men and fat children sat and looked out at the world. The beach hotels were still visible, towering into the air. Beyond and between them, the ocean shone.

I stopped at a coffee shop in a little strip mall, out of sight of the beach and the sea. It was dark in there and air-conditioned. I shivered and read a copy of *Time* magazine. The Arborite tables glowed and the pots of salad fixings beneath the sneeze-guards gleamed with freshly sprayed mist. I was wearing shorts and was so cold my legs turned blue.

I had resolved not to telephone the woman I had been missing but, traitor to my pride, I ended up writing her a letter. It was sufficiently detached, I thought, to make it clear how fine I was. I called some other friends, all of whom were mutual, and bragged about the crossing. I made the gale so fierce that even though lashings on the genoa were numerous and competently tied, they broke and, were it not for my heroic lunge for the sail, that would have been it, the boat would have capsized for sure.

Then, flush with the pleasure of talking to friends, and holding my calling card in one hand and my address book in the other, I dialed her number.

"Oh my," she said, "it's you."

"I crossed the ocean."

"You're in Japan?"

"Well, half the ocean. Hawaii."

"Wow. What's it like?"

"Like *Hawaii Five-O*. Lots of hotels. Women in muumuus, loud shirts, shorts."

"So you're okay."

"I'm great."

"Listen, I can't talk long, I'm on my way to a play."

"Okay."

"But I can talk for a few minutes."

"I don't want to make you late."

"I have a few minutes."

"I'll call back later."

I walked back to the boat, wincing. Roland was standing there looking at the *Sea Mouse*. I told him I wanted to go for a drink. That was when he introduced me to the Lighthouse.

Roland was known at the bar and we found a table in the back and sat down. He told me I looked distracted. I told him I was still getting used to being ashore. He said that he knew nothing about sailing, what it was like out there, at open sea. I told him I had only just learned what I knew. "Like me and fixing my boat up," he said.

"Yes," I said, though I thought there was a huge difference. He had thrown himself completely into his project — for better or worse. I could land a job back home any time I wanted and had taken someone with me who knew all about this boat stuff. He was made of sterner stuff, I thought, and said so.

He said I was flattering him. I denied it. We ordered drinks. I thought about the phone call I had just made.

Roland knew two waitresses: Teri and Toni. Teri surfed the north beaches and once had seen a tiger shark attack. She could speak Japanese and wanted to open a English language school for Japanese business people. Toni was less effusive, less beautiful and easier to talk to. They both liked Roland, found him eccentric, I think, and unthreatening. They took turns sitting down with us and chatting about Roland's boat. They asked me my story and I told them about drinking rum into the early morning with Peter Ericson and his theory about the Vikings spreading the lore of navigation across the uncharted seas. They thought he sounded insane. I told them I thought they had a point. Teri wore a bougainvillea bloom in her hair. Toni said she had always wanted to be out at sea, by herself, clean air, no noise, no problems. We all nodded.

The next day Roland came by the *Sea Mouse* with Eric, a friend of his, and asked me if I wanted to go get something to eat. We walked down to catch a city bus. They had found coupons to a suburban bar that let the possessor eat all he wanted at the buffet as long as he bought a drink. I slunk down in my seat and tried to figure out how I was going to get out of this. Eric was flirting with a young woman a few seats in front of him who was trying hard to brush him off. He leered at her like a lizard. She rang the bell and got off at the next stop. I nearly did as well.

Eric was in his mid-forties and looked older. He had the scanning-all-around mannerisms of someone who has been in trouble and he affected a greasy and exuberant familiarity with me that had me putting my wallet into my front pocket and sitting straighter than I had since basic training. We finally got off the bus and walked into the mall that led to the bar and presented ourselves and our coupons to the doorman. It was a secretaries and salesmen place, all suits, yellow ties and lacy blouses. Cologne hung over the crowd like a pall. Frosted hair and bravado circled one another in courtship dances. The doorman looked at us and our fresh-from-the-boatyard clothes and sandals, then asked if we had any money. Eric put his hand on the man's shoulder and laughed. The man bristled. Roland presented our coupons. The doorman asked where we had gotten them. Eric gave the man ten bucks. We went in.

We sat at a table for six and even as the place filled, people kept their distance. No one even asked to borrow a chair. We went to the buffet and piled our plates high with barbecued spareribs and sat down and ordered beers. Eric started telling his story.

He had been married in Florida, he claimed, and had a home and a little boy. He had been working as a house painter when he got involved with a coke operation. He was mostly just a user, paid a quarter ounce or so for doing deliveries or for keeping lookout. Then one day, he said, he was on the beach and he found a big bag of coke that had been thrown either from a plane or a boat out at sea and had washed up. He took it home and hid it in his garage. He told the guy he'd been working for about the bag and made a deal to sell it to him. There was a double-cross and then there was some shooting and police. He told the police who and what he knew and did only a short jail sentence. But his wife divorced him. The day he was done his jail time he hightailed it to Hawaii and changed his name. He was living on Roland's boat for the time being and had found work painting in one of the malls along the ocean. He was worried, though, because he'd had to take a urine drug test the day before and he wasn't sure he would pass it.

It is difficult to interpret a story like this, when you know that the teller is basically lying to you. Eric was persuasive when he said how much he missed his wife and his son. I was sure he'd had a family and now he didn't. I was glad she'd seen through him and gotten away. Assuming she got away.

But he was a snake. There's a snake under almost any rock you care to tip over, on the waterfront of Honolulu. But *Roland* wasn't a snake. As I watched him listen to Eric's story, I wondered how these two had wound up living together. I imagined it started with Roland feeling lonely, in his little rotting boat, no phone and his friends all afraid of the waterfront. Then someone knocks on the hull.

I admired Roland's devotion to his once-beautiful boat. But his withdrawal into that devotion brought Eric into his life, which could only ever lead to unkindness. One way or another.

It took us two weeks to get around to buying the new gear we needed. Every morning Don and I made lists and resolved to get our errands done. Then we headed out in opposite directions and didn't return until late at night, usually drunk. Every day I promised to make some phone calls to the sailmakers and to rent a car so we could spend the following day doing boat things. Each evening I returned, having spent the day reading magazines in the overly air-conditioned coffee shop and the evening at the movies. Don got sidetracked, too. I don't know how he passed his days; he seemed as embarrassed about his lack of will as I was about mine.

We had both constructed fantasies about ourselves that emphasized self-reliance and disdain for cities and their enervating conveniences. And here we were, clinging to Slurpees and audio-visual stimulation like some South Pacific version of Beavis and Butthead.

I asked Don one morning what he thought our problem was. He looked across the table from me, the same hollowness around the eyes. "We're just tired," he said. "We've only been here a couple of weeks. We're still pretty determined. We just wish we were more determined than we are."

And he got up and walked down the dock, not to reappear until late that night. Drunk again.

Finally we went together to a rent-a-car agency in a strip mall and then drove out to the sail loft that Don had worked in that winter he stayed here on his boat. We needed to repair several of our sails, which had suffered from my education in heavy-weather sailing.

The loft was in an old warehouse in Kehii Lagoon. An industrial park next to the airport where all day long 747s roar a few hundred feet overhead and the whole earth shakes. The ground is littered and parched. Even though it's only a few miles from Waikiki, it's difficult to imagine that it's on the same island. This is where the people who aren't rich keep their boats. There is a passel of small stores selling used marine gear. The people who live on their boats here do not own anything else. It was exactly what we were looking for.

At the sail loft, we climbed some stairs to an open wooden-floored warehouse space; it was satisfyingly musty-smelling and dark. There were six sewing machines in pits in the floor and, around them, stretched sails that were pinned to the floor by awls. A Filipina sat in one corner whirring away and did not look up. In the office a fat man sat on an old chair talking on the telephone. It was very dusty and very hot. The fat man looked over his shoulder at us for a moment and then kicked his office door shut. We could see him inside, his back to us, still talking.

Some time later, he emerged buttoning up his shirt; Don introduced us. The man's name was Gerry. Don reminded him that he had worked for him for a year and Gerry pretended to remember. "Oh yeah," he said, "I thought you looked familiar."

"It's nice to see you again," Don said.

"Yeah. Hey, do you want a job? My apprentice just quit to spend the winter on the North Shore surfing and I'm backed right up on my orders. Five bucks an hour. Maybe six?"

"How long do you think you want to stay in Hawaii?" Don asked me.

I looked back at him, surprised, and then at Gerry and back at Don. This would be a terrible place to get stuck. I said I wanted to get going within a few days. Don actually looked disappointed.

"Sorry, Gerry. But can we rent one of your machines for an hour or two, to sew up our own sails?"

"Yeah. Twenty-five bucks an hour, clean up your mess," Gerry said, retreating into his office.

Don stretched out our tattered sails and planned their repairs. He seemed so at ease that I wondered again what it was that had stopped him from taking these qualities home to the chickens. He showed me how to run the machine.

This was the first sewing of fabric I'd been privy to since I was in junior high and was forced to take home economics. I learned that sailmaking is a gracious and beautiful craft that revolves around the business of making curved objects out of flat material and assembling them in a manner that will allow a twenty-four-thousand-pound boat to be pulled along by them. More arcana. I liked it.

Soon the fabric was flowing past Don steadily and the torn seams were joined once again and the sails looked nearly new. We paid Gerry on our way out.

We spent the rest of that day driving right around Oahu, looking out at the sea on our left. We stopped at the surfing beaches and sat down in the sand and drank beer as we watched bronzed young men sliding down the hills of water that broke furiously and then crawled up on the beach. Both of us wanted to be surfers. By this time we had the complexions, if not the deltoids. We watched them until late in the afternoon and then we got into the car and drove back to Honolulu. It was night when we got back to the boat and, at last, it felt like it was time for us to be getting ready to head back to sea. Either that or resign ourselves to spending our lives wishing we were surfers and had larger physiques. And that sandy blond hair they all seem to have. And the lingo. It was a pretty close run there for a few hours.

The next morning we launched into our errands with vigour. Our lovely ash improvised reaching pole from Anacortes had broken the first time the sails had become backwinded and so we decided to buy the more expensive metal one. We also bought electrical wire and extra line and a new anchor. Then we drove to Costco and bought groceries to fill the boat, cans and cans of an iced-coffee drink that we had developed a taste for and plastic bottles of rum and whiskey that smelled like lacquer thinner. Our larder was full again. We were pleased that the gear we'd broken coming down could be replaced. In the Marquesas, we understood, one could buy coconuts and bananas and fine Bordeaux and Camembert, but a new anchor or sail was impossible. So we were lucky to have stopped here.

That night Roland and I walked to the Lighthouse. He had spent the day working on his deck, which leaked terribly with every rain. He had been at this task for weeks and was confident that he had finally solved the problem. He hoped it would rain soon, just so he could know.

Teri and Toni were both working and again they took turns sitting with us and talking about the ocean. They both wanted to go to Tahiti by sea, they said. Teri had been surfing that afternoon and had decided that she wanted to live the rest of her life on the water in a swimsuit. Toni said wait until you're thirty-five and see if that's as appealing. To you or anyone else. Teri laughed. Sort of. Roland and I concentrated on being amiable.

Roland talked about waitering. He had done it for twenty years and quit because he thought he wanted to do something larger, he said. By which he meant fixing up his old wooden boat. "But what's wrong with waitering?" he asked. "Nothing," he said, answering his own question.

The poor guy, I thought.

"I know Paul Theroux," he said. "I saw his books on your boat. He came into the restaurant I worked in all the time."

"He lives here now?"

"Yes."

"What's he like?"

"He tips well. And eats alone a lot."

"Figures," I said.

"From his books, you mean," Roland said.

"Yeah."

"In person he's different. Still cranky, but in a different way. Of course, I just fed him soup."

"Did you read what he had to say about Hawaii, in *Happy Isles*?"

"Yeah. Of course, he *did* move here."

"He must have liked it a little."

"Or liked disliking it."

"Like with his friends."

"And his food," Roland said, rolling his eyes.

I phoned my parents from the bar, forgetting about the time difference, and woke them up. They were pleased to hear from me, had wondered if I had set to sea again without calling them. No, but soon, I said. Then my mother told me that they had gotten a telephone call from a man who said he was a friend of Catherine's and who was wondering if they knew where she was. What did you tell him, I asked. What *could* they tell him — they didn't know her. I told them it was a divorce going badly. My father asked how I thought her husband got *their* number. I told him Catherine knew it, and had used it to find out where I was. I guessed Frank had found it written down somewhere. "This is very strange," my mother said. My father asked me to do anything I could to stop the man from calling again. I phoned Catherine at the number she had given in East Hampton. The woman who answered said she had no idea where she was. I asked if I could leave a message. She said no.

I went back to the table. Roland said he was getting tired. I told him I'd get the bill. He thanked me and left. Toni came by. She said Teri had been asking her when I was leaving.

"Maybe tomorrow," I said.

"Too bad."

"I could postpone."

"Don't be too available," she advised. I spent the rest of that evening smiling widely and invitingly at Teri. She smiled back a couple of times and then avoided looking at me. I stayed there until closing. When I paid the bill Toni handed me her address and told me to write her a letter from Tahiti. I said I would.

"Good night," I said.

I looked over at Teri. She looked puzzled. Then she looked away.

The next morning Don woke me up with a cup of coffee. He looked like he hadn't slept that well. I stared at my reflection in the shaving mirror. I didn't look like I had slept very well either. We looked better than this when we were at sea. Which was saying something. I asked him if he could think of any reason we shouldn't just go then. He said he couldn't.

Then one of us inhaled. The laundry that had been fermenting in the forepeak still needed to be done; it was our last excuse. Don gathered it up in green garbage bags and loaded the bags into the dinghy. He rowed the boat full of pungent clothes over to the fuel dock and laundromat. I started putting breakable things in lockers. It cheered me up immediately. That was a great morning, stowing charts and whistling.

While Don was sitting in the laundromat, a wizened brown man with speckled shorts and a French accent walked in and disdainfully began stuffing his shirts into a washing machine. He sat down beside Don, who had been enjoying the show. He raised his eyebrows at Don, who thought he was flirting, at first. They began exchanging news. His name was Roger, and he had just sailed up from the northernmost of the Line Islands, Palmyra, a thousand miles south of Oahu. He had lived alone there for the last two years. It was very hard, all that time by himself. But he survived. He was strong. And now he was here for a few months, in civilization. If you could call this civilization. He sniffed loudly. Don offered him his handkerchief.

The owners of Palmyra, who lived in Honolulu, paid Roger to stay on the atoll and look after the place. Which was to say, make sure nobody else tried to live there. Which was fine by Roger. He preferred the solitude. It was pure.

Since the end of the Second World War, Palmyra has been a calling point for visiting sailors, about three million frigate birds and no one else. In the mid-seventies there were two widely publicized murders there that spawned a book and a movie. The book was called *And the Sea Will Tell*, by Vincent Bugliosi, which Don had read. (He told me the story as we had drifted toward Hawaii. Staring up at the sky and daydreaming, I hadn't caught all the details. Which was fortunate, as Don told the story three or four times and each time I learned new things.)

It had taken two years on the atoll for Roger to start longing for company more permanent and voluble than visiting yachtsmen. Those *imbeciles*, as Roger termed them, were usually taciturn, remote and too self-involved to carry on a conversation. The first few times a mast had appeared on the horizon, he'd watched hopefully. Then the arrival would come ashore and be unabashedly *disappointed* to see another person, especially one with pretensions to authority, on what was meant to have been an uninhabited atoll. "And I 'ave been dere for two years, talking to de seabirds and dey want me to apologize for spoiling dere trip, most of de time dey won't even leave me any food, just set off after a day or two. Such poor *mannaires* ..."

Then a Canadian sailor named Derrick had arrived on the island and had agreed to supervise while Roger returned to Hawaii to do maintenance on his boat — on the condition that Roger would return within four months and that he would send him some food, as Derrick was running low, and Roger had no supplies to leave him. Derrick also agreed to feed Roger's dogs, which weren't allowed into Hawaii — quarantine and all that.

Roger seemed much more concerned about the welfare of his dogs than he was about Derrick. He asked Don if we could stop off in Palmyra to deliver food to his dogs. And to Derrick.

Don thought it sounded like a great idea. He had always wanted to see the place and here was his chance. He told Roger to come over and see me.

I was sitting in the cockpit of the *Sea Mouse* when Don came rowing back excitedly to the boat. He explained Palmyra all over again, and the place sounded like magic to me. A basically unsettled atoll full of ghosts and relics, a few hundred miles above the equator. Who'd have thought a place like that could still exist? Before Roger ever showed up we had resolved to go there.

When he finally knocked on the hull, I poked my head out and said, "You must be Roger. We'd love to go."

"You must be very careful entering the reef, eet ees very dangerous."

"Have you seen any ghosts?" I replied

"Everyone asks me about the bodies. I think they are in little pieces on the sea floor."

CHAPTER SIX

THE OCEAN SOUTH of Hawaii was very different from the one we had crossed to the north. Don and I both wondered why it was so different — whether it was the fact that it was three weeks later in the season or whether in these waters the winds were just that much more constant and strong. Or whether Hawaii had changed our perspectives. We certainly acted differently. We maybe exchanged twenty words the first two days at sea.

Thirty-five days at sea, only to fetch up on a shoreline of strip malls and McHappy burger wrappers swirling on the pavement: Don and I had gone nowhere. The gloom between us made my gut ache and I stared all around at the sea. I wanted to put my head between my knees and forget all of this. Then a wave rolled the boat from side to side and dishes flew everywhere, smashing all around Don, and both of us clung to whatever was near. The power of the wind and the sea pressed on us like a clamp and, thankfully, made our moods seem trivial.

The first night out, the wind howled steadily at nearly thirty-five knots. No sooner had we cleared the harbour at Waikiki than the boat flew up into the air and down into the trough of the next wave. She did this all night long. We had lost our sea legs and soon we were again nauseous and perspiring. I said that I'd prefer to stay up top and Don nodded and went below, lay down on the cabin sole and covered his head with a blanket. I wondered if he wasn't only making his seasickness worse, but he seemed uninterested in conversation so I left him alone. Later that night, I stuck my head down the hatch — I was thinking of making some tea — and I heard him breathing quickly and jerkily, his whole chest shaking. I retreated back into the cockpit and did without tea for the rest of the night. We had spent perhaps a thousand hours within a few feet of one another, yet I could say nothing. The morning came and I stayed up top, out of Don's way, and shook the reefs out of the sails.

The wind remained very fresh and the boat heeled over to her gunwales and stayed there. Don, lying on the cabin sole; the *Sea Mouse* on her gunwales; me in the cockpit — all of us groaning. We made a hundred and sixty miles that day; it was astounding. The water roiled under the stern and behind us were whirling eddies, spinning and slick until lifted by the next wave train.

"Do you think you're carrying too much sail?" Don called up.

Onward we pounded south, with the wind off our stern and the boat just flying. It seemed impossible that this could be the same vessel that had dribbled its way over from the mainland a month before. Speed in a sailboat at open sea is potent: it is obvious and frightening. The horizon tilts over thirty degrees and ocean starts flying through the air, but there is surprisingly little noise. There is just the wind, which predates the fact of your speed and would be there anyway, and there is the water rushing by the boat, gurgling as it goes. Every other fast thing is loud and exhausting. But sailing fast on the open ocean is like nothing else. When the spray is too much, you go below for an hour to heat up some soup and make some coffee. The boat goes just as fast. It could go on for months. After a while it's easy to feel like a passenger. You just have to hang on.

How hard you have to hang on is partly a function of the strength of the wind, but much more importantly of the angle at which the boat tries to proceed relative to the wind. Every aspect of the experience of being at sea on a sailboat is nuanced by this angle. On this stretch we were doing a close reach — the wind was coming at us nearly perpendicular to our course, just a little in our face. On this tack the *Sea Mouse* charged through the ocean and was stable and comfortable at a nearly constant heel. When we had come down the coast of Oregon, the wind had been right in our faces, and we had been heeled over on our sides for weeks at a time, beating.

The spirit of a boat on a beat is one of forbearance; the boat proceeds slowly, slamming into oncoming waves and nearly stopping completely against the largest of them. Water sweeps back over the boat from the bow and everything and everybody becomes wet. If this was what sailing was like all the time, there wouldn't have been a sailing keel laid down since Watt's day. When we were on a beat for long stretches of time I found that I stopped brushing my teeth and writing in my journal. Instead of cooking we ate beans out of a can and rinsed the spoons in the sea and threw them back in the drawer.

Which is to say, you can go against the weather, but after a while it will take its toll. That sounds whiny, back on shore.

When the wind strikes the boat from slightly behind, is nearly perpendicular to the course but a bit to the stern, this is a broad reach. When the wind strikes the boat from directly behind, this is called running. Most of the open-water work done by small boats is in the direction of the trade winds, westabout, and so the preferred tack is the easiest course: the dead downwind run. On a run, a sailboat seems to move the slowest. Think of it like a river current. Travelling with the current may feel slow, but it is the fastest and easiest way to get anywhere. There is less struggle but more progress. It is the same with the sea and the wind.

The spirit of a boat on a run is one of ease and peace. Running, the *Sea Mouse* flew two headsails only, one from each of her twin forestays, and sailed as straight as a toy pulled on a string. The boat scarcely needed to be steered with her sails set like this and in fact it was difficult to persuade her to maintain any course but dead downwind. With little boat motion, and only the gentlest of winds moving across the deck, this was the country-club-afternoon-cocktail-party of ocean tacks.

On a reach (wind perpendicular to your course) the boat heeled dramatically, and took seas on the beam, from the side, and went very fast. It was often wet, and the *Sea Mouse* was not quite so easily balanced as when she was running but, still, it was possible to set the sails and the wind vane so that she was steady enough. You must remain attentive, however, and gin gimlets are out of the question.

For most of the first two weeks back at sea, the wind was steady off the quarter (broad reach), and the seas were reasonable; the wind vane worked for days at a time, without needing correction. These days were strange. The boat steered herself, surging along quite clearly of her own volition. The sense was that of being on a horse that knew its way home and wanted to be there badly. Our only purpose was to keep the coffee hot and watch for a wind shift or sea change. Which, in the trade winds, is uncommon. We were going exactly where we wanted to go; if there was a concern it was only whether we were going so fast that the rig was being strained. Day after day the boat surged along needing neither attention nor guidance; it became hard to imagine that it ever would. This was a dangerous way to think.

The point when a lot of wind becomes too much wind is a difficult but very important moment to identify. My inattentiveness became clear when the sail started to rip. We were a week out to sea. What on earth was I *thinking* anyway, carrying that much cloth in that wind? At least it wasn't the mast that went. It might have been worse. Idiot.

Most boats at sea will carry five or six headsails to suit precisely the sea conditions. The *Sea Mouse* had two. Since the wind had ripped the big one, we acknowledged the prompt to put up the smaller one. Sailing strategies on the *Sea Mouse* were rarely a sophisticated matter.

I dug out the sail palm and needle and began sewing up the tear. It went so much slower by hand in the cockpit than it had in the sail loft in Hawaii. The sail bunched up in huge wrinkles and my stitching was clumsy and childlike. I chewed on my lip and wrestled to line up the edges of the ripped seam.

The wind grew stronger and spray swept across the deck. The sail nearly went over and into the sea but I caught it at the last moment. The sail was packed away. Too bad. The wind picked up further and veered around until we were beating. I doused the mainsail. The boat settled in on its side and plowed along, slower despite the growing wind because of the mounting seas it kept slamming into. Don finally came up top.

The seas were now too big for the wind vane to steer; we took turns at the helm and were quickly exhausted. After a day and a half of this we pulled down the sails and went below and slept. As we closed up the companionway hatch behind us the rigging shook the whole boat so hard the vibrations could be felt through the hull. For the first time since we had left Oregon behind, I felt cold. Don made tea. We drank it and lay down. It always took me a long time to fall asleep in heavy weather. I wanted to think about something other than sail trim and compass headings. For a while there I was as worn down by the sea as I had been by the artillery regiment. As I had done on my couch on the prairie, I waited for it to pass. Unlike then, it did.

In Hawaii I had bought more Chatwin: *What Am I Doing Here* and *Anatomy of Restlessness.* I bought more Paul Theroux, Jonathan Raban's *Coasting, The Travels of Marco Polo* and Herodotus' *The Histories.* I found a bruised paperback called *Great Novels of E.M. Forster,* which did not include *A Passage to India* and so was suspect enough that it had wound up in the sale bin at the Honolulu Book Store along with calendars that featured the Beaches and Bathing Beauties of the Aloha State. I had carted these books down to the boat by the bagful and Don had looked at me and asked where I thought I was going to put them all, the *Sea Mouse* looking more and more like an overfed *Sea Hamster.*

Before coming ashore in Hawaii, we were already deep into the jungle, at least in our own minds. The cognitive dissonance presented by frozen-yogourt shops on every corner was confusing and disappointing. *We* were adventurers. Where were the gates of Lhasa? Where was Oxiana, under the dunes? After we docked, Don had scampered down the dock to call the Hawaiian friends he had been describing to me affectionately for thirty degrees of latitude and twenty of longitude. I was left standing there, wondering where the prayer platforms were, looking around for something unfamiliar. This will sound naïve. But we had been on the ocean for over a month. I expected the foreign and exotic beauty of the fantasy landscapes from my winters on the artillery base.

And this disappointment was what had left Don so quiet too. In the years since he had last seen his friends, he had come to remember them as exotic and welcoming intimates, not at all like his friends back home, so predictable and familiar. His Hawaiian friends were adventurers too. They did interesting things. Like us. Sailing to see them.

But Don had found those friends working as security guards and bartenders and struggling and failing with their marriages. Over the course of the two weeks we spent there, it wore him down. He didn't complain while we were tied to the dock, but once at sea, it came out. You had to wonder if there was any escape, he said. Whether every place is just like the last one.

"*Place, shmace*," I thought, staring out at the turquoise ocean. It isn't the arrival, it's the journey. And more precisely, the *journeyers*. Us, that is. "Three thousand miles across the North Pacific," I remembered thinking a few days after arriving in Hawaii, straightening the part in my hair and pausing to pluck a long nose hair, "not too bad." Puffing myself up like a tenth-grade tough, I strolled along the dock in Waikiki, casting dismissive glances at all the other pretty boats. "Dock queens," I pronounced them, as I ostensibly examined a detail of rigging design on someone else's boat and paused to exude a little more confident experience and raw throbbing virility. When people spoke to me in the bars by the dockside I took about ten seconds to launch into the gales of the North Pacific. A dentist from Michigan made the mistake of asking me to tell him more and, God help me, I spent an entire afternoon *braying* to him about the relative merits of split rigs versus sloops. I was just starting to get into the Appropriate Mental Attitude for Long Distance Passage-Making when he extricated himself and fled. I looked around and saw irritated faces everywhere within earshot. Briefly chastened, I left that bar and did not return. It took about five minutes for my preposterously swollen ego to reinflate. What Don put up with.

Ego and the traveller: at the end of the twentieth century, even the choice of the word "traveller" drips with vanity. All of us are tourists who can get home from anywhere we want in about eight hours. There is nowhere we can go where our shiny faces, hideous Tilley Hats and too-large nylon packs would be unfamiliar to those being toured. Even if we imagine a place to be exotic, we're not, not any more. But this was an insight unavailable to me at the time. I was sallying forth into the void, seeking knowledge and experience only dreamt of by the Barca Lounger set. Think about those obese, myopic and ancient dogs one sees in the yards of marginal farms, in hill country or the northern edge of the prairie. Trotting out around the rusting cars and gasping furiously at the imagined threat of visitors and at leaves moving in the wind. And young men and women stride off from the suburbs with satellite-navigation systems to guide them across the mountains or the ocean, clad in Gore-Tex, and as safe as anyone not actually *in* a La-Z-Boy.

Out at sea again the self-conscious posturing finally let up a little in the face of rubbery-legged nausea and the absence of an audience. I returned to my reading. I had never been more preoccupied by Chatwin's idea of what the traveller represents to the settled than now, when I had pronounced myself a traveller and not at all settled. And no longer confined, either to a small military-owned bungalow on the Manitoba prairie, or otherwise. Chatwin and his contention that the traveller represents redemption to the houseowner appealed very much to my vanity. I, for one, was pleased to redeem any number of sallow-faced suburban homeowners.

I wanted to bask further in Chatwin's approval and the transcendent superiority of my new existence. I launched into reading all I had been able to get of Chatwin, as we charged south to Palmyra. The bright sun and windburned days receded as I entered another more interior landscape. At sea, I could adopt whichever posture I wanted. There was no one around to roll their eyes and snort. Except Don. Who was thinking about his own stuff.

Chatwin spent much of his adult life walking through deserts in the Andes and Patagonia, Australia, North Africa, China and India. He wrote of these travels with authority, as though he had been born on a migratory trek somewhere on the steppes. The same refrain is repeated over and over: admire the pastoralists, the nomads, and pity yourselves, soulless city-dwellers, owners of objects too heavy and valuable to carry on your person. *Be more like me.* This is from *What Am I Doing Here*.

I went to the Sudan. On camel and foot I trekked my way through
the Red Sea hills and found some unrecorded cave paintings. My
Nomad guide was a Hadendoa, one of Kipling's fuzzy-wuzzies. He
carried a sword, a purse and a pot of scented goat's grease for anointing his hair. He made me feel overburdened and inadequate; and
by the time I returned to England a mood of fierce iconoclasm had
set in.

The complex mixture of ideas that makes Chatwin's ethos so
appealing is present in this short excerpt. Firstly, the nostalgia for
vanished existences — the same thing we find in Tolkien tales
about cabins in the forest — his guide "carried a sword," even. And
the repudiation of materialism that echoes religious asceticism
("trekked my way through the Red Sea hills"), and finally the
promise of veiled and foreign beauty. Scented goat's grease for
anointing his hair. You can practically hear the shouts in the
bazaar, smell the charcoal fires roasting spits of sheep. I closed my
eyes and inhaled deeply.

Don emerged from below to come sit in the cockpit and watch the
ocean fly past. He was still very subdued. I distracted myself with
Chatwin but Don was braver. He seemed to be determined to
understand why he felt the need to move so badly and why he felt
so badly on the move. It was as blue and bright as a postcard from
Greece. We exchanged glances. He stared out at the horizon. I
went back to my book.

It's so easy to fall in love with the author when one loves his book.
I came away from Chatwin persuaded, sold, converted to his religion of restlessness. A whole other way of valuing the world seemed

suddenly clear; that it was a tenable worldview, and possible to live by, was evident in the life of this man Chatwin. Walking through the rain along the coast of southern Chile, and thinking about revolutions. Disdaining possessions and valuing truth.

I should never have read about Chatwin except as he described himself. But out on this ocean, after leaving Hawaii, I also read Paul Theroux's *Granta* essay published shortly after Chatwin died. Theroux seems genuine in his affection, but spends the largest part of the article excoriating Chatwin for all manner of faults — chiefly the details of his life he withheld from the reader.

Later, I read more Theroux and understood that his dyspeptic and corrosive storytelling is directed more typically at himself, and that this is his art, his approach to what he thinks is worth recording. Chatwin's ghost, then, may be flattered that Theroux thought him worth the effort — Naipaul probably isn't. One might have hoped that shared experience would prompt Theroux to be sympathetic to his friend and colleague, but that would be missing the point. There is no collegiality among travellers — each resents at some level or another every other pink-faced ugly-hat-wearer. Each wants to be the only person there, the only person ever to have been there. The urge to travel begins in this desire to get away from people like you. Self-contempt and misanthropy are the parents of peripateticism. The end of the millennium is filled with each.

From Theroux's cruel essay it emerged that Chatwin's life undermined to a great extent his own ideals about mobility and spirituality: he was himself an obsessive collector of objects. In his last few years, he went on lavish sprees in shops in London and Paris, buying jewellery and paintings he couldn't possibly afford, and that his wife would be compelled to return. He was sick then, and dwelling on his manners is ungracious, but the real point is that it was *objects* he was turning to as he became more ill, by all accounts objects of beauty and precision. This is what he had written elsewhere, in *Anatomy of Restlessness*:

Luxury hampers mobility. The nomad leaders knew that overindulgence threatened their system. Civilised ways were insidious. Attila drank from a wooden cup and Chingis Khan lived in a yurt to the end of his days.

Chatwin's relationship with possessions was complicated — he delighted in luxury, its hampering of mobility notwithstanding. In his writing, he reviles what he loved — his misanthropy, like Theroux's, does not spare himself.

As a young man, Chatwin worked for Sotheby's. *What Am I Doing Here* and *Anatomy of Restlessness* both include lively anecdotes from his years with Sotheby's, as an autodidactic art appraiser. At an astonishingly young age, he reminds us, he became a director of that institution. He describes the certainty that he developed very early on, in the judgment and superiority of his "eye."

He is coy about the circumstances behind his departure from Sotheby's; he describes a mysterious ocular ailment that caused him to awake one day "half-blind." No organic cause could be found. Like some Victorian consumptive, our young hero sets off to find health in the open horizons. It wasn't the only time Chatwin described himself as suffering from an improbable-sounding illness; before he died he explained his wasting away as a consequence of having become infected by a Chinese bone fungus. When he died of the more familiar, more lethal AIDS, the lie that may have sounded exotic to him just seemed pathetic and obvious. It is almost as if he didn't want to be believed.

Chatwin was entitled to dissemble about his health — these matters are private. And there is nothing to say that because an author has been untruthful, his book must be too. But as I learned more about him, I became uncomfortable with how completely I had accepted the man's ethos. Chatwin proposed a new way of living and of valuing the world. *Move*, he urged, and the worst of you — your possessions, your position — will be left behind. The best will follow you. Lying about his illness, especially in the early years of the plague, protected him — and his wife — from a malignant and despicable social revulsion, preserving his position. His possessions — well, it is hard to begrudge him the comfort he found as he became confined to his wheelchair and lost his hair. Still, once a prophet has staked out the turf of asceticism, it is always upsetting to watch him return to the tent. Even if you're sitting happily inside it. Much the worse if you've left the tent yourself, and are trying to remain outside.

I reread the introduction to *What Am I Doing Here*: "The word 'story' is intended to alert the reader to the fact that, however closely the narrative may fit the facts, the fictional process has been at work." On the first pass, the statement had hardly seemed outrageous: travel writers *are* the original impressionists. But as I sat there, in the bright hot equatorial sun, sailing south and away from my friends and the places I knew, a question began to gnaw at me about the man and his beautiful ethos and the degree to which it was built on a fantasy of what he wanted his life to be. I had the same fantasy, after all. Chatwin wrote that introduction near the end of his life. Perhaps he was perplexed by how dependent he had ended up being on the city and the place he had found in it. A place that had been accorded him because of the books he had written, condemning the city.

I sat there on my bouncing boat with an intimation of disquiet — if even Chatwin couldn't realize his ideal, what was *I* doing here, emulating him?

In *Granta* Theroux describes Chatwin, "never much of a mountaineer," at a dinner at the Royal Geographical Society, "speaking animatedly about various high mountains he had climbed." Beside him was Lord Hunt, leader of the first successful Everest ascent, and Chris Bonington, conqueror of Nanga Parbat, both of them entranced. "He had plans for further assaults and expeditions — all of them one-man affairs, no oxygen, minimum equipment, rush the summit."

The fact of their entrancement was perhaps what mattered to Chatwin — their experience and knowledge of this world notwithstanding, they were cast into a reverie, a dream world, by him. He was a storyteller.

And in pushing people to climb mountains or sail across oceans storytellers are a part of those adventures. And, anyway, it wasn't like he never left his cork-lined room. He walked across deserts. And moved readers to make all manner of trips themselves.

Chatwin died in 1989 in the arms of his wife. Many people who knew him did not know that he was married. In his autobiographical writing, no reference whatever is made to his sexuality. In the *Granta* piece, Paul Theroux wrote:

> I used to look for links between the chapters, and between two conversations or pieces of geography. Why hadn't he put them in?
>
> "Why do you think it matters?" he said to me.
>
> "Because it's interesting," I said. "And because I think when you're writing a travel book you have to come clean."
>
> This made him laugh, and then he said something that I have always taken to be a pronouncement that was very near to being his motto. He said — he screeched — "I don't believe in coming clean!"

After Don and I had exchanged a total of about five sentences, and a stack of books had been read and placed back on the shelves, the air of intensifying silent preoccupation was at last interrupted by a shriek of wind. A jet of rain flew out of a wall of cloud that had not been there twenty minutes earlier and the boat lurched far over to one side. Don dashed up the companionway and I followed and we raced to the mast to douse the main and genoa and barely made it and the boat righted and the squall just howled. We got below as the air temperature fell and the rain beat the water all around into a froth. We were both soaked and panting.

"Holy smokes," I said.

"Where did that come from?"

"Man, I have no idea."

"It's nice to have something to do for a change."

"How far are we from Palmyra?"

Don got up to plot our position on the chart.

"A hundred miles."

"Jeez, I'm glad something woke us up, we could have plowed right into it."

"Listen, I'm sorry for being so mopey, I don't know what's got into me."

"Shit, don't worry about it, I thought *I* was the one being anti-social."

Night fell and the rain continued like loose change in a washer, the whole cabin top vibrating with its force.

In the morning, we hoisted a small headsail and the mizzen. We crept along and the next day, by the GPS position, we were fifteen miles from Palmyra. We searched the horizon for any sign of land but there were only grey line squalls marching across the sky.

If we were not where we thought we were then the GPS wasn't working and we could be anywhere. Not such a good thought on such a big ocean. Think about *that*. Sudden paralyzing doubt. A low atoll like Palmyra is only visible for ten miles or so, at sea. Think about the navigators with only an astrolabe and no chronometer trying to find an island like this. They could have gone around in circles for weeks, listening for surf by night and scanning the sky by day. And they did. Think about how well we would have done, reading *Celestial Navigation in Ten Easy Steps*, holding the sextant awkwardly and trying to judge the angle from sun to horizon to within a few sixtieths of a degree.

We crept closer and watched very carefully for palm trees and breakers and then finally Don pointed and a grey-green fringe appeared on the horizon. It looked like a streak of mould on the surface of the water.

CHAPTER SEVEN

Wreckage Washed Up

> *In the great quietness of these winter evenings there is one*
> *clock: the sea. Its dim momentum in the mind is the fugue*
> *upon which this writing is made. Empty cadences of sea-*
> *water, licking its own wounds, sulking along the mouths*
> *of the delta, boiling upon these deserted beaches — empty,*
> *forever empty under the gulls: white scribble on the grey,*
> *munched by clouds. If there are ever sails here they die*
> *before the land shadows them. Wreckage washed up on the*
> *pediments of islands, the last crust, eroded by the weather,*
> *stuck in the blue maw of water ... gone!*
>
> LAWRENCE DURRELL, *Justine*

ROGER HAD BEEN careful to draw in the unmarked hazards on our chart of Palmyra. The pass through the reef into the lagoon was dangerous. "You must enter this pass at a heading of forty-three degrees north magnetic," he told us, stabbing the chart with his forefinger for emphasis. He wrote this on the chart.

"Gotcha. Forty-three degrees," I said.

"Magnetic," Don reiterated. Roger appraised us. He was investing a considerable sum of dog food in this voyage.

"There are many broken boats on the reef here, sailboats and freighters, fishboats too. This is not a marked harbour. You must be very careful."

"Very careful," Don said, nodding.

"Of that reef," I added helpfully.

And now here we were. We crept along the outside of the reef looking for the entrance and darting back out to sea when we spotted coral heads until finally Don was certain he had found it. I remained at the helm and waited for the sickening crunch of keel on coral. When we emerged into the still waters of the lagoon we exhaled. We studied the shore. Palm trees hung together over the shining white sand at angles that would not be stable come the next big blow. The sand was unmarked and there were no lights and no buoys. It was very quiet. We wondered if Derrick was still there. It had been more than two months since Roger had left. Looking more closely, we could see white-with-bird-shit concrete blockhouses among the trees. Uninhabited but not unspoiled. Eerie.

Then, at the far end of the lagoon, we saw a little blue boat at anchor. As we cautiously moved toward it, a small rowboat was launched from the shore and a long-haired fat man in his fifties rowed toward us with evident enthusiasm. He was grizzled and deeply tanned and his boat was only just able to hold him. He looked like a hamster riding an oyster shell. He bobbed steadily closer to us.

We motored until he was alongside. He tied up and we helped him aboard. He grinned and grinned. We told him we had food for him, and for the dogs. Derrick said, "Praise Jesus." He showed us where to anchor and we shut off the engine and stood there on deck and studied the island. "Welcome to Palmyra, boys," he said.

"This isn't like anything I've ever seen before," I said.

"I've dreamt of this place for years," Don said.

Derrick looked around at the islands surrounding us. "Me, too." Less enthusiasm, there.

He was from Comox, British Columbia, and he was both delighted and abashed to have company. We climbed into our dinghy and followed him ashore and then sat on the beach and looked around. The *Sea Mouse* rode at her anchor gently. Palmyra is a ring of coral-sand islands surrounding a lagoon. The only thing that

keeps the land above water is the coral reef, which breaks up in big
storms and sends boulders of coral rolling onto the shore. These
boulders, and the sand they quickly turn into, are Palmyra. During
the war the US Navy built a causeway that linked all the islands like
a string through pearls and created a road around the lagoon. The
causeway has subsequently eroded and now a rowboat is the only
way to travel between the islands. The elevation is nowhere more
than fifteen feet above sea level. It would be a bad place to be in a
hurricane.

Palmyra was discovered by the *Betsey*, under Captain Edmond
Fanning, in 1798, after the ship nearly plowed into it in the night.
Fanning did not land, or name the place, but contented himself
with not becoming its understimulated and coconut-eating first
inhabitant. He continued on past, breathing a heavy sigh of relief.
The first landfall was made in 1802 by the crew of the *Palmyra*, an
American trading vessel en route to Manila, under a Captain Sawle.
His crew spent a week exploring. His dispatch relaying news of the
discovery took four years to reach home.

> New island, 05° 52' North, 162° 06' West, with two lagoons, the
> westmost of which is 20 fathoms deep, lies out of the track of most
> navigators passing from America to Asia or Asia to America.

The next landfall was made by the survivors of the *Esperanza*,
a Spanish pirate ship loaded with Incan treasure. Wrecked after a
battle with another ship, its crew managed to off-load the treasure
onto Palmyra. After a year, the survivors built two rafts and set sail
in different directions. One raft was never heard from again. The
other was picked up by an American whaler, with only a single
survivor, who died of pneumonia shortly after his rescue. He lived
long enough to tell his tale, however, and ever since the fate of the

treasure has been speculated upon. No remnant of it has been found.

In 1862 the island was annexed by the king of Hawaii, Kamehameha IV. When Hawaii was in turn annexed by America in 1898, Palmyra was included. In the years since it has mostly been ignored, the lack of fresh surface water impeding its settlement. In the early part of the twentieth century it became the private property of an American family in Hawaii. It was the descendants of this family that had hired Roger. In the thirties, Pan Am used it as a refuelling stop for its Clipper flights to Samoa. When the Second World War broke out, the US Navy built a large base on Palmyra, with a five-thousand-foot runway from which it conducted anti-submarine patrols. The only action the island saw during the war occurred three weeks after the attack on Pearl Harbor, when a Japanese submarine surfaced and shelled a dredger that was building the harbour. The sub was chased away by the shore battery and for the rest of the war bored sailors and pilots played basketball and drank beer and read of the conflagration sweeping the globe.

After the war, the American family who claimed private title to the island sued the navy for its return and was successful. The navy pulled out any equipment it could salvage, and all its men. Within a very few years the little city that had been built there had been reclaimed by the jungle.

When open-ocean sailing became popular after the war, Palmyra became known as a beautiful and very strange waypoint between Hawaii and Samoa. Sailors began making landfall there, and soon the remnants of the old base were covered with graffiti and bullet holes, calling into question Chatwin's notions of the redemptive power of long journeys. Today the buildings from the war have mostly been razed. There are plywood dormitories, however, that were built in the 1970s to house Polynesian workers brought over from Fanning Island, a hundred miles to the east, hired to clear the airfield of the encroaching jungle. These dormitories still stand but the jungle is now creeping up on them. The windows have been broken and rat feces covers the floors. The metal bed frames are rusting. Mildewed pornography lies scattered on the floor, sodden and chewed by the rats.

In the two months he had been there, Derrick had been everywhere on the island. He promised to show us the interesting places in the morning. Mostly, he said, it was desolate. Coral-sand shores and coconut trees, thousands of rats and seabirds. Unrelenting wind and sun. Machine-gun blockhouses, crumbling from the salt water used in the mortar. Don and I thought it sounded intriguing.

"I don't know why you keep using the word 'desolate,'" Don said.

"You'll see in the morning," said Derrick.

The marines had built a cistern to collect rainwater and it still worked. A pipe ran from the cistern to, of all things, a white porcelain bathtub, which sat in the jungle surrounded by ferns and palm trees. You could bathe in fresh and sun-heated water, surrounded by seabirds and coconut crabs. I dug the dead leaves out of the tub and plugged the drain. I turned the tap and rainwater filled the tub. Salt and oil peeled off my skin like a cast-off carapace. I even shaved, in halting bleeding swipes. When I stepped out and dressed I found Don waiting with a towel over one arm. "*Desolate*?" he said. "The man has obviously never seen downtown Nanaimo on a Sunday morning." I smiled and it hurt my abraded face. Don charged at the tub.

Sunset that night over the lagoon: the isolation felt far more profound here than it ever did on the boat. No matter how bleak its surroundings, the boat always carried with it at least the prospect of company. The island, however, had been alone for all but the six war years.

We ate spaghetti in the dark, sitting on the concrete ramp the military had built. Seabirds roared out a steady cacophony and we leaned back on that astonishingly motionless platform, looking at our boats bobbing at anchor.

The remains of the military's stay on the islands were everywhere. Concrete machine-gun emplacements stuck out of the soil, broken crockery, too. Rusting derelict jeeps provided shelter to scurrying rats, which were everywhere. I could see them in the tops of the palm fronds; most of what moved on the island was small, brown and sizably betoothed. Derrick told us that when he had first arrived on Palmyra, he had looked forward to sleeping ashore, but he changed his mind after one night in the hammock.

Palmyra is six degrees of latitude north of the equator; eight degrees north and south of the equator runs the intertropical convergence zone in a band east and west around the world. The merging of the northeast trades of the northern hemisphere with the southeasterlies of the southern creates a stable weather pattern that stays constant even during hurricane season, a band of safety even while the tropical oceans to the north and south churn like a Moulinex. All year long here, it's like summer on the prairie: bright humid wet mornings and towering clouds by lunchtime and cold rain and lightning before supper. The sky closes in and darkens in minutes, right before one's eyes, throat feeling swollen and tight. Then the wind comes. An hour, or two, of wild skies and then everything breaks and the night is clear and cool. Stars like powdered quartz. On the prairies this weather is particular to mid-summer and is experienced as a short and strange time of the year that lets the farmers fix their machinery and rest between hay cuttings. On the ocean this daily progression of weather replaces the sense of seasons, and the whole island turns itself to the sun and then the expected rain. The sense of a year is replaced by the sense of a day, and it's very strange to lose the larger scale of time. Alone on an island populated by rats and coconut crabs, ruined buildings all around — as paradises go, it has a decidedly post-apocalyptic feel to it.

Derrick had spent the first half of his working life as a photographer in the air force, he said, launching into his story without prompting. After he got out of the service he spent twenty years working in a pulp mill on the coast of British Columbia and cultivating an intimate relationship with rye whiskey. He'd hurt his back a couple of years ago and his union got him a disability pension. He retired and his wife fell in love with her boss at the telephone company; in the space of one confusing year she divorced him, his daughter stopped acknowledging his existence, his son started patronizing him. His intimacy with rye whiskey became a passion.

"Oh boy," we thought — just as *we* had finally stopped the long melodramatic gazes out to sea.

He was wiped out financially; she got half his disability pension. The house was sold before he knew it and the only thing he could afford was to live on a boat. So he did. Then he woke up one morning and thought, "Holy Cow," and quit drinking.

Clearly a man of enthusiasms, Derrick devoted that day forward to living as piously as he was able. Bible meetings replaced draught nights and ultimate fighting gave way to prayer-session group hugs and suddenly his life had Meaning. He sat on his boat one night and it came to him: he'd sail down to Mexico to spread the Word. So he did.

But in Mexico they had no use at all for a unilingual Anglophone itinerant lay preacher and they got this across to him pretty quickly. The language barrier notwithstanding. So he loaded up his boat and pointed her at Hawaii. Thought he'd go right around.

About a week out to sea he suffered one of the mishaps that sailors fear the most. He lost his rudder. He told us this and we stopped smirking. At first it was just bent, and he reinforced it with an aluminum pole and that worked for a little while. Then one morning he woke up and the entire apparatus had fallen into the sea.

A boat is three things: a hull, a rig and a rudder. Anything else is optional. This is profound solace when electronic devices are failing, seawater has gotten into the fuel and the curry paste has gone off. But the loss of any of these three essentials is catastrophic.

If you had a choice, the rudder sounds like the one you would choose to lose. It sounds like it would be the easiest of the three to jury rig. Derrick tried everything he could think of to improvise a rudder, but a keel boat under sail generates tremendous forces and he broke lashing after lashing. On the whole, he said, a broken mast would have been much easier to repair. Even a small hole in the hull would conceivably have been tolerable. A small hole.

Without a rudder it isn't possible to sail close to the wind; it becomes very difficult to follow any heading at all except for vaguely downwind. The prevailing wind in the tropical ocean is out of the east — returning to the mainland wasn't an option. He could only go west. He controlled his northing and southing by letting his boat lie facing either north or south when he went to sleep at night; he'd drift six or seven miles in whichever direction. It was pretty crude steerage. He had an outboard engine and about thirty miles' worth of fuel. After a month out there, he wondered if he was going to be able to hit the islands after all, he was drifting so far south, or whether his desiccated corpse would drift all the way to Indochina. It got him thinking.

On day sixty-one the Big Island poked up just above the horizon. Derrick pulled the starter cord on his little outboard engine. It turned over and coughed. He pulled it again and blue smoke chugged out over the sea. He pointed himself as best he could at the little green lump on the horizon.

His son had reported him missing. The coast guard had stopped looking for him. He said his faith was only ever stronger when he was out there, but that afternoon, it was fine, coming in like that. He'd lost thirty pounds and he'd read the Bible right through, a couple of times. Every night he'd listened to evangelical radio shows out of Ecuador, first to the English and then to the Spanish segment. He'd tried to learn Spanish that way; you'd have thought he had enough time, he said, but he failed. He did learn how to pray though. He got really good at praying.

Then he talked about this woman he met in Mexico while he was getting ready to go. She was Asian, he said. He said he thought he'd like his next wife to be Asian, they're so nice. But he couldn't marry a woman who wasn't a Christian. He'd met a few women since he started sailing and he told us about them — lonely and mostly troubled it seemed. He had wanted to help them, he said, without a trace of self-consciousness. I tried to picture it: Derrick, six-two, two-forty maybe, fifty-five or sixty, grizzled beard and a pugnacious manner that was all the more evident for his evangelical enthusiasm.

When Don and I rowed back to the *Sea Mouse* that night I asked Don what he thought of him. Don shook his head. "I just hope we're not like that, to other people."

"Evangelical Christians?"

"Jerks who are convinced we've figured everything out."

"We're not much like him, Don."

"We're guys out in a boat, going to deserted islands."

"Yeah, but we're half his age, and this is adventure for us, not salvation."

"We're all here for the same reasons."

The next morning after we rowed ashore, Don disappeared into the island by himself, saying he wanted to explore it alone for a while. I was lying in a hammock looking up at the clouds when Derrick walked up. "Gonna sleep all day?" he asked.

"I wasn't sleeping," I said. "Just looking at the sky."

"Where's your friend?"

"He's off exploring."

"I hope he doesn't get lost."

"It's not a big island, Derrick."

"It's big enough. There's strange things around here."

"Like what?"

"Like bodies," he said, trying to be mysterious. It worked.
"Where?" I asked, sitting up.
"Around."

In 1974 a man named Buck Walker and his companion Jennifer Jenkins sailed their leaking and marginally seaworthy sloop, the *Iola*, to Palmyra from Hawaii. There were some things the police wanted to talk to Walker about that he didn't want to get into — drugs mostly. In Palmyra they met an older couple, with the improbable names of Mac and Muff Graham. They had sailed around the world in their boat, the *Sea Wind*, which was by all accounts a beautifully built and well-equipped vessel. Mac Graham, in photos, has the patrician air of Fred MacMurray in *My Three Sons*, and Muff looks rather like June Cleaver with a two-pack-a-day habit. Buck Walker and Jennifer Jenkins, on the other hand, looked like people you'd see hitchhiking in the rain on the West Coast. Anything but patrician. The two couples didn't get along.

The most compelling evidence of the antipathy between them is that Muff's skull finally washed ashore in 1981, sealed inside an aluminum trunk. It bore marks of having been burned with a torch. Jenkins and Walker had shown up in Hawaii with the Grahams' boat a month after the Grahams stopped answering hails on shortwave radio. Initially, the young couple was charged and convicted for theft of the boat. But on discovery of Muff's skull, they were then charged with murder. Jenkins hired Vincent Bugliosi (who was also the lawyer who wrote *Helter Skelter*) to defend her. Bugliosi persuaded a jury that Jenkins just didn't know what had happened to the Grahams, that Walker told her they had both drowned when their dinghy tipped, and how was she to have known he was lying? Walker got life; Jenkins' trial became *And the Sea Will Tell*, Mr Bugliosi's book, which relates all these events in self-aggrandizing and prurient detail.

In Bugliosi's book there is a chart of the island, mapping the events described, the locations of the camps, where different arguments erupted. Palmyra is a small place and so every feature is readily identifiable. Those who visit the island find staying there like sleeping in an apartment that has been the site of a gruesome tragedy. Everyone notices the bathtub for instance. The place has history that revolves around events other than these, but nobody ever talks about anything else.

Walker is still in prison, in Washington. Jenkins is free and lives in Southern California. The *Iola* has not been recovered. No trace of Mac Graham has ever been found and presumably the remainder of Muff's body is rolling around the sea floor someplace off Palmyra.

"So, Derrick," I said, "why would you go out and do that? Sail across the ocean just by yourself?"

"It brings me closer to God."

By this time it was nearly dark and the surface of the lagoon was still except for the ripples from the manta rays that glided through.

"How, exactly?"

"There's no distractions out there, it's just you, and if you're ready to receive Him, God. It's easy to see Him out there. He is obvious."

"Other people distract you from God?"

"No, *I* distract myself from God sometimes when other people are around. Being weak."

"What do you mean?"

"Well, I don't always do right by other people when they're around."

"You chase Asian women."

"I get proud and want to impress people and sometimes I get angry at them."

"Me, too."

"Oh, I do worse."

Which might have just been the zealot's insistence on the most extravagant confession.

"So if you're not around anyone, you can't hurt them."

"Everything starts with your relationship to God. Between you and Him, that's what matters. If that's clear, you'll treat everyone else well. And they'll be good to you, mostly."

Derrick and his wife had lived for many years on an acreage just outside of Comox. His wife raised goats there. She was crazy about those things; she sold milk in town and the kids to other farmers. Occasionally they butchered one, but she felt awful whenever they did. The goats drove Derrick crazy, got into his hunting gear, shit all over the lawn, bawled late into the night. He worked shifts at the pulp mill and was entitled to come home to a clean and quiet home, not to have to *compete* with goats for her attention.

He did a lot of things to hurt her in the time they were together; cheated on her, hit her, blew his pay on liquor. But the worst thing he ever did was kill the goats one afternoon when she was away visiting her parents.

Self-isolation to save oneself from one's own evil: ascetics disdain most of all themselves. This makes them interesting until one learns that perhaps they ought to, and then one wonders if they are being hard enough on themselves. People who would stomp out onto the heath to rave at the wind are often not likeable. And why would they be? It's not a succession of good and compassionate decisions that leads someone to decide they may not take pleasure again.

Roger's two dogs were wary of Don and me and only a little more trusting of Derrick. They had been on Palmyra now for two years at least, and they were not accustomed to people. Roger fed them fish that he speared in the lagoon. Derrick had been doing this, too, but had been chased out by sharks twice. He was relieved to see the dog food. A week before Don and I had arrived the dogs had chased a rat into the water. It had led them on a chase over the coral at low tide, until one of them lunged at the rat and tore his scrotum open on the coral reef. When Derrick learned I was a doctor he asked me if I would have a look at the injury. He wondered if I should just castrate the poor thing.

Derrick and I spent a morning chasing the dog around the island. Like in Jack London's *To Build a Fire*, the dog kept wisely out of the way. The closest I could get was about thirty feet. Finally, I studied the dog with binoculars. The scrotum was ripped open, certainly, but from that distance I couldn't see any infection. Derrick and I sat among the coconut trees and debated what we should do. "Optimally, that should be cleaned up and repaired," I said. Derrick nodded. "But I can't see doing it on that dog with just you and Don holding him down."

"It's hard to watch him suffer like this."

"We could put him down."

"Sometimes he looks like he is in agony and sometimes he seems fine."

"You could just wait and see how it goes."

"Does he need antibiotics?"

"He needs surgery. If that scrotum abscesses then antibiotics won't make much difference. If it heals in from below without abscessing, antibiotics won't make any difference either."

"How likely is it that it will heal over without getting infected?"

"It's a mess."

"Goodness."

"Do you have something you could use to put him down, after Don and I leave?"

"Yes."

Derrick and I walked around the island. We looked at the destroyed airfield the navy had built, and the detritus of aircraft that sat on the tarmac, penetrated by shoots of trees and shrubs. On the far side of the island the wreck of a sailboat lay on her side on the reef. She had run ashore about six months earlier, after her skipper, a singlehander, had set the wind vane to steer and had gone to sleep. The skipper had stumbled ashore, pulling a crate of beer cans with him. He sat there weeping and drinking beer as his boat was smashed to pieces on the reef. Roger found him the next day and had set about bringing gear off the boat. The skipper, according to Roger, just sat there drinking. Another sailboat stopped in Palmyra en route to Samoa a few weeks later and the skipper had joined them. When the skipper tried to take the salvaged gear from his boat with him, Roger had claimed it as his own.

Derrick and I watched the sad little boat swaying in the surf, her mast bent forlornly. Even now, you could tell she had been a pretty boat. "That was unkind of Roger," I said.

"Roger is a troubled man."

"You gotta wonder about someone who would choose to live here by himself, indefinitely."

"Yes," Derrick said.

The next day I pulled the torn headsails to shore. I sat down on the concrete seaplane ramp and began stitching. Don stayed on the boat and tidied up the galley. Derrick wandered up from somewhere and sat down beside me. He had brought a thermos of coffee and he poured me a cup. I said thanks and kept sewing.

He asked me where Don was; I said he was on the boat, cleaning up. Derrick thought that Don was in spiritual crisis. He recognized it. I told Derrick about Don's wife. Derrick said that you have to acknowledge your own sin, as the starting point. I told him that I thought sometimes people just fall out of love with one another, no sinning involved.

"Doesn't happen."

I lifted up my head. "To you, maybe."

"It's a sin whenever someone falls out of love."

"It's *regrettable*, certainly."

"It is the origin of all sin."

I went back to my sewing. Derrick started going on about the Song of Solomon. I don't remember what he said.

Don disliked Derrick intensely and was very uncomfortable around him. And the island itself, which he had dreamed about for years, seemed to disturb and sadden him. He retreated from Derrick and me whenever he could. I asked him at night what the matter was. He said he didn't know.

"This place isn't as nice as you expected, is it?" I asked.

"It's as weird as I imagined, but I don't know, maybe if we were alone here, maybe then it would be better. It isn't physically any different from what I expected. This is what atolls are like. I don't know what the problem is."

"Derrick?"

"He drives me crazy. He's so desperate and pushy. He starts talking and just assumes you want to hear it. He doesn't pay any attention to the person he's talking at."

"I guess he's lonely."

"Well, he drove everyone away from him at home and just 'cause he's out here doesn't mean the same things aren't gonna bug people here."

"You wouldn't want to end up like that," I said.

"I don't know how you would," he said.

I spent most of the three days we were there sewing up the genoa. Derrick sat with me and helped. His stitching was tighter and more even than mine. He showed me how to seal the knots with contact cement. We had finally negotiated a conversational course clear of religion. We talked about diesel engines and how to swag wire-end fittings, about which islands had the cheapest harbour fees, how to anchor in a tropical storm. I mentioned that I'd been in the army and he told me again that he'd been in the air force. He had learned how to really drink there. We had even been posted to bases twenty miles apart from each other, thirty years apart in time. I told him I thought that the army was mostly stupid. He agreed. Sitting there sewing and talking, he was kind to me. He told me he still missed his wife. He said he still had nightmares about their fights, about beating her up.

Before the marines came the lagoon had been open to the sea in each direction. In the gaps between the islets that made up the atoll the surf washed up over the reef and into the lagoon, and flowed out the pass. Since the now-crumbling causeway was built, the water is not exchanged and the coral in the lagoon is dead and dying. There are still the manta rays and white-tipped sharks and red snapper; it's really just the coral that's affected for now. There are no permanent inhabitants to chronicle these changes, so it's hard to know how profound they are. Derrick was going to move on in another month or two. The only reason he was confident that Roger was coming back was the dogs. When Roger did return, it wouldn't be for very long. His boat was steel and rusting. Like him.

In the meantime, the coral refiltered the same deoxygenated water over and over again. The lagoon paled with deadened white coral heads and the sea rumbled on the outside edge, surf exploding high into the air against the reef. Ashore, the rats and crabs scuttled over one another in the ruins of the gymnasium, searching for coconuts.

"It's a hard thing to figure out, how you can make things better after the fact," Derrick said.

"Atonement," I said.

"Yes."

We had delivered the food for Derrick and the dogs and the sails had been resewn and hurricane season was drawing nearer. Already the short-wave was speaking of tropical depressions forming off Fiji. On the other hand, it made sense to stay a few weeks. We had finally found our anti-Manitoba, after three thousand miles of open-ocean sailing.

"We *could* hang out here with Derrick a little longer."

"That's certainly attractive."

"He would tell us some more about his religion, I'll bet, if we asked him."

"I really want to make Tahiti before we have to stop for hurricane season."

"Hurricane season starting about now, of course."

"Well, before we get too deeply into hurricane season."

"I don't want to stay here."

"When do you want to leave?"

"Today."

"Okay."

Derrick asked us what our hurry was. He confided in me that he thought we were moving on because he'd offended Don somehow. I reassured him, and wondered how many times in his life he had looked that lonely and vulnerable. It was just that we wanted to get to Tahiti, I said. "Why do you want to go there? It's crazy expensive, they speak another language and they make you post a thousand-dollar bond just to stay three months."

"I've always wanted to go to Tahiti."

"Well, I'll be sorry to see you two move on." And he gave me an awl that he had fashioned out of a sail needle and a bit of wood.

"It's for when you need to make a guide hole for the needle. When you're sewing really thick sail cloth."

"Thanks, Derrick."

"Take care of yourself."

We weighed anchor and motored out of the lagoon. We were a mile off the reef when the radio crackled: *Sea Mouse, Sea Mouse, Sea Mouse, this is Tara, radio check, over.*

Tara, this is Sea Mouse, we read you five by five, over.

Roger Sea Mouse. Good luck, boys.

Roger that, Tara.

Tara out.

I have always found the dialogue of correct radio procedure stirring. Such restraint. Such dignity. I fingered the awl he had made for me.

We pointed the boat south.

CHAPTER EIGHT

THE WINDS WERE FRESH and we moved south quickly. The grey-green mould streak of Palmyra sank below the horizon. Strange and otherworldly, its limited beauty was all the more striking for its lack of any resemblance to anything we had imagined. That is to say, it was nothing at all like Gilligan's Island.

Which is really what we were looking for. We wanted to drink mai tais out of coconuts and leer at Mary Ann and Ginger and never get sent any bills. We wanted to go where privilege and security endure, and alabaster-skinned movie stars shriek "*cannibals,*" at movements in the jungle and run into the arms of the skipper. (We both wanted to be the skipper.)

On Palmyra Mr and Mrs Howell would have been stewed and eaten. Their bones cut up and thrown into the sea. The professor's rarefied knowledge would have held no currency there, and the skipper would have used the professor's glasses to start fires. They all would have feared the beasts in the trees. Palmyra is not for human beings. There is no ground water there. People only turn up because they think it is uninhabited. Of course it is inhabited — by all the people looking for an uninhabited island.

South of Palmyra the *Sea Mouse* entered the doldrums, in the aforementioned intertropical convergence zone. The doldrums is a pattern of weather that hangs either on or just south of the equator. The air is thick and wet and thunder showers erupt periodically with momentarily vigorous winds that shake sailors loose from their torpor, panicking as they scramble for the halyards, to douse the sails in the suddenly roaring wind. More often, much more often than that, the air is entirely still, and a sailboat will roll and pitch with her sails hanging slackly from the spars. Elsewhere, when becalmed, there is an expectation or at least a hope that the centre of whatever high-pressure system one's caught in will wander on, but here there is no such hope. This is permanent and static air; it scarcely moves except to discharge electricity, and it's like this all year round, all around the world. There are no seasons here, even hurricanes do not enter the doldrums, will not cross the equator, won't draw a line on a map and say "I want to go there and there."

The word "doldrums" has come to be synonymous with depression or stagnation, a leap not difficult to understand the third or fourth day that one rises in the morning to creaking and sagging sails.

Wind

> *The wind, the wind. It has nearly as many names as moods: there are siroccos, Santa Anas, foehns, brickfielders, boras, williwaws, chinooks, monsoons. It has, as well, unrivaled power to evoke comfort or suffering, bliss or despair, to bless with fortune, to tear apart empires, to alter lives.*
>
> JAN DEBLIEU, *Wind*

The prevailing winds on the ocean arise from two causes. The most important of these is the warming of the air along the equator. The warmed air rises, and the vacuum left behind draws in the cooler air from the north and the south. If the earth didn't rotate, these winds would always flow due north in the Southern Hemisphere and due south in the Northern. But because the earth rotates, the angular speed at the equator is greater than it is farther north or south and, as a consequence, the air rushing to the equator is deflected to the west. In the Northern Hemisphere, it is easy to sail south or west or both; below the equator it's easy to sail north or west or both. It is always difficult to go east.

More circumnavigations are born of these meteorological phenomena than of a desire for a sense of completion, of the poetic beauty of a completed circle. Not that this undermines the beauty. When practicalities conspire to assist the completion of a beautiful thing, the right response is gratitude, not skepticism.

Further away from the equator, toward either pole, this pattern changes again, and westerlies prevail. They do so mainly in the guise of storms, however: nasty cold-fuelled gales marching in sequence around the globe, lined up one after the other on satellite photos like columns of bush fires.

Hurricanes are the most feared weather pattern and the most talked about, but these northerly and southerly gales can achieve a violence that makes survival in a small boat at sea just as unlikely as in a tropical storm. And the westerly gales are far more frequent than hurricanes, and are reliable and devastating features of both the northern and southern waters. Hurricanes gain their reputations as much by their relative rarity as by their acknowledged capacity for senseless rage. The gale seasons of the north and south are the larger problem to the open-ocean sailor. There isn't much difference between forty-foot seas and eighty-foot seas to a small boat — dead being, pretty much, dead.

In contrast, sailing in tropical waters even in hurricane season is almost always peaceful. The trades blow out of the east and are so constant in direction and strength that we went days and days without ever having to adjust either the sail trim or the rudder. On the radio we listened to the American weather service following the tracks of the Mexican hurricanes across the Pacific, out toward Hawaii. All we knew was peace and ease. Farther north, the low-pressure systems had mounted and the frequency and severity of gales described seemed entirely of a piece with what we had seen up there. Northern waters seemed inclined toward outbursts and we had no difficulty imagining the extremes of that unrestrained anger. Near the equator, on the other hand, the character of the water itself seemed gentler. That it was capable as well of incomprehensible violence seemed incongruous, like the grey and gentle man next door who always astonishes the neighbours.

Hurricanes are best understood not as phenomena of air but of water. Water temperatures greater than eighty-two degrees Fahrenheit nourish them and water cooler than that depletes them. Hurricanes are fed by rising columns of cooling wet air, and as the water within them condenses out as torrential rain, tremendous energy is released — rain driven as if from a pressure washer. Hurricanes are common and devastating in the Caribbean, on the Pacific coast of Mexico, in the southwestern Pacific and in the northwestern Pacific. They exist in all tropical waters except the south Atlantic, and they are very uncommon in the southeastern Pacific; cold water currents usually keep those areas too cool for their formation. They are called cyclones in the southwestern Pacific, Bay of Bengal and Arabian Sea; typhoons in the northeastern Pacific and hurricanes in the lands settled by the Spanish — the Caribbean and Mexico.

All of this makes for a great deal of discussion and worry, especially when you are out there. The wind blows from the east. It rarely rains. All there is to do is sit still and read about meteorology and imagine the worst.

I would have done well to have read a bit more about meteorology before deciding to go to Palmyra. It is possible to make a reasonably fast passage from Hawaii to Tahiti, but to do this it's necessary to reach eastwards to the equator, and to make as much easting as possible before the northeasters switch around to the southeast. Once south of the equator, proceeding due south is difficult and southeast nearly impossible. Tahiti, a quick glance at the globe would have demonstrated, was southeast of Palmyra, and just above the equator.

All of which is to say, if you're in Hawaii and intending to sail to Tahiti, don't stop in Palmyra unless you have a very large fuel tank or are not at all given to long sigh-filled sessions of staring at the sea. The pleasures of languor notwithstanding.

Once through the doldrums, the trades freshened again and blew warm and constant. Constantly from exactly where we wanted to go. The *Sea Mouse* tacked widely across the ocean, trying to claw its way closer to Tahiti. Our hopes for a two-week passage were soon abandoned.

The southeast trades blow in from the neighbourhood of Easter Island, the bit of dirt the farthest from any other anywhere. The ocean just goes on and on, from the South American Cordillera almost uninterrupted to the Marquesas, and even those are only a matter of a few hundred square miles of land interrupting millions and millions of square miles of sea.

Any understanding of the Pacific must begin with an appreciation of its scale. In size it is to other oceans as the Himalayas are to the Appalachians. In area it is larger than all the land masses of the earth combined. Initially, it seems easier to sail across this ocean because of the absence of land masses — there is less to run into in the night, there are fewer shallow shoals, and fewer vessels lying poorly lit and fishing in the dark. It is open ocean. Freighters travel along the line between Long Beach, California, and Yokohama, but elsewhere the ocean is empty. A sailboat goes many weeks between sightings of other boats and this is probably the only warm ocean of which this may still be said. Eventually the enormity sinks in, and the progress made even on good days is insignificant judged against the length of the trip.

Don now spent most of his time up top, looking out at the sea. When we both felt talkative we chatted about movies and motor-cycles and what the clouds looked like. The nights were as warm as buttered toast and it was much more comfortable to sleep in the cockpit than to lie in a sheen of perspiration below. And so we found ourselves looking up at the stars and wondering about the world.

Within our discussions of the merits of four-stroke engines and the deficiencies of American beer, there was an encoded conversa-tion about our disappointment in Palmyra. We had both found the island strange and unnerving but Don had been profoundly shaken by it and, leaving it astern, he didn't return to normal. He was dif-ferent and puzzling — he spoke more slowly and more confi-dently. He often went below when I was atop and he stayed in the cockpit when I went below. I assumed I was irritating him. When he did speak, and when I finally listened to him carefully, another explanation emerged.

He saw, in his reaction to the isolated and desolate beauty of Palmyra, a way forward and out of his unhappiness. He talked about how much he wanted to go to an island where he could get to know the people, and become for a little while part of their community. I thought to myself, "Now he wants to join the Peace Corps." I was still mired in Therouxian misanthropy, and was content to make fun of Derrick and me and Don, and miss my ex–girlfriend and ache. Don had moved beyond me somehow; he read the US Navy's description of South Pacific harbours and wondered aloud what they looked like. "Probably plenty of Coca-Cola signs," I said, amused with my own cynicism. Don didn't notice.

The southern stars had been creeping up on us as we crawled south. The big bear disappeared behind us and the cross rose up in front. It became unnecessary to consult the compass; whichever of us was on watch would lie with his head in the corner of the cockpit watching the stars above the mast. As long as the Southern Cross was halfway between the forestay and the starboard shroud, the *Sea Mouse* was on course. As before, if her sails were balanced and trimmed, she would follow whichever course was set as if she knew the trail. The distance to Tahiti fell very slowly, and we again had to abandon the ritual of calculating our daily progress. But these were glorious days and nights. We were suspended there in an existence that came to have a sense of completeness about it, independent of departure or destination. Tahiti was an abstraction; it came to feel normal to lie out there under the sun and just stare at the clouds and feel the swell of the sea. Losing the sense of dawdling, of being delayed by our thirty- and forty-mile days was an improvement. It is so hard to abandon the sense of schedule — until it abandons you in the face of large and implacable settings. The ocean just goes on and on and contains its own momentum, a rhythm unimpressed by anything else. One bright mid-afternoon the wind finally did pick up and soon we were making better time. I made myself comfortable in the cockpit and looked at the sails all full and the boat heeling over, the water rushing past quietly.

Languor is underrated. It is not possible to be immobile in modern urban society except by dint of constant effort. Holding on tightly to the riverbank and fighting the current is not languor. Nobody likes that. But bone-lazy idleness, hours and hours spent staring at the sky and remembering books and birthdays and great kisses: this is a pure pleasure that eludes the productive in all their confident superiority. Languor is sunny and hot. It is at home near the sea and is best appreciated in environments of beauty and limited promise. It contains within it the idea of boredom, but is also coloured by idle fancy, and the understanding that some things proceed best with limited attention. Fishing, for instance. If you're always reeling in and checking your bait, you'll only worsen your chances. Relax.

In the army there was boredom as profound as that which occurs at sea, but there was, as well, a self-consciousness that required one eye to be on the tent flap lest some prancing major strut in, on the lookout for idleness. You can't be hiding or feeling guilty and be languid at the same time. Long sea passages have the attributes of being both profoundly idle and of providing the illusion that something is still being done. When I have been idle without any purpose whatsoever, I have not been able to read — the immobility gave rise to agitation, and agitation does not much lend itself to making one's way through Tolstoy, for instance.

A principal pleasure of making a long ocean passage lies here, in the opportunity and the mental inclination to be able to just read and read, without guilt or distraction or lingering anxiety that something is not being tended to. A glance at the sails and the compass establishes that all that can be done is being done. Back to Chatwin.

The carrying device of *Songlines* is a lovely idea. The land was created by wanderings of the original beings, who dreamt as they wandered, dreaming the world into existence. The paths of these wanderings are recorded in the songlines, which describe the geographic pattern of the original wanderings, and the first dreams that lent reality to the world. Each separate path — the path of the bandicoot, or of the spiny anteater — is maintained by the clan of that creature, chapters of which are present in each tribal group. A given chapter is entrusted with the maintenance of the portion of the song that describes the path as it crosses the land that lies within their knowledge.

A member of the clan of the fire ant, for instance, may decide that he wants to wander the length of the songline. He knows enough of the song to take him only so far; then he must find a member of the clan of the fire ant in the tribal group next to his, and they sing their songs to one another. When one leaves off, the other picks up, telling the stranger the path to take. After travelling some distance, the wanderer will find that he no longer understands the language of other members of the clan of the fire ant. No problem, Chatwin tells us, for the directions are contained not only in the lyrics but also in the harmonic and melodic structures of the song. Onomatopoeia made literal.

It turns out that this is hyperbole, sadly. But isn't it a lovely idea? Knowledge and explicit communication through music, through pitch and melody and harmony. The music of a journey. Oh my. And the delightfulness of the idea is an accomplishment — as was the entrancement of seasoned and worldly mountaineers by the expedition proposals of an inexperienced climber.

Chatwin describes a man he travelled with named Arkady. Biographers have never clearly identified who Chatwin meant by Arkady, if indeed there was any one man. Part of the time that Chatwin was wandering the outback and researching his book, he travelled with Salman Rushdie. (Chatwin at one point maintained that Arkady was in fact Rushdie.) When I read this in Rushdie's *Imaginary Homelands*, I was pleased, reassured that there was evidence that the man in fact existed at all, that someone I had heard of had met him. So not everything about the man was created, it wasn't all some metafictional life project.

The idea of the "dreaming tracks" or "songlines" captivates me as much as it does Bruce. How could writers fail to love a world which has been mapped by stories? I find myself envying him his subject.

He talks about it constantly and we go in for long arcane passages of supposition. What happens when two songlines cross? Do the songs acquire common lines? Or does one line "burrow" while another "flies"? The London Underground map appears in my mind. I keep nagging away at the idea of junctions ...

Like Theroux, Rushdie considered himself Chatwin's friend. But even though he is more restrained, perhaps *because* he is more restrained, his discussion of Chatwin is damning.

Later, after the book is published, Bruce tells someone that "of course" I am Arkady. This isn't true. I know one person in Alice Springs, like Arkady of Russian descent, also highly knowledgeable about aboriginal religion, who is a much more obvious model. Nor do I recognize a single one of our conversations, in *The Songlines*. The truth is, "of course," that Bruce is Arkady as well as a character he calls Bruce. He is both sides of the dialogue.

Chatwin's elevated version of the escapist idyll — the redemptive power of nomadism and all that — was as manufactured as a trailer-park fantasy of actresses in grass skirts and limited guile. I wanted my mai tai. What good is an escapist fantasy if it doesn't really exist out there somewhere? It's like lotteries — they represent hope because even though the chances of winning are effectively zero, they *aren't* zero. Fantasy is only potent if the idea is allowed to persist that somewhere out there it really is attainable. But these days, does anything worth escaping allow you to?

At night in those warm waters, the wake of the *Sea Mouse* would glow silver and white with the bioluminescence of the dying plankton in her wake. Bioluminescence occurs in turbulent water; the turbulence sheers apart the cell walls and membranes of plankton. The contents of those cells are released into the water, including the phosphorus, which is what every living thing uses as its most immediate source of energy. When the phosphorus hits the water it releases all its energy in a brief flash. Millions and millions of disintegrating plankton form a light that the eye may observe, and marvel at. In the waters of Genoa Bay, in British Columbia, in the weeks before we left, I had seen phosphorescence of this kind. It was so bright that as I walked gently along the dock the minuscule ripples in the water created by the vibration of my footfalls were lit up in bright and rapidly moving circles that spread out so quickly one might think small and frightened fish were moving in unison.

Sometimes, when the water was still enough, our wake would stretch behind for what looked like many miles, glowing dimly off to the horizon. I often looked up from my books (I read in the cockpit at night with a flashlight, like some nine-year-old under the covers) and watched the line of faintly glowing water brighten behind us as my eyes accommodated themselves to the dark. The Southern Cross, creeping up in front of us, the glowing wake pointing north; there was light all around us at sea.

As we slowly proceeded south and further out of the intertropical convergence zone, the wind gradually rose, remaining always in our faces. We were beating once again. The contrary wind itself was not so much an obstacle — in flat seas it is possible to go very fast nearly into the wind. But, as the seas grew, the bow of the *Sea Mouse* would bury itself ponderously in the oncoming waves and the entire boat would shudder and slow, rising up and out briefly then slamming headlong into the next wave. This was hard not just on the crew but on the boat.

Two weeks out of Palmyra, I was below staring at the locker full of dried foodstuffs when I heard a loud crack and felt the whole boat shake. We both ran forward and hung our heads over the bow, looking for evidence of a collision. The chainplate anchoring the forestay had abruptly bent and almost broken. We doused the sail immediately and tried to figure out why we hadn't been dismasted. The slack forestay sagged and swung in the swell. The mast lolled around drunkenly. We shook our heads. Purists disdain engines, but fortunately there were no purists aboard.

We looked at the chart and calculated the distance to the nearest landfall, in the Northern Cooks, one hundred miles away. It was described in the *Sailing Directions of the South Pacific* by the US Navy:

Penrhyn Atoll (9 00's 158 00'w.) Lies about 330 miles WNW of Vostok Island, and is the largest and most northerly of the Cook Islands N group. Numerous low islets, some of them several miles in length, stand on the reef surrounding the lagoon; they are covered with coconut palms which reach an elevation of about 15.2 m (50 ft).

The atoll is about 12 ½ miles long in a SE to NW direction and is about eight miles wide. North-West Bank, with a charted depth of 6.7 m (22 ft.), extends about 1 ½ miles NW from the NW extremity of the atoll.

The winds at Penrhyn Atoll are usually E, with occasional N and NW winds between December and March. Hurricanes are said to form in the vicinity of the atoll, but winds of hurricane force are unknown here.

Omoka (9 01's, 158 04'w.) (World Port Index No 55720.) is situated on the S side of the West Pass, within the lagoon. The Resident Agent lives here. A channel leads from the fairway of West Pass to Omoka; it will accommodate vessels with a draft up to 4.3 m (14 ft.). There is a stone wharf here suitable for vessels up to 150 ft. in length with a depth of 4.3 m (14 ft.) alongside. There is anchorage off the village in 18.3 m (10 fm). There is anchorage in the lagoon in 15 fm, sand, with the flagstaff at Omoka bearing 230, distant 1 ¼ miles.

We started up the engine. It would take the very last of our fuel to get there.

CHAPTER NINE

PENRHYN IS A LOW ATOLL like Palmyra and, like her, she only crept above the horizon when we were practically upon her. A fringing reef stood well offshore and the pass through it was narrow. It was early evening by the time we were close enough to approach and so we elected to stand offshore that night and motor through in the morning.

All night long we took turns napping and checking our position to ensure we weren't drifting in the wrong direction. In the morning we arose to find that, even so, we had drifted twelve miles east of the atoll. We were practically out of diesel and in motoring back to the island we used the very last of it. The engine began to cough a mile away from the entrance to the pass. In desperation we added kerosene to the fuel tank and the engine ran long enough to get us through. Lamp oil. We burned *lamp oil* as fuel to get through. Breakers the size of semi-trailers erupted on either side of us.

The atoll consisted of a thin rim of land encircling a six-mile wide lagoon. This rim is itself broken into eight *motus*, or smaller islands. The islands are nowhere more than three hundred yards wide. Five hundred people lived in the little harbour town of Omoka, the larger of the two settlements, alongside and upon the sea. They settled here about fifteen hundred years ago, having arrived from Tahiti in outrigger canoes. All the activity on the island revolves around the reef — within it, in the lagoon, there is an oyster farm that employs some people. The remainder fill their days fishing off the reef for tuna and mahi mahi, and in the lagoon for smaller fish. Everyone would understand how it feels to arrive safely after trouble out on the ocean.

We set the anchor and then we stood on deck surveying the atoll and the little town visible through the palm trees. It looked exquisite. There was a metal-roofed church that shone in the sun, and quiet little paths along which scooters silently (from that distance) sped. Children were running after one another screaming soundlessly and small, neat houses were visible through the trees, painted pale blue and orange and purple. Don and I fought over the binoculars and finally became so excited we were jumping up and down.

We piled into the dinghy and rowed ashore. We met a cluster of relaxed-looking and shirtless young men sitting on the beach. "Are you from the yacht?" one of them asked, having just watched us pull in, anchor and row ashore.

"Yes, hello, what a lovely island this is," I replied, bowing and scraping to anyone who might potentially be of assistance in fixing the bent chainplate.

"Well then you have to go back to your ship and wait for the customs man to clear you in."

"How will he know we are here?"

He smiled. The young men sitting with him began laughing quietly.

"He will see you." We nodded, still grinning maniacally, and turned around and rowed back to the *Sea Mouse*.

"You know they're having us on."

"Shut up."

"The customs inspector is sleeping in his hammock and wouldn't notice if a coconut crab climbed aboard and shit on his nose."

"Shut up."

We sat on the *Sea Mouse* and stared forlornly at the town before us, imagining the taste of a cheeseburger and a cold beer. We debated how long we should sit there until we tried again. We studied the young men on the edge of the great stone jetty jutting out from the beach. They appeared immobile, staring fixedly out at the lagoon. At us. Don figured that eventually they would tire of their joke and one of them would row out to tell us to come to shore after all. I was not nearly so optimistic.

"Ice cream."

"Ice cream would be nice."

"Ice cream and cold beer and a cheeseburger."

"You are a walking heart attack, man."

"Shut up."

"You shut up."

Eventually a small boat motored out from the beach. Through the binoculars we could see a prosperous older man in shorts and a mostly unbuttoned shirt sitting in front of an equally prosperous-looking younger man, also in shorts, manning the engine. The boat sat so low in the water it looked like a submarine about to dive.

The Customs Officer had brought with him a little satchel. He held it up as they approached. They tossed us a line and we helped them tie alongside and climb aboard. The Customs Officer was named Desmond. He and the other man, whom he introduced as his brother, came below. The *Sea Mouse* looked and smelled like two men who considered themselves easygoing had been living and perspiring in tropical heat for a thousand miles. From the expressions on Desmond and his brother's faces it appeared they were used to a slightly higher class of yacht. They both breathed through their mouths.

"Can I make you tea?" I asked. They nodded yes. I made tea.

Desmond and his brother collected a few dollars from us and stamped our passports. Desmond asked, "Do you have any tobacco on board?"

We shook our heads no.

"Any firearms?"

No.

"Any alcohol?"

Don and I looked at each other and I rose and dug out the plastic quart bottle of the least savoury rum imaginable that we had bought in Hawaii, at the Costco, right next to the automotive aisle. I held it up. "We do have this," I admitted. Desmond looked at it, unscrewed the cap and sniffed it, and then hurriedly screwed the cap back on. He cleared his throat and looked us in the eyes, taking in my dishevelled hair and Don's shaven pate.

"Now, boys," he said, lowering his voice, "do you have any narcotics on board?"

"Oh no, sir," we said in unison. "Would you like to have a look around?" I invited him, gesturing about the cabin. He sat there and took in the heaped and pungent clothes, the soiled sea cushions.

He shook his head no.

Desmond concluded his business with us pretty quickly after that and returned our passports. He told us that he'd cleared us for entry from a customs point of view but that we still had to be cleared by the department of agriculture inspector, another relative. We were to await that man's visit before going ashore. "You don't have any fresh produce aboard, do you, boys?"

"Nothing fresh," we replied in unison. He looked at the galley, and nodded. And then he and his brother climbed back into their boat and went ashore. We waved goodbye. They waved back.

We waited another hour but there was no department of agriculture inspector. We stared at the shore. Finally it was too much and we climbed back into the dinghy, which could only hold the two of us if one of us huddled over the other while he rowed. Children on the beach saw us rowing awkwardly in. They joyfully swam out into the surf to meet us fifty or sixty feet out and gripped the gunwales of the dinghy. We were certain they would tip us.

"Hello!" they cried.

"Please let go," we implored, smiling tightly. More of the lithe grinning children crowded around us and smiled widely up at us. One boy tried to climb aboard and we shrieked, "Please let go!" and the boat turned sideways with the mass of children adhered to it like multitudes of clinging hyenas hauling down a zebra, the oars waving ineffectually in the air. Together we all careened into the beach, the urchins screaming with pleasure. Don and I felt like grouchy old people, but we affected happier countenances and pulled the dinghy farther up the beach, with several of the older boys helping us.

We asked them if there was ice cream. They told us, "Not until the freighter comes," in maybe two months. We looked at one another. We asked them if there was a restaurant open.

"There is no restaurant," one boy said, "but you can buy tinned food at one of the shops."

We nodded and looked around. The place was as perfect as a model of a South Pacific paradise in a bubble glass with sparkly sand that you could shake up and then watch settle. There was a cool fresh breeze blowing in off the reef and the whole village was shaded by fifty-foot coconut trees that sprouted in regular intervals along the laneways. Occasionally an adult appeared, walking slowly along one of the shaded lanes, who smiled and waved. We waved back.

We badly wanted to eat something other than the curried egg noodles that had been our staple most of the way from Hawaii. We began looking for the shops the boy had told us about, but all there appeared to be were small neatly tended houses, and that metal-roofed church. We walked back to the beach and asked the boy where the shops were. He was delighted to guide us and took Don by the hand, pulling him off in the direction of one of the little houses we'd passed. I followed. Don grinned at me.

The boy knocked on the front door. It was locked. No one answered. He ran around to the back and Don and I followed. The boy woke up an old man sleeping in a lawn chair. The man stirred himself and apologized. Don and I were embarrassed to have woken him up. He led us into his shop from the back door.

Don and I studied the nearly empty shelves. The old man gesticulated, "The freighter has not made it in since three months now." There were a few packages of batteries and a box of wooden matches, a few cans of butter and a few dozen bags of fluorescent-orange Cheez Doodles. There were bottles of Coca-Cola in the cooler and there were one-pound bags of sugar and salt and some larger bags of rice and flour. We bought one of everything and thanked the man and walked outside, swigging our cold Cokes and scarfing back Cheez Doodles until our lips and faces and the better part of our chests were powdered with glo-orange crumbs, our bellies leaden with congealed salted glue. We were very happy.

On the boat we had read that there was an airport to the west of Omoka that had been built by the Americans during the Second World War. We had read as well that the people of Penrhyn used an old crashed American bomber from that era as a source of aluminum for manufacturing their own combs and household implements. Don told me that he'd like to walk out there and it was clear he wanted to go alone. I waved goodbye and he walked west down that little road. It was the first time in a month and a half that we had been more that a few yards from one another and it felt refreshing, but strange.

I found another little shop, at the other end of town, and I walked in and looked at the similarly sparse shelves and tinned and dried foodstuffs. The cheerful fat man behind the counter told me he was the Chief of Police, and was a relative of Desmond. I told him I had met Desmond. He knew that. I asked him where the department of agriculture inspector worked. He pointed to a small building beside the wharf. I bought some more Coca-Cola and some suspect-looking canned kippers. The Chief of Police asked me if I had any guns on board. "Oh no," I told him.

"It would be okay if you did," he said, "you would just have to store them with me while you were here."

"Well, I don't."

"Okay. Do you want a cup of tea?"

"Sure."

We walked across the road to his office. It was not clear to me whether his motives were personal or professional. I wondered if this was going to be some *Midnight Express*-body-cavity-search-interrogation situation. The Chief of Police opened the unlocked wooden door. The office was painted crocus-blue; it is the only crocus-blue police station I have ever seen. There were pieces of paper scattered on the floor. The afternoon breeze appeared and the pieces of paper stirred and shifted back and forth, returning pretty much to their original resting place. There was a portrait of Queen Elizabeth II on the wall, and a cuckoo clock. The Chief of Police plugged in a hot plate and put a pan of water on to boil. He carried two chairs to the front porch of the police station and sat in one, motioning to me to sit in the other.

"You come from Canada?" the Chief of Police asked.

"Yes."

"Is it nice there?"

"It's nice. It gets pretty cold sometimes."

"It's never cold here."

"I like it here."

"There are many jobs in Canada?"

"Yes."

"Like New Zealand."

"But colder."

"Yes."

"I've been to New Zealand," the Chief of Police said.

"Did you like it?"

"Yes. There are many shops there. But people are in quite a hurry."

"It's a problem," I agreed.

"I like it better here."

"Me too."

"You've been to New Zealand?"

"No. In the larger sense, I meant."

"Oh."

A boy appeared on the street, pulling a wagon with his sister in it. As they passed, the little girl waved at the Chief of Police. He waved back and said something in Polynesian. The boy grinned and said something back. I grinned. We all grinned. It was very sunny. We watched people walk up and down the street. The Chief of Police's wife waved from inside the shop. We waved back. The water on the hot plate came to a boil. The Chief of Police got up and made us each a cup of tea.

After another half hour or so of sitting there, the Chief of Police asked me where I was sailing to after I left Penrhyn.

"Tahiti," I said.

"Will you be coming back here?"

"I don't know, maybe."

"If you do, will you bring me some .22 shells?"

"Okay."

The Chief of Police's wife appeared in the doorway of their shop and glanced over at him and then disappeared again.

"I should get back to my shop," he said. "It has been nice meeting you."

"Thank you for the tea."

"You're very welcome."

There was a phone at the government office that could be used to make collect calls. I telephoned my parents. My mother answered. She was relieved to hear from me. It was the middle of winter there and they missed me. That detective fellow had phoned again, but hadn't left a message. I missed them too. Yes, I was having a really wonderful time. I said goodbye huskily and hung up.

I walked back to the beach and looked at the *Sea Mouse* bobbing at anchor. She appeared content to me. I sat down and, sedated by my full belly, I fell asleep under a coconut tree.

I woke when Don sat down beside me.

"It's very beautiful here," he said.

"It sure is."

"I'd be happy to stay here if you wanted."

"Well, I'd still like to make it to Tahiti eventually."

"Were you still thinking about leaving the boat down here someplace and flying home to work?" My money had been running low and during our starlit chats out at sea I had mused about the possibility of doing that.

"Yes."

"I could stay down here with the boat in Penrhyn while you were gone."

"That sounds like a good idea."

"Maybe I'll find a wife here."

I craned my neck around to look at him.

We had been sitting on the beach for over an hour. A thunderstorm began forming in the eastern sky and Don suggested that we should get back to the boat to watch the anchor in case the wind came up. We stood slowly and were walking to the dinghy when the rain hit and suddenly it was very dark and cold. The wind rose about a second after that, stirring up a steep chop on the lagoon — it was too rough to row out to the boat. We ran to the warehouse on the stone wharf to take shelter.

Another outsider, from the look of him, was standing under the wharf looking out at the lagoon. He had long greying hair pulled back in a ponytail and wore a Harley-Davidson T-shirt and speckled cotton shorts. He looked like he was either a real rough forty or a pretty good fifty-five. He was deeply tanned and drunk. He spoke out of the side of his mouth. "You're in the boat that just pulled in, are you?"

"Yes, pleased to meet you." I told him my name, and he reciprocated.

"Hugh, but you can call me Bobby Peru."

"How long have you been here, uh, Bobby?"

"About a month."

"Where did you come from?"

"Hilo."

"We came from Honolulu, by way of Palmyra."

"How long did you take?"

"All told, thirty-four days."

"Well, I was thirty-one, and went more directly, so you did well."

"It felt pretty slow."

Sharp white-capped waves were now sweeping across the lagoon, and the boats at anchor were all bucking and pitching wildly. The rain was falling nearly horizontally now and the palm trees were bowed over like reeds. We stood and watched our boats carefully. We had to talk loudly to be heard over the wind and rain.

"I was stuck on the equator for eleven days, no wind at all," Bobby yelled.

"We spent quite a bit of time becalmed too. It's sort of reassuring to know we're not the only ones who go that slowly," I yelled back.

"Well, you've picked a nice place to come."

"It looks like it."

"This is the first weather like this that I've seen here."

"In a month?"

"Yeah."

"What do you do here?"

"Drink, mostly," he had to yell, over a gust of wind. He grinned.

"Are there bars here?"

"No. You have to get a permit from the church deacon — you probably already met him, his name is Desmond — to order it in on the plane. They won't give me any more permits, so me and some of the boys here have been making bush beer out of coconut milk."

"What does Desmond think about that?"

"Oh, he doesn't like it too much."

"How many people are with you?"

"I'm singlehanding."

"How do you find that?"

"It gets to be a drag when I'm becalmed."

There was a third sailboat in the harbour, a steel boat about the same size as the *Sea Mouse*, French-flagged, and a little battered-looking. I asked Bobby Peru, "Have you met any other sailors while you've been here?"

"A few. They're mostly not very sociable. There's that French family out there. There are five people on that boat. Makes me think singlehanding isn't so bad."

I looked around the veranda under the warehouse, then walked closer to the wharf and looked at the *Sea Mouse*. I couldn't remember her pitching so violently in any of the storms we'd been in. On the other side of the warehouse, I saw, was the French family. There were indeed five of them, and they were working on their skiff, which they'd pulled up under the veranda. The father and his son, who appeared to be nearly an adult, were sanding a fibreglass patch they had applied to her bottom. I waved at them, and the mother, smoking a cigarette and watching their boat pitch at her anchor, waved back. There was a daughter who was taller than any of the others who looked at me a moment longer and then quickly away. The younger boy wore very thick black glasses and was rolling his own cigarette; he looked about fourteen. It seemed to me that the confinement together on their little boat, all those thousands of miles from France, had fused them. None of them strayed more than a few yards from the others. I looked at the daughter and her brothers and the father and the mother and wondered how intimate it was possible for a family to be before it became destructive. Where I was from, children that age generally loathe their parents. This family adhered to itself like a clump of molluscs. I wondered what any of them thought about their lives. When the trip was over, what would be fractured?

I walked back to the wall of the warehouse and sat against it beside Bobby Peru. Don was staring at the anchor line, though the wind was letting up and we were less worried than before. I studied Bobby's boat; she was a Hans Christian 38, and very beautiful. Even from shore I could see her Aries wind vane and roller-furling gear. They looked brand new. I looked at Bobby. He didn't.

"Hey. Do you and your friend want to come to my boat for supper tonight?" Bobby asked.

"Sure," I said.

When the rain and wind let up, Don and I rowed back to the *Sea Mouse* to inspect her anchor gear. There was a note sitting on the table. It read: "I came here and there was nobody home so I disinfected it. Enjoy your stay." It was signed but the name was difficult to decipher. Printed under the signature was "Cook Islands Department of Agriculture." The boat smelled of industrial pesticides. Which is to say, better. We closed the cockpit hatches to keep the stuff in, let it do its work.

Don sat down in the cockpit and looked at the lagoon stretching out all around us. "I've never even imagined a place as beautiful as this," he said. He looked to me like he was in love.

I agreed, brushing insecticidal dust from the cockpit bench before sitting down.

"It's hurricane season now," Don said. I adjusted my cushion for maximum comfort and lay down on it.

"Maybe we should just stay here."

I kept adjusting my cushion.

Hurricane season. Generally described as running from early November to late March, it exists as a statistical phenomenon more than as a seasonal certainty. Hurricanes may occur any time of the year in the tropics and, dissipating, they may extend themselves as far north as Canada. So you never really know when you're safe. But as a matter of frequency, January and February are bad months to be in the open water in the South Pacific, and December and March are dicey as well. Storms would be coming. And in storms such as these it is better to weather in a good place than a bad place. We were seven hundred miles from Tahiti.

He had a pretty good point.

When we arrived at Bobby Peru's boat that evening for supper, he seemed about as drunk as he'd been that afternoon. "Bobby Peru, this is a lovely boat you have here," I said as I climbed aboard.

"You can call me," he rasped, leering at us from the companionway, "the Pey-roostah!"

Don and I looked at each other.

"Hello, Pey-rooster," Don said.

"Welcome aboard, boys." He turned and went below. We followed. He poured us glasses of wine. "This is the very last of the good stuff," he said. "From here on in, it's bush beer." Don produced our plastic bottle of Rio de Costco rum.

"Well, it looks like we're gonna have a party," the Pey-rooster declared.

His boat made the *Sea Mouse* look dowdy even to my eyes. Despite Bobby's own state of dissolution, his boat was clearly loved. Her cabin framing was in polished teak and huge thick teak knees supported the cabin top. The galley gleamed with polished stainless steel. He showed us her head and shower, a *shower*, and her forepeak, which was crammed with an inflatable boat still in the wrapping, a thousand charts, scuba gear, everything Don and I had fantasized about. The boat had obviously been very expensive and he had nearly as much invested again in the gear. He was cruising in fine style. Don was a little perplexed by the unwrapped inflatable boat.

"Bobby, why haven't you ever used this inflatable, tried it out at least?"

"I have one in the water, you saw it when you came on board."

"Oh yeah."

Later, when Bobby was in the head, Don leaned over to me, whispering, "He's got a quarter million in boat and gear here."

I looked at him blankly.

"The man isn't a stockbroker."

I nodded.

Dinner was pasta with a tomato cream sauce; we ate better than we had since leaving Hawaii. Bobby and Don discussed wind vanes. Bobby was very frustrated with his, which he'd named Ingrid, as it was manufactured in Sweden. He wasn't at all convinced that it really worked. He had repaired it himself, repeatedly, and had been tempted to throw it into the ocean. We told him the story about our "Richard," which we had come to regard as sort of a placebo wind vane. Don asked him where he was headed.

"I'm going right around," he answered. "Want to see my charts?" We nodded. He brought out his charts of Samoa and New Zealand, the Torres Strait, Diego Garcia, the Red Sea, the Suez Canal and, just in case, the charts of South Africa's coast. "This is going to be a great trip," he said.

"A solo circumnavigation. That will be great. Have you read Henderson's *Singlehanded Sailing*?"

"No."

"By his account there have only been a few hundred done."

Bobby looked a little disappointed. "Never heard of the book. Really, a few hundred? I'd have thought fewer."

"He lists them. I've got the book on the *Sea Mouse*. You can look at it if you like."

"So how come you're doing this, Bobby?" Don asked.

"Well, I owned a bar in Seattle and I had some trouble there with all the bureaucrats and everything, so I told 'em all to fuck off, you can't mess with the Pey-roostah!"

"So you left."

"Yeah."

"Just like that?"

"Sure."

"What was your bar called?"

"It doesn't matter. How did your two sorry asses wind up out here?"

Don told him that his job had been getting to him and then one day he'd heard that I was looking for someone to go sailing with and he just left. I said something about always wanting to see the Southern Cross.

"Just like that Crosby Stills and Nash song."

"Which one?"

"Never mind."

I looked through his bookshelves as we sat there. There was Slocum, and Moitessier too. There were many volumes of the war poets, Sassoon, Graves and Rupert Brooke. I picked one up and began flipping through it. "I was a medic in Vietnam," Bobby said. "I love those guys." He put on music then, opera. And I looked at him and wondered if he was trying to impress us and of course he was, as we were trying to impress him. Which was a little disappointing. We had all crossed the same ocean, and we each knew that it could be hard out there. You'd have thought the breast-beating might have let up for at least a little while.

We got into the bottle of very bad rum and kept talking. I sat in a corner of the boat, my back to a bulkhead. Don did likewise. "So why do you want to go to Tahiti?" Bobby asked, from a third corner.

"I dunno," I said, "it's just always seemed like an interesting place."

"When you arrive in Tahiti they make you post a bond of a thousand dollars. It's like you've been arrested and you're before the bail judge."

"Well, I've just always wanted to go."

"Don't be silly. Stay here, we'll have a hoot."

Don added: "We're well into hurricane season now. Who knows what we'll get hit with on the way."

"It would feel to me like I was quitting if we didn't go there."

"Have more rum," Bobby said, filling my glass, "we'll get you to see reason."

"I was in the army, too," I said, seeking escape.

"Oh yeah? Which unit?"

"The Canadian army. An artillery regiment."

"The *Canadian* army?"

"Yeah."

"Did you see any action?"

"No."

"Don't talk to me about the fuckin' *Canadian* army. I was in *Vietnam*," Bobby said, leaning forward for emphasis. I wasn't seeing reason just yet, I was thinking. I looked over at Don.

"What was that like?" Don asked.

By four in the morning we were nearly through the two-quart bottle of rum. Vietnam had been terrible. Something about booby traps, malaria, VD. A little heroin situation. But it was after Bobby got back that he had screwed up his life. He spent a few years driving his bike around, hanging out with people he knew were trouble, never feeling like he was a part of anything. Then, for a while, he was seeing this woman, and he thought he was going to do okay.

"Either of you two married, girlfriends, anything?"

And then all that came out, in one long monotonic ramble, from each of us in turn. The kerosene lamps were out of fuel now and it was just the tropical moon shining through the portholes that lit the boat below.

Yeah, well, like he was saying, things were looking pretty good there for a while. They had a sweet little thing happening. But he messed it up. He was just too used to living that other way. In the States it's an old story, guys coming back from Vietnam. And sometimes it sounds like they use it as an excuse for any trouble they get into for the rest of their life. Lots of those guys would have gotten into their share of trouble anyway. But the thing is, it wasn't really anything that happened to him in the war that put things on a bad track. It was what he did in response to it that had been the problem. "A medium-sized thing happens and you do a big thing as a consequence and from there on in, it's the big thing that happens. So best to think about the responses you pick," he said. "Like you two and your girlfriends." We both looked up.

"Wife," Don said.

It was past sunrise. The tropical morning sun was very bright and Bobby and I were sitting up top. Don was down below sleeping. Bobby asked me how old did I think he was. I said forty. He was briefly pleased and then his mouth tightened when he realized I'd lied. He said forty-eight. In the morning light he looked like Willie Nelson but fatter and greyer, sixty, actually. As I thought this I was surprised to realize I had it together enough to try and spare his feelings. If only I'd had it together enough to stand up and pull Don into the rowboat, I'd have rowed home. I looked at him.

"Stop feeling sorry for yourself," he said. "You're in the catbird seat."

I nodded. I leaned over and was sick into the lagoon.

The next afternoon I woke and the cabin of the *Sea Mouse* stank of rum and garlic and all I could do was hold tightly to the edges of my berth. I listened for Don. He had gone. I stood up and looked around the boat. It wasn't exactly clear to me how or when we had made it back from Bobby's boat. It was very hot. In three weeks I would be thirty years old.

I walked up top and looked around. I could see the *Sea Flea* on the beach, and a boat rowing toward me. A greeting rang out. It was Bobby waving a bottle of something. I looked ashore. I looked at the children playing on the beach. I looked back at Bobby.

He hadn't been to bed yet. I helped him climb aboard. He had found a bottle on his boat that was keeping him going. He offered me some. I shuddered. He crawled below and lay down on a sea berth. He said I looked unhappy. I told him I was hungover. He asked what time it was. I said one in the afternoon. He shook his head. "Imagine that."

I asked him if he knew where Don was.

"Saw him rowing ashore a little while ago," he said, and passed out.

I tied my sandals together and looped them through the belt on my shorts. I climbed into the water and swam ashore. When I arrived on the beach the children helped me to my feet. They asked me if I was all right. "Fine, kids," I said. I staggered to a palm tree and sat beneath it. I put my sandals back on. I wrung out my shirt and put it back on. I walked through the town and stopped in at the Chief of Police's store. I bought some twine and fish-hooks. He asked me if I was feeling well. I told him I had just gone for a swim to cool off. My clothes were dripping. He asked me if

I wanted some tea. I said thank you, maybe another time. He said, have a nice day. I said, you too. I walked on.

I came to Desmond's metal-roofed church. It was quiet and no one seemed to be around. The island was only a few hundred yards wide here. You could see ocean on either side, through the trees. It was warm but the dark clouds in the sky promised rain. An eight-year-old boy walked up to me and asked me where I was going. "I'm looking at the church," I said. He asked me if I was from the yacht. I said yes.

"Nice yacht," he said. I looked out at the *Sea Mouse*. Great orange rust streaks ran down her sides and the tattered headsails sat on the foredeck in bunches. The forestay hung slackly from the mast.

"Thanks," I said.

"Have a good day," he said. I would, I said. He walked on. In the yard of one of the houses a young woman was doing laundry. I waved to her. She waved back and grinned. I walked to the beach and sat down. An old man was standing on the beach. He asked me where I was from. I told him.

"Welcome to Penrhyn," he said.

When I was in the ninth grade my English class studied the novel *Mutiny on the Bounty*. I was disaffected and bored, high most of the time, and to me that novel couldn't possibly have been less interesting. I read aloud to the class the passages I was given, as each of my classmates did in their turn. I giggled inanely over the scenes that struck me as funny, although the binding of the book seemed hilarious as well, as did the holes in the tile of the dropped ceiling, and the idea of chalkboards and of brassieres. Bruce McLaren, the English teacher, clicked his tongue with irritation at my reddened eyes and vacuous smile. He often stared out the window as we went through these desultory exercises in time-filling. This was in Selkirk, Manitoba, a steel-mill town north of Winnipeg; my classmates and I understood that we were destined for lives in which stories of Englishmen arguing with Englishmen on wooden boats would not much matter. I remember the girls, bored-looking with heaped on eye makeup and pores like albino oranges and the boys in frayed jean jackets, the names of rock bands scrawled upon their backs with felt pens, their lanky greasy hair and inadequate hygiene — all our thoughts on anything that was not this. We were all in deep storage, maturing like wheels of cheese in some warehouse, until the day we were fit to unwrap for the purposes of steering a forklift for the Manitoba Rolling Mills or driving a cash register for the Safeway. Tahiti had nothing to do with any of us and it was testimony to the stupidity of this mother of a school and of Bruce McLaren that we were reading *Mutiny on the Bounty* at all.

It made no impression on me. I was not left with a lingering sense of the exotic grandeur of the world nor of the capacity of humanity for cruelty and betrayal. When the summer came and we turned our books in, I did so with relief and disdain. I don't remember where we went that night to drink until we vomited into the grass and I don't remember who fought whom. I know that between drunken car crashes, hunting accidents and hastily explained accidental overdoses, half a dozen of those children were dead within a decade. Which wasn't the direct result of my not having been moved by *Mutiny on the Bounty*, but may have stemmed from the same root cause, which is to say: that awful place.

Overlooking Main Street in Selkirk is a forty-foot-high fibreglass catfish painted a shade of green evocative of the indelible stain meat inspectors use to declare beef Unfit for Human Consumption. He is called Chuck the Channel Cat and proclaims Selkirk to be Catfish Capital of Canada, a feat more remarkable for the alliterative poetry of the phrase than its accuracy. The Red River behind the town is brown, polluted and wide; most weekends, it is true, there are a handful of Bayliners and Lunds bobbing out there with fishermen who sip rye whiskey and smoke and lie and catch pick-erel and sauger, and the odd catfish, yes, which they usually throw back. Evidently Principal Pickerel Place and Sauger Central have already been claimed.

When the town council approved the construction of Chuck in the mid-eighties and began promoting the town's embryonic tourism industry with its "reputation" for catfish, another Manito-ban town, Emerson, protested, as it already claimed title to Catfish Capitalhood. A dispute ensued, which culminated in the mayors of the two towns arguing their cases on a national call-in radio show. Selkirk won. It was the town's finest moment. People spoke of it for days afterwards.

On winter nights, one of my friends, the one who had a car, picked each of us up in succession and whoever had bought pot that week rolled joints as we drove the three miles to the north end of Main Street, where the Indians lived. Then we turned around and drove back past Chuck, to the south end of Main Street, where the 7-Eleven was. Then we turned around and headed back north, past the little strip mall on Eaton Avenue, past the Chinese restaurant and past the Liquor Commission.

There is no shortage of cheap land in Selkirk. The buildings are all low and the parking lots expansive, usually lying between the street and the businesses themselves like protective moats. The win-ters are astonishingly painful and nobody walks anywhere except those with recent DWIs or repossessed cars. It is so thoroughly car culture here that the sight of someone walking is cause for sus-picion. Sometimes men and women will be seen walking on the highway into town from the Scanterbury Reserve thirty miles to the north. There was also a man who dressed like the sailor in the Old Spice commercial who walked everywhere, but other than that, only crazy people walked out of doors.

About ten thousand people live in Selkirk. Nobody ever moves there except for RCMP officers when they are transferred and the occasional retired farmer who has sold his land and is tired of shovelling a mile-long driveway and wants to be able to walk to the Riverboat Café.

My friends were Ross Paddock, who owned the car, Darryl Bailey and Frank Parkes. All of us were power-mechanics majors in high school and most of the time we smelled of wheel-bearing grease and gasoline. Ross and I, in pictures from that time, wear eyeglasses that compete with each other's for hideousness. We were all so skinny our limbs jutted out as if we were stick insects with dreadful complexions. Girls did not like us. We thought this was because we were ugly and smelled bad. We were right.

Apart from the steel mill, Selkirk is a bedroom community of Winnipeg, in every way like the vast sprawl of suburban towns that stretch across North America, ugly and placid and convenient. It is in no way rugged and really hardly even rural, but at one time it had been. The abandoned steamers that used to ply Lake Winnipeg sit rusting and rotting in the sloughs that lie off the river. Some of the old men who live in Selkirk were trappers and fishermen when they were younger, and there were reminders, in the McCleod Hardware store — gear for such pursuits sat unsold and dusty on the back shelves — of a time that struck my teenage sensibilities as having been more heroic and less banal. At the time I didn't know the word banal, and would have said, "fuckin' retarded."

So while I didn't read *Mutiny on the Bounty*, I did read *Field & Stream* and *Outdoors* and, in a prelude to the escapist fantasies that occupied me as a soldier, imagined living in a cabin by myself in the bush a hundred miles north of town, catching trout (which I knew only from these magazines as something to be prized — in Manitoba there are jackfish, or northern pike, and pickerel, or walleye.) I studied the advertisements. Trucks, rifles, smokeless tobacco, fishing gear, rye whiskey; various representations of the Marlboro Man fingered whiskered chins and stroked especially appealing representations of the proffered merchandise. That state of whiskered wherewithal was all I wanted.

My father's chin, on the other hand, was as cleanly shaven as a city man's face would be. He wore a suit instead of a sheepskin coat and had never chewed tobacco in his life. Although he had once smoked a pipe. I have subsequently discovered my father to be a kind and patient man who is full of love and deep strength but at that time he was a mystery to me. Like so many of the fathers in that town, he had accepted the fifties model of grey-flannel masculinity and he was up every morning at six and gone by seven, commuting into the city in necktie and blazer. He returned late in the evenings and worked on reports at his desk in the basement. When he emerged to watch television with the rest of us, he quickly fell asleep in his big chair. I remember looking over at him, rasping over the dialogue of *Three's Company*, his head lolling to one side.

My idea of adulthood, of what I should be trying to become, was formed by those sportsmen magazines: self-reliant and silent, a good shot and an able judge of cover. If I could be those things, then at least I could live among trees and mountains and streams. Clearly, I was not a particularly bright adolescent. But it seemed very clear to me that the alternate model — necktied and exhausted — would strand me in some Selkirk, commuting through flat grey cinder blocks and gas stations and Chinese and Canadian food restaurants.

I saved my money from the gas station I worked at, and I bought a shotgun and a hunting licence. I practiced trying to use snuff, and gagged and spat into wastebaskets, wondering what I was doing wrong. Those sunburnt guys in the ads always looked so serene. I browbeat my father into coming home early from work a few evenings in the fall so that we could walk together in the publicly owned marshes north of town looking for grouse.

We spent hours and hours out there, tramping about and getting straw stuck in our shiny shoes. We might have, in the course of all that time, seen maybe a half-dozen grouse. On at least a couple of occasions I discharged my shotgun, but only as an afterthought to their thumping escapes — I disturbed not a feather and I think my father and I were both relieved. He was equally relieved when hunting season ended and he could return to work where people approved of him because he was conscientious and tried hard, and where they didn't go on inexplicably about smokeless tobacco products in an accusing tone.

After a few years I stopped reading *Field & Stream* and I stopped fantasizing about owning chaps or living in a cabin, but I was left with the idea that such a model of existence represented a way out of the flat, dull fluorescent-lit torpor of Winnipeg's suburbs. Self-reliance, stoicism and a sufficiently rugged-looking hat could save your soul.

When I discovered travel literature I was in the army and deeply dissatisfied with my surroundings — I took solace in the clear skies of Newby's Hindu Kush and Thesiger's Empty Quarter, just as I had before sought escape from Selkirk in reading about hunting whitetail deer in the Adirondacks. I read O'Hanlon and Theroux and Cahill and was very grateful that distraction like that was available, as I had long since accustomed myself to being the only openly dissatisfied one, at least in that officers' mess, on that base.

Later I read Sallie Tisdale's insightful essay in *Harper's* on the remarkable rise of travel literature and what she contends is its obsession with manufactured danger and exoticism. It became clear to me that there are millions of people living as discontentedly as I was. I was the rule rather than the exception. These people live in Selkirk and Orange County and Etobicoke and just outside Houston and anywhere at all where long stretches of tedium are interrupted by Boston Pizza joints immediately adjacent to video arcades beside 7-Elevens serving Slurpees and Hoagies to shift workers headed home and too tired to cook.

I sat there on the beach in Penrhyn until my stomach settled enough to be hungry. Then I walked back down the road. An old woman asked me if I was looking for my mate, as she put it. I said yes. "He's out at the airstrip, talking to Lester," she said. "Lester is the weatherman here. Would you like some lunch?"

"I'd love some," I said.

"Come with me," she said.

I walked with her to her house, which was small, concrete and very neat. She made us jelly sandwiches and lemonade. Her granddaughter appeared from somewhere. She had just come back from school in New Zealand. She was sixteen and so beautiful my chest tightened. We talked about school, and Canada and what she thought about New Zealand, which was, basically, that it was "way more interesting than here." We finished our lunch and the old woman cleared away our plates and thanked me for coming for lunch. I thanked her. She laughed and shrugged.

Her granddaughter walked me back to the beach. There were some boats that had come in. "The fishermen are back," she said. "One of them will give you a nice fish." I asked her where they fished. She said, "Some of them stay in the lagoon and dive for oysters, and some of them go outside the reef and fish for big fish out there." The biggest of the boats looked about three times the length of the *Sea Flea*, maybe eighteen feet long. On the open ocean, through surf like semi-trailers. We walked closer and she introduced me to the fishermen. I smiled. A toothless man of maybe thirty handed me a tuna. He was wearing a torn T-shirt that said Seattle Seahawks.

"Thank you," I said.

"Pleasure," he said. He went back to cleaning the rest of his fish. My guide waved goodbye and disappeared. I set down our supper in the *Sea Flea* and waited for Don to return. When he did, I showed him the fish. He just shook his head. We stood there, looking around at the island, and the people going about their business and hardly noticing us except to smile shyly.

We set to work on the broken forestay chainplate, in preparation for leaving. It wasn't that hard to repair, we found, with the boat motionless at anchor in the lagoon. It took about three hours. After finishing, we rowed ashore with all our fuel jugs and hitch-hiked to the government office to pay for our fuel. The woman behind the desk phoned her brother, who came down and opened the warehouse where the diesel was stored. We filled our jugs. A flatbed truck appeared and drove us back to the beach, where we loaded the jugs back on the *Sea Flea*. Don and I, the jugs and the almost-awash dinghy inched our way to the boat. We refilled our fuel tank. We had nothing stopping us from continuing on to Tahiti. It was like wolfing down chocolate mousse. We should have taken our time. Without speaking, Don began lifting the anchor. I started the engine.

CHAPTER TEN

WHILE WE HAD STAYED on Penrhyn, the trade winds had not abruptly altered their eternal pattern. They still blew straight out of the southeast, the direction we wanted to go. We hoisted the sails and began a series of long ocean tacks, east and then south, proceeding by successive approximations toward Tahiti. Moving from northwest to southeast, we would transit the length of the Society Islands, named for their congeniality, the Iles Sous le Vent, Bora-Bora, Huahine, and finally Moorea, before coming to Tahiti. All these temptations en route.

Three days out the wind slackened until we were almost becalmed. Averaging a hundred miles a day, it would take us a week or so to cover the seven hundred miles to Tahiti. This, of course, assumed that the wind would be present and favourable some of the time.

When the wind was entirely absent, we started the engine and motored. This kept our daily average up for several days. One night I was on watch and thought I saw a ship in the distance. Concerned that he couldn't see us, I switched on the *Sea Mouse*'s running lights. The winking lights approached no closer than a few miles. I settled back in the cockpit, relieved, and fell asleep.

The next morning, the batteries were completely dead. Both banks — I had set the battery switch to "all" just to sabotage that built-in safety feature. I looked sheepishly at Don. He rolled his eyes and we dug out the portable generator we had brought along for just such a circumstance. It wouldn't start.

We took apart the carburetor, cleaned it and reassembled it. It still wouldn't start. We changed spark plugs and polished the points. It still wouldn't start. We repeated step one. We cleaned out the fuel tank. We took apart every electrical connection and polished them all with emery cloth. We repeated step two. It still wouldn't start.

We sat there in the boat, bobbing slowly up and down in the South Pacific Ocean. Tahiti was four or five hundred miles to the southeast. With no batteries our engine would not start. There wasn't any wind at all.

I looked at some of the books that Bobby Peru had traded us. There was Douglas Oliver's *The Pacific Islands*, published by the University of Hawaii, and a passel of backpackers' guides to one thing or another. I learned this:

Tahiti was discovered by Polynesians sailing westward from the Marquesas around 800 AD, as a part of the explosion of exploration and colonization that had so impressed Peter Ericson. The Polynesians were originally from what is now Indonesia, and had arrived in Samoa by 1000 BC.

A frenzy of expedition launchings began a few centuries into the Common Era. As the Roman Empire was ossifying and sclerosing, huge ocean-going catamarans, capable of holding a hundred adults, were being built and launched from beaches in the Samoan Islands. Canoes such as these were observed and described by Captain Cook, and the utility and grace of these vessels is obvious in his descriptions. From Samoa they reached the Marquesas in around 300 AD. The pattern of this exploration was not systematic; large, fertile and close-at-hand islands remained unsettled while far more distant and inhospitable lands were discovered. After who knows how many months at sea, relieved and, no doubt, skinny men and women stumbled ashore, looking for fresh surface water, for fertile soil. Sometimes they found them. Sometimes they didn't. (If Hawaii was found, then presumably Palmyra was, too, at some point or another. No surface water, no fertile soil — no historical record of habitation. I wonder how long it took them to put the boat back in the water again. Imagine the arguments.)

I thought about the men and women who sailed to Easter Island. Rapa Nui, they called it, the navel of the world. Windswept and cold, with all of New Zealand undiscovered a few weeks' sail to the south, with prevailing winds blowing right there — but at least it was land. Even closer — only a few *days'* sail, the Cook Islands. Hawaii and Christmas Island were reached in further months-long voyages, against contrary winds, around 500 AD. New Zealand, the Tuamotus and the Cook Islands were reached in the following five hundred years.

It seems astonishing that anyone even talks about Leif the Lucky. Christ, he was practically in *sight* of his discoveries. Which were, of course, already well inhabited. From Iceland to the coast of Greenland is a few hundred miles; from Southern Greenland to the coast of Labrador, a few hundred more. From Easter Island to the western edge of Melanesia is eight thousand miles. In open wooden boats, without charts.

Eventually we gave up trying to fix the generator. The batteries were dead and without them the engine simply wasn't going to start and that was all there was to it. We read novels and turned the tuning knob of the short-wave radio. Whenever the wind came up we leapt to raise the sails and, slowly, we edged closer to the Happy Isles.

Making open-water passages in a small sailboat is like descending into a tunnel. At any given time, between any two bodies of land, there must be a handful of sailboats progressing from one to the other. The circumstances of weather and current are probably similar for each, but in the course of the passage, these boats remain ignorant of one another. The departure is made with dozens of masts visible astern but they slowly sink below the horizon, and then there is only your boat, and yourself. You may know that those boats you left behind are planning to follow you in a few days, but that knowledge has no relation to your circumstances at sea. Out there, it is as if the world has disappeared.

When you arrive at your destination, there will again be a forest of masts in a large harbour — and the people on those boats will know well the sorts of trouble you've had with fickle winds and squalls. But they will not know the particular squalls you have known, and so there remains the impression that only *you* have made that particular trip, that only *you* became quite that lonely out there, frustrated with winds that always blow in your face.

December 27, 1994
My thirtieth birthday. Spent the day reading — Chekhov, a novel by Kim Chernin. An account of the fall of Saigon by James Fenton — and listening to the short-wave. Only a hundred miles from Bora-Bora, 230 from Papeete, but going so slowly, not even 2 kts, averaged out. Getting easting remains very difficult but there are few alternatives to enduring.

I am worried about going into the pass, which faces west, in Bora-Bora, with no engine and no charts. It might be the wrong thing to do; perhaps a few more days worth of endurance and getting to Papeete proper will be the right thing to do. We shall see. We shall see. I use that phrase often, here.

After two weeks of bobbing up and down, one day Don idly reached for the start cord of the generator, and for the ten-thousandth time, gave it a tug. I was sitting below when I heard the generator sputter to life. I went up top and Don was sitting there dumbfounded. We charged the batteries and started the engine. In a couple of hours we were on our way, making four knots straight for Tahiti.

The inculcation in the minds of Europeans of the idea of Tahiti began through literature, with the books of Melville. His novels *Omoo* (1847) and *Typee* (1846) concern whaling voyages to Tahiti and the Marquesas, respectively. *Typee* is the better known of them and is based on a month he spent in the Taipai Valley of Nuku Hiva, one of the Marquesas, after deserting from his whaling ship, *Acushnet*. By describing the Marquesan island as "paradisiacal" he ushered in the era of men and women as pallid as lard fantasizing about warm winds as they huddle and cough in the northern winters. Within a generation of Melville's departure, the population of Nuku Hiva (ten thousand or so) was shrunk by ninety per cent, dead from European diseases, war and alcohol. Much of the appeal of Eden depends on the absence of others. The South Pacific steadily grew more and more paradisiacal.

In the last six years of his life, Robert Louis Stevenson travelled and lived in the South Pacific. He chartered a yacht, the *Casco*, in San Francisco in June 1888, and proceeded to Tahiti, via the Marquesas. (Which was just what I'd intended, the little matter of the anchor being lost overboard having torpedoed that.) Stevenson stayed four months in a little village on the south shore of Tahiti and described it as "The Garden of the World." His *Tales of the South Seas* further propelled the idea of Tahiti as paradise.

Paul Gauguin arrived in 1891 and is probably more responsible than anyone for turning the place into an icon in the imaginations of the snowbound. In fact, he didn't much like the place and moved on pretty quickly for the Marquesas, which he found less French, and less restrictive. This may have had something to do with his fourteen-year-old mistress — but the details are sketchy.

Just as much of the exploration of the Arctic happened as a consequence of the search for the lost Franklin Expedition, the next wave of writers came to Tahiti in search of Gauguinia. Rupert Brooke came looking for lost paintings in 1913–14 and W. Somerset Maugham came to research *The Moon and Sixpence* in 1916. He found a Gauguin painted on a house door. He bought the owner a new door and took the painting home with him. (Chatwin, in his Sotheby's years, sold a Gauguin that had been in Maugham's estate when he died. I wondered whether it was that door.)

When *The Moon and Sixpence* came out in 1919, the idea of Tahiti was cemented into the minds of book-reading cold people. Charles Strickland, a protagonist modeled on Gauguin, is presented as a half-mad tortured genius driven by demons, baffling to all around him in Europe, whose struggle to achieve his own greatness is frustrated until finally he makes his way to Tahiti:

> Here, on this remote island, he seemed to have aroused none of the detestation with which he was regarded at home, but compassion rather; and his vagaries were accepted with tolerance. To these people, native and European, he was a queer fish, and they took him for granted; the world was full of odd persons, who did odd things; and perhaps they knew that a man is not what he wants to be, but what he must be. In England and France he was the square peg in the round hole, but here the holes were any sort of shape, and no sort of peg was quite amiss.

Maugham's description of the island expresses a sense of graciousness and complex beauty:

> Tahiti is a lofty, green island, with deep folds of a darker green, in which you divine silent valleys; there is mystery in their somber depths, down which murmur and splash cool streams, and you feel that in those umbrageous places life from immemorial times has

been led according to immemorial ways. Even here is something sad and terrible. But the impression is fleeting, and serves only to give a greater acuteness to the enjoyment of the moment. It is so like the sadness which you may see in the jester's eyes when a merry company is laughing at his sallies; his lips smile and his jokes are gayer because in the communion of laughter he finds himself more intolerably alone. For Tahiti is smiling and friendly; it is like a lovely woman graciously prodigal of her charm and beauty; and nothing can be more conciliatory than the entrance into the harbour at Papeete. The schooners moored to the quay are trim and neat, the little town along the bay is white and urbane, and the flamboyants, scarlet against the blue sky, flaunt their colour like a cry of passion. They are sensual with an unashamed violence that leaves you breathless. And the crowd that throngs the wharf as the steamer draws alongside is gay and debonair; it is a noisy, cheerful, gesticulating crowd. It is a sea of brown faces. You have an impression of colored movement against the flaming blue of the sky. Everything is done with a great deal of bustle, the unloading of the baggage, the examination of the customs; and everyone seems to smile at you. It is very hot. The colour dazzles you.

Throughout this, and throughout the writings of Melville and Stevenson, too, runs the idea of the Polynesians as Rousseau's noble savages, uncontaminated by late-Industrial-Revolution Europe. Implicit is the possibility that Europeans, by venturing there, could recapture a state of grace. Look at Gauguin, after all. This is another of Maugham's Europeans, cast upon Tahiti:

Our life is simple and innocent. We are untouched by ambition, and what pride we have is due only to our contemplation of the work of our hands. Malice cannot touch us, nor envy attack. Ah, *mon cher monsieur*, they talk of the blessedness of labour, and it is a meaningless phrase, but to me it has the most intense significance. I am a happy man.

The idealization of Tahiti has always required a certain amount of willing self-delusion. To carry off his representation of paradise, Maugham has Gauguin/Strickland die of leprosy after painting his masterpieces one after the other in a steady stream, loved by his young wife, and happy. That word again. But Gauguin hated Tahiti, considered it nearly as suffocating as Europe and retreated to the Marquesas, and then even further, to the less-settled northern side of the island. He quarrelled with the local police, who objected to his public drunkenness — and when he finally did die, of alcoholism, he had been sentenced to a short prison term. The locals quickly forgot him. They only remembered him again when more shiny-faced people arrived to make a fuss over his grave. He left a son behind, as does Strickland, but while the fictional son is content and at ease with his life, Gauguin's son drank himself to death with the same determination as his father.

After the homicidal spasm of the world wars undermined any idea of the perfectibility of man as represented by modern Western city-dwellers, escapism bloomed. Exit routes have included the hairy-footed shire, techno-Utopianism and various cults of comet-dwelling and political personalities. Maugham, Stevenson and Melville had all helped to prepare the ground for this.

It was after the war that the idea of the South Pacific as an attainable goal, as, inevitably, paradise, really began to capture the popular imagination of North Americans. Demobilized sailors and marines returning to Peoria and Tallahassee and Muscle Shoals brought stories back with them of peace and ease and limitless physical beauty stretched out under warm blue skies. Suddenly everyone was longing to live on a desert island and sip papaya punch under the shade of a banyan tree. *South Pacific* was set on one of the *Iles Sous le Vent*, Bora-Bora, and brought home to non-combatants this picture of an idyll. A whole industry began to form around the manufacturing of a paradise as represented by plastic palm trees and ukuleles and grass skirts. The comic-strip desert islands with the one coconut tree became a modern icon and Gauguin became better known for his flight to paradise than for his paintings.

Tahiti. Vanilla came from there. Great coffee, too. Both things I liked. I'd have bet there wasn't an ugly mall on the whole island. Everything starts with the idea that the place you live in is beautiful. Then you don't deface it. Waterfalls plunging off green mountains, down sheer cliffs and straight into the sea.

Moorea appeared on the horizon like Doom Mountain, craggy and shadowed and sharp. Then it began raining and the wind veered to the north and increased steadily. The *Sea Mouse*'s progress slowed and we spent hours running the engine and tacking back and forth against the wind. I went down below to make tea and was so tired I fell asleep on the table. I woke up to Don touching my shoulder. When I came up top he pointed at Tahiti, rising up through the fog. We sailed closer and saw the entrance through the reef into the harbour. We transited the pass. All along the beach we could see white buildings lining the road, with cars and bicycles moving slowly back and forth.

This is from Rupert Brooke's poem, "Haunting," written in Papeete in 1914:

In the grey tumult of these after-years
    Oft silence falls; the incessant wranglers part;
And less-than-echoes of remembered tears
    Hush all the loud confusion of the heart;
And a shade, through the toss'd ranks of mirth and crying,
    Hungers, and pains, and each dull passionate mood, —
Quite lost, and all but all forgot, undying,
    Comes back the ecstasy of your quietude.

CHAPTER ELEVEN

BOULEVARD POMARE runs along the Papeete harbour, and small cafés look out upon the ocean with an equanimity found nowhere in Paris, but with all the *hauteur* of that city and the fierce and impeccable waiters too. I walked inland away from the beach and drank in the scent of the mountain and car exhaust and coffee roasting. We had overturned the *Sea Flea* in the polluted harbour and I was soaked and filthy, but I had been soaked and filthy for months now and this was very fine. I gaped to either side and felt shivers of pleasure and cold sweep up and down me.

Tropical storm Victor had hit that morning as we had been anchoring, had blown up in earnest only a few minutes after we had cleared the harbour entrance. As we had tried to get the anchor to set, we had been driven repeatedly almost up on the beach, each time motoring out into deeper water and better bottom; the transmission chose just that moment to stop working. It had been the worst four hours of the trip, and it seemed certain that the boat would be blown ashore. But the crew of the boat next to us, four hippies from Marseilles, had come to our rescue with a spare anchor and chain; they had worked hard with us, and finally it had held. Don and I thanked them over and over again; embarrassed at our effusiveness, they had withdrawn.

We stayed on the boat in the rain, looking at the shore, jumping to our feet again and again, certain that the anchor was dragging, but it was not, and we calmed ourselves slowly. Eventually we climbed into the *Sea Flea* and rowed ashore, separating as we hit the beach, drenched and smelly.

I kept walking until I came to the customs post where I handed over both our passports. As I stood there smiling maniacally and trying to endear myself to officialdom, my French vanished. *Please don't ask to inspect my boat, monsieur. Just stamp our passports and let me go get the mail.* The inspector indulged my attempt to speak in the only civilized language, and we stumbled and tripped and he repeated each question and I grunted and spat out the vanishing words but the only phrase that stood out in my mind was *Voulez-vous coucher avec moi, ce soir* in a falsetto disco beat. I struggled to stamp that out of my head, and I only barely escaped that office without propositioning the *gendarme*, and the consequent jail term and beating.

I was walking in the rain, with a piece of cardboard held over my head, to get the mail when a car came to a quick stop beside me. A young woman unrolled her window and asked me where I was going.

"*Voulez-vous, uh, à la poste,*" I replied. She opened the door and told me to get in. This was not Paris. She asked me where I was from. I told her about the boat, about crossing the ocean, she clicked her tongue and said — this delighted me — "*ooh la la.*" We grinned. We arrived at the *poste*.

"*Merci*," I said.

"*De rien*," she said. I got out.

"*Au revoir*," she said, and sped off.

I stood there grinning. Goddamn. Ta-hi-ti. Look at me.

That night, Don and I ate supper in a café: mahi mahi *grillé*, red wine and beautiful bread. Then cheese and coffee and cognac. Piles of opened letters sat beneath the table. The *poste restante* box had been filled by our mail and the mustachioed man in uniform had informed us that had we been another week arriving, it would all have been sent back. Just so we knew who to be grateful to. Thank you, sir, we told him sincerely. We clutched our bales of letters and looked at each other. We each wanted to be alone. We parted, sympathetically.

I walked by myself away from the sea, into the interior of Papeete. The *gendarmerie* lay on the edge of the town, its back to the mountain. Fog rolled down and off the mountain and there was rain falling further up the slope. I walked past the barracks of the Foreign Legion and toward the Catholic cathedral. Its bells were pealing and the ringing echoed through the town. It began to rain again and I hurried to a café.

Poste restante is an institution worth thinking about. You can write a letter, send it out to a place that a friend may be travelling through — and it works. Standing in dusty antique post offices around the world and holding out one's passport hopefully — it is impossible to express the pleasure of getting a letter in such circumstances. At home one imagines oneself crowded and confined, longing for anonymity and room to move. But after a few months at sea there is only one desire: *Avez-vous des lettres a moi, monsieur?* We are not so easily disentangled after all.

I sat in a little café facing a quiet street of ochre- and yellow-painted single-storey buildings and watched the rain fall like fruit.

My letters sat at my feet in an elastic-banded cube. The waitress brought me a sandwich and a *café au lait* and it was about as far from the army and Selkirk, Manitoba, as there is. *Tahiti*, by sea.

As I sat in that café I remembered Catherine and the Café de la Palette and the fight we had there. The narrow streets that sprouted off Boulevard Pomare reminded me of where she had lived. I remembered telling her that I would not take her to sea, that I was determined to see Tahiti and would not compromise. As if Samoa or Pitcairn would have been unthinkable — we both recognized the argument as the convenience it was, and for that reason Catherine did not try to persuade me.

And now I was repaid by a barrage of recollection. Her voice was clear in my ear and I could smell her scent and I had no idea where on the planet she was, except not where French flags flew. Not here. I remembered her devotion to her son and her self-destructive impetuousness and her fine and compelling imagination, her magnificent letters.

Letters. I looked through my bale of correspondence. A woman who loved one of my friends had written to me, and in her muted and dignified ache I felt all the sadness of the autumn return, but less corrosively. When I thought about my ex–girlfriend I still winced — that had not changed. I recalled her strange and fragile beauty and the open-eyed fear and delight with which she looked out at the world. I missed her. But I did not call her this time. It was clear that she and I were better off for parting and that aching is part of the beauty of the world. Like rubbing a bruise and remembering the leap that led to it.

In the café were legionnaires, with their *kepis* hung on the hat rack. For a moment, I was Huckleberry Hound in the Sahara, mourning his sweet Clementine. The soldiers were as I remembered the artillerymen in Shilo, boisterous and large. I read my mail. I wanted to be a legionnaire. I wanted my own *kepi.*

Paris is a city of the cold northern European plains, and it has winter, and chimneys rise from all the old roofs. When rain comes and doesn't stop, the leaves fall and people aggregate together and endure. Tahiti is not like this. It is warm here even when it rains, heating a house is not a problem and endurance is not as necessary. But still, in the city of Papeete, which is one hundred thousand people, the influence of Paris may be seen, her nature intuited in the cobblestones and the winding roads and the blue street signs and the funny little pharmacies. The officious bureaucrats bustle through the streets, as they do back home, in the only civilized city in the world. And of course they long for Paris. In their homesickness it is possible to feel affectionate toward them in a way that is not possible in Paris.

Parisian accountants in the South Pacific longing for decent opera and a million Shriners in the heartland reminiscing about Bora-Bora, their own youth and quietude. All of us wishing we were elsewhere.

En route here, I had told Don that I wanted to fly home to make some money to repair the transmission, and reprovision the boat. Don said he would wait for me in the South Pacific. At one point he had wanted to spend hurricane season in Fiji, but after seeing Penrhyn, he was rethinking that. I told him it was up to him. Once I started thinking about going home, I began to long for it. I knew the foreign and physical beauty of Tahiti, and felt it, but I wanted to go home. Don didn't. He wanted to live on Penrhyn Atoll. As we outlined our plans for the remainder of the winter, I think we both wondered if we would in fact see each other again. It seemed likely, but not certain. I worried that I would become mired back in Canada, and that leaving again to sail home five thousand miles, under any circumstances less desperate than those that had pushed me out here, would seem impossible. It wasn't clear that Don would be sailing home with me. It seemed more likely at that point that he would remain in the South Pacific. Each of us was gravitating toward his fate; I wished I wanted his more than I wanted mine. Back to the strip malls. Maybe I could

open a little practice in one. Share a receptionist with a dentist.
Pick out my own wood-veneer panelling.

A week later Don and I said goodbye at a café facing Boulevard
Pomare. We had rowed my little leather suitcase and my pack ashore
and had tipped again in the surf — *haolied* is the transitive verb
used, from the noun which means "pale ones." My bags smelled
of the Tahiti harbour and so did we. Then the rain started falling
on us at our patio table but we remained there, letting the effluvia
wash off. Don was quiet. He said he was happy, but he seemed
torn, uncertain whether he wished he was going home, or whether
this deeper and solitary plunge appealed to him more. He said he
thought he would make friends with the hippies. There was a pause.

I told him thank you.

He said you're welcome.

I said that I would write.

"You better."

CHAPTER TWELVE

*We want to be set free. The man driving a pickaxe into the
ground wants to know the meaning of his pickaxe blow.
The pickaxe blow of the convict, a humiliation for the convict, is not the same as the pickaxe blow of the prospector,
which gives stature to the prospector. Prison is not in the
place where the pickaxe blows fall. The horror is not the
physical. Prison is where pickaxe blows fall without purpose,
fall without bonding the man to the community of men.*
And we yearn to escape from that prison.

ANTOINE DE SAINT-EXUPÉRY, *Wind, Sand and Stars*

IN WINNIPEG it was thirty-two degrees below zero and the
air had a crystalline sharpness to it that I recalled immediately.
When I stepped out of the airport to find a cab I couldn't
breathe. After I piled my bags in the back seat, the cabbie turned
to me and said, "What's that smell?" I asked him to drive me to a
late-night diner where my friends often spent time. When I stumbled in, there they were, sitting at a table. We all smiled. That city
is so cold in the winter, and still it blazes with the warmth of a
bread oven when you return.

I found work quickly. Within a few weeks I had two jobs —
one was in an emergency room in the city and the other was in
Rankin Inlet, on the coast of Hudson Bay. It was a strangely fractured time, flying back and forth between the city and the Arctic.

I rented an apartment and phoned the army, which had kept my belongings in storage since I had taken my release. For the first time in two years I had all my books and papers around me.

When winter storms blew up I stayed awake listening to the potency of the wind. Weather was newly disturbing to me. Living on the prairie, I had always enjoyed storms. But now, when the wind screeched at night I would awaken terrified, and run into the living room/cockpit, searching for landmarks against which I might judge whether the anchor was dragging. I had lost the ability to take pleasure in the unreasonable urgency of storms, and the sense of safety and warmth that they lent to shelter.

But slowly the sea retreated and when I awoke frightened at night I learned to remain in bed, to put a pillow over my ears. I settled into a kind of moon-faced and viscous ease. My friends and I had dinner parties for one another and we ate elaborate meals of baked salmon and roasted garlic and wild rice. Those evenings I thought less often about asceticism and the redemptive quality of journeys through deserts on foot.

I met my ex–girlfriend for lunch one day and she told me of her impending marriage. She said she thought that she should tell me directly, not let the news seep to me through embarrassed friends. "Why ever not?" I wondered, forgetting for a moment that my own cringing cowardice in such matters is not universal. I smiled and kept eating my mandarin orange salad.

It was a little like eating lunch with a piece of devotional sculpture. She was preposterously gracious. She smiled with benignity and indulgence when I told her that I had missed her. Sympathetic but not encouraging — perfect. It had been a hard winter for us both, she said. I did not know what had made her winter hard, but nodded anyway, trying to be as empathetic as she was.

At sea, I had tried to believe that I was distorting her in my memory, that I was only missing a construction of some masochistic need of mine to pine, that I was exaggerating her kindness and loveliness. But it wasn't so.

This did not ease matters in the subsequent weeks for me. She finished her salad and checked her watch. I tried to stop it with telepathy.

She told me about a man she knew in Rankin Inlet, an Inuk who had travelled as a boy to Winnipeg for a series of operations; in the year and a half he had had to stay in the south he had lived with her family, who grew to consider him an adopted son. She gave me photographs of them together as children for me to take to him and I looked at her in these photos, two years old and just as beautiful, and I took them, and a letter she wrote up to the Arctic and gave them to her brother. I envied his enduring affiliation with her.

Rankin Inlet is on the west coast of Hudson Bay, about four hundred miles north of the treeline. Like the other little towns in the Arctic, its buildings cling like barnacles to the sheets of rock that line the coast and slope slowly beneath the ice like a doorjamb. The buildings are mostly modular affairs manufactured in the south and then loaded on barges and shipped north during the brief summers. Here and there is an older wooden building — a church, an old shed built by the Hudson's Bay Company, the nuns' residence — made out of timber shipped north and sawn and erected on the spot. These buildings have a self-respect about them, a feeling of belonging that is lacking in the other dwellings. The name of the area, Keewatin, means north wind, and that wind scours the flat land like a sandblaster. Left to themselves, these buildings would blow into the sea faster than even Palmyra's did. This is a topography that has always enforced transience, as much as humility.

I spent much of what remained of the winter and spring travelling to the little Inuit towns that line the coast of Hudson Bay.

Coral Harbour, Arviat, Whale Cove, Saniqiluaq in the Belcher Islands — I remembered these towns from before I went sailing and I was eager to see them again. The Inuit are fundamentally a maritime people, and I now imagined myself an acolyte of that religion. When I arrived in these little towns it took me about five minutes to tell the nurses and janitors of my acquaintance where I had been. I rolled up my shirt sleeves to show them my tan. They laughed at me and rolled up theirs.

In Repulse Bay I saw the town priest to check his blood pressure. Louis Fournier was an Oblate priest from Normandy who had lived among the Inuit since 1948 and thinks and dreams in Inuktitut. I had met him before and had come away awed at his commitment to the people of Repulse Bay and at his profound humility and strength. He was nearly eighty and had none of the patrician severity that I had always associated with Catholic priests. He had a greenhouse abutting his church and grew flowers in it. He considered the sexual mores prescribed by the Vatican to be unworkable, at least in the Arctic, and found his own accommodation with his people in matters of desire and passion. When I visited there, he would invite me for a lunch of caribou stew. My fractured French would be trotted out and he would pretend to be able to make sense of me for a little while. Gradually we would switch to English as our conversation grew more engaging. I usually brought him pipe tobacco and bottles of burgundy. "For the church," he would say, as he accepted them. Minutes later the wine would appear in our glasses and we would drink to the Holy Spirit.

This time I told him about my sailing trip. I told him about Derrick on Palmyra Atoll, and about Don, in search of a wife.

He told me how, in the fifties, he had grown dispirited about his role in the life of the Inuit and the part he saw the church playing in their cultural assimilation. The people were coming in off the land rapidly then, were giving up their dog teams, had already forgotten how to make the *qayak*, and were becoming increasingly dependent on *kablunauk* pilot biscuits and tubs of lard. In Arviat and Baker Lake there was terrible famine; the caribou had changed their migratory path and the people were dying. At the same time tuberculosis was epidemic. It was hard to see how anyone was better off for contact with people like Louis Fournier.

He confessed to his bishop that he thought he was unable to continue in the order. The bishop suggested that he take a retreat and meditate upon his frustrations. Fournier saw his crisis as a result of the practical effects of his work, but the bishop persisted in his spiritual solution. Fournier loaded up his dogsled with ammunition and food and set off to Baffin Island to contemplate his future. He stayed out on the land for a year, living in an *iglu* in the winter and a tent in the summer. My little jaunt through tropical seas seemed abruptly less impressive to me, but this was not Fournier's intention in telling me his story.

Fournier found a small valley to live in and he built a little camp for himself and his dogs. He gathered together a cache of seal and caribou. He told me his days were simple and he knew peace out there. The role of the church and his own role within it did not become immediately clear to him, but he enjoyed the solitude. While it lasted.

Within a month of his arrival he had visitors. Families on the land came upon his little camp and joined him. The Inuit have no vocabulary for a desire for solitude; under the open frozen arctic sky, there is only pleasure in meeting others. Fournier went on hunting trips with the men and together they all feasted on the seal and the caribou. They remained with him. He did not ask them to leave. He did not find any epiphanies forming within himself. He played with the children. His Inuktitut became more fluent. He did not meditate much.

For a time he considered setting off on his own again. This was a nomadic people, and in their own tradition, when bands became too large for an area's game to support they split up. Aggregation was not inevitable. He made plans to leave. He told his companions he would move on. He didn't. His companions would not leave him alone. They understood more of isolation, loneliness and self-sufficiency than anyone and they would not leave him alone. In the end he returned to Repulse Bay.

We ate our stew. I asked the priest what he thought he achieved on the land. He changed the subject. I suspect that in his inability to truly isolate himself Père Fournier had found his insight. He has not left the people since. This might have been a transformation of the sort that Moitessier experienced. It is difficult to know for certain because Fournier himself deflects any direct questions on this point. He has remained in the Arctic, however, and is only at home there, in his little house in Repulse Bay and in his little church. He grows irises in the greenhouse. The house is piled high with liturgical literature from France. The crucifix in his church is two crossed narwhal tusks.

I met a dying doctor in Rankin Inlet. He had practised for years in the Arctic, flying between villages, tapping on bellies, delivering babies and draining pleural effusions. I came across his clinical notes in the charts of many of the old Inuit men and women I met and treated. They spoke of him affectionately but with some puzzlement. Up there, the pattern of teachers and physicians and nurses is one of relentless rotation; almost nobody stays for more than the two or three years that the contracts stipulate and the Inuit grow weary of explaining their circumstances over and over again to yet another fresh foreign face. One assertive young woman told me that southerners just came up there like a visit to the zoo, to see oddities, and are relieved to get away again to brag about having been there.

The dying man had tried to become a part of that place. He knew Louis Fournier. He spoke of the priest as the man he would have liked to have been. To have belonged to these people.

But the doctor was already ill when he had arrived a decade earlier. He was too frail to hunt much or to spend winter nights on the tundra, and so, despite his desire, he did not become a member of the community. The people who stayed in their houses, like me, reading and listening to the radio, declared themselves to be marking time and waiting for their return to the south. The only thing that distinguished the old doctor was his persistence there. He had fallen in love with the people and had committed himself to them. But there are acts and qualities necessary for intimacy to be sustained. Strength, for instance. The weak do not often love well. He could not do the things that men in that land did and so his admiration for the Inuit had remained a distanced regard.

And so he drank himself into dissolution and had been compelled to retire. He referred to the matter as his disability, suggesting perhaps that his back had given out on him. I visited him in his house and, in the course of many long conversations there, I did not challenge him on the point.

There was a woman he lived with, his wife, a white schoolteacher who had stayed in the town nearly as long as he had. These two fell into a tender and wildly self-destructive embrace. Each accelerated the other's drinking and they were both aware of what the end would be. By the time I met him, he was too infirm to live alone and so neither of them left. His liver was failing and he came to the nursing station periodically to have me drain the ascites — the fluid oozing from his diseased liver into his abdominal cavity — so that he might breathe more easily.

He was sometimes delirious those days, from the accumulation of toxic protein metabolites in his blood. It was thought to be an important point, to establish just how confused he was, as a measure of the severity of his liver failure. Sometimes he phoned the nurses to talk and whispered gibberish to them for many minutes before his mind cleared and he was able to say what he wished. These were painful encounters for the nurses, who had worked with the old man when he had been healthier and had loved his kindness.

The doctor was an intelligent man and his early life had been full and promising. He had been born in Burma, the son of a Royal Navy dentist, and had studied medicine at Cambridge. There had been some service in the Royal Navy, and then he had come to Canada, with a young family. He worked in British Columbia for a time and then, in the wake of a disintegrating marriage and the first voiced suggestions of his overfondness for alcohol, he had returned to university to study anthropology. Chatwin had done the same thing after the mysterious "ocular ailment" had ended his time at Sotheby's.

In the course of the doctor's studies he conducted excavations of pre-European contact camp sites in the Arctic. He told me he was moved by the inhospitality of the tundra, by the fact that the land made no pretense of welcoming or sheltering people. He loved the gentle men and women who struggled there. After he graduated, he returned to medicine, but only as a means to live in the north. He explained this to me as I inserted a needle into his abdomen, hoping not to puncture his bowel; at times, he was hard to follow. In the middle of a long and elevated conversation about art and literature it became suddenly clear that he thought I was his brother, three thousand miles away in England.

As we both watched the amber fluid seeping out, looking remarkably like the whiskey that was its causal origin, the old doctor and I chatted about travel literature. He had long ago read Joshua Slocum and Chichester. The idea of frontier had captivated him, too, had drawn him into abandoning his marriage and lucrative medical practice in the south, drawn him to the Arctic and the winds there, just as his own papery skin and brittle bones were beginning to fail him.

I mentioned Bruce Chatwin's writing and his eyes lit up. "*The Songlines*," he whispered, "is a very beautiful book, full of subtlety and subtext. Poor Chatwin has been called so many names over that book and what he must think." With a mind to the warnings about the doctor's confusion, I asked him if he knew where Chatwin lived presently. The doctor looked up at me, and knew that I knew Chatwin was dead. He said so and then he looked away from me, out the window. I looked at the snow blowing over the cold rock, ashamed.

I visited him in his home. His wife was often away at conferences and he was lonely. His house was like a cave cut into the snow, though it was as dark, dry and dusty as a broom closet. There were boxes stacked everywhere that had not been unpacked in the five years he and his wife had lived there. Empty whiskey bottles stood on every horizontal surface alongside overflowing ashtrays with cigarette ash heaped in little piles around them. He was sitting on his couch and reading Yeats. He was pleased to see me, he whispered, and invited me to sit down beside him. He spoke to me about the Irish poets. He would have liked to have had more time, he said, to study them. It took many minutes for my eyes to adjust to the dark and for that time it was like I was blind and speaking to a hermit in a cave. It was so smoky in that room my tongue stuck to the roof of my mouth every time I inhaled.

There were some American snowmobilers in town who had come across the tundra from Churchill and were headed north, as far as Repulse Bay. We had both read an interview with them in the local newspaper. I asked the old doctor why he thought these people were travelling through the Arctic, whether he thought that they represented something of Chatwin's sentiments about nomadism and the possibility of redemption through movement. He pursed his lips at that and said, no, he didn't think they were interested in that at all. He thought they wanted to conquer the land, to show themselves and their machines equal to the power of the tundra. I said that I thought vanity could initiate actions that might in the end have something more noble about them. He asked me if we were still talking about the snowmobilers. I said I thought so. He nodded. He said that he thought that the motivation for travel was very important. What the person was looking for made the only difference between tourism and travelling.

I said I thought we were all tourists, now. He said he supposed I was right.

"So should we all just stay home?" I asked.

"Yes," he said. "But we should think harder about where we choose to make our homes. And how we live there."

"But what about Chatwin and his idea about the effect of living in one place, in cities, and in houses, any sort of permanent habitation."

"Chatwin is getting at a fact of our history. He is talking about our origins on the savannah. He thought that at some level we still long for that, and maybe he is right. But that has nothing to do with jetting off to some strange place for a few weeks or months and staring at the people who live there."

"Can anyone really be a nomad any more, and wander around self-sufficiently and endlessly? Chatwin didn't make his clothes out of what he found in the desert. He made forays out from a base and took what he needed with him."

"That is making an expedition, my boy, not being a nomad. Not in the anthropologic sense."

"So nomadism demands self-sufficiency as much as it does motion."

"It's the principal difference between nomads and urbanites, I think."

He paused to cough and light a cigarette. "It's an important idea. Cities wouldn't make people so crazy these days if their inhabitants weren't confined to cities, and shackled to all the other city-dwellers, by necessity. Specialization, anthropologists call that. Super-specialization, these days."

"Maybe Chatwin wasn't talking about nomadism at all, but about cities."

"Oh yes. And the thing is, he is entirely a product of cities himself. That Sotheby's business, and all the talk about his moleskin notebooks and his education. His admiration of nomads is really just more of this educated and privileged Briton's self-contempt, of the sort that became wearisomely prevalent in the early eighties. As if the man's own intelligence and erudition weren't an extreme of super-specialization. He wouldn't have lasted long as a root-grubber himself. Have you seen pictures? The man was a *wisp*."

"But no one is self-sufficient any more. Chatwin wasn't and nobody else is. No one feeds and clothes themselves just off the land. No one remembers how."

"The Inuit were doing it until thirty years ago."

"But even they don't any more."

"You're right."

We sat there in silence. Then he asked me if I would have a drink. I said yes.

One day in the nursing station I found, in a stack of medical update tapes on evolving strategies in the treatment of otitis media and meningitis, a videotape that had been made when the old man had worked in the hospital in Churchill, four hundred miles to the south. In it he gave a long lecture on the history of the Inuit and their culture as it existed in the pre-contact era. He was already frail when the tape had been made and his thin hair stuck up in elf-like tufts around his ears. But his delight in the topic was evident and his eyes sparked as he described the sophistication of the technology developed by the people.

I learned that at almost the same time as the Polynesians were discovering New Zealand, the Thule culture of the far north was sweeping across the Arctic, a similarly maritime and relentlessly mobile folk, with sophisticated technologies of boat-building and whaling and seal hunting. They were the first to use the *qayak*, and the *umiak*, the large open boat with which they travelled the northern coasts, wandering incessantly, in search of caribou, and bowhead whales and ring and bearded seals.

As with the Polynesians, this exploration and colonization had proceeded in a sudden explosion of activity. In the space of a few generations, the *qayak* and the *umiak* spread eastward across the Arctic sea and were sailing along the coasts of Greenland, thousands of miles from where they had originated, near Alaska. Thousands of miles farther than the Vikings had had to travel from Iceland.

Like the Polynesians (who gave us the English word for the custom) the Inuit tattooed themselves, and the women in particular wore elaborate facial tattoos that marked their marriages. In the hospital in Churchill there was a framed photograph of a woman who had dark blue-black lines tattooed on her face, spreading from her jaw to her cheeks in nearly the same manner as the Polynesian style. She was one of the last who wore them. It was not possible to hang this picture on the wall, as the woman was thought to be a shaman and the other old people had been frightened of her. The photograph sat behind a chair in the nurses' lounge.

She looked tiny, this old woman from Baker Lake, and she wore a hospital housecoat. Over the tattoos on one wrist was an ID bracelet, and behind her the shiny polished white walls and floors of the hospital were exactly as they are today. It was only a few years old, this photograph. The woman was dead of lung cancer now, was already dying when the photograph was taken. She would have been born in an *iglu* or a tent and would have been married before the First World War, before the priests came to kill the old gods. She would have been astonished and delighted with kerosene lanterns and oil furnaces, would have been among the last to consider them optional.

The Inuit embodied Chatwin's idea about nomadism as completely as any culture, and I wondered, as I worked up there, why he had never travelled to the Arctic. The tundra is so fragile that neither the caribou, nor the creatures that eat them, can stay in any one place for more than a few weeks. The delicacy of the land is such that it is quickly depleted, overgrazed and overhunted; all creatures who live here have to migrate, and not in pursuit of epiphany.

The people lived for weeks and months at a time on the sea ice in houses made of snow. Their mobility was never hampered by the luxury that Chatwin describes as the principal impediment to a realized life; the idea of the Inuit is the idea of nomadism and spareness itself.

I asked an old man whether he missed those days on the tundra, whether he thought his life was better in town than it had been on the land. He laughed and said, "You know, *kablunauks* are always talking about how warm the *iglu* is. The *iglu* is made out of snow. It can only get so warm and then it falls in. *Iglus* are *cold*. I like living in my house."

Other people I met told me that they did miss the time on the land. They missed the sense of constancy, the sense that the knowledge and experience and wisdom of the old people were valuable and important. They understood the caribou, and they knew how to find their way on the land. Now, they complained, the old people felt irrelevant. The young hunters took the GPS devices with them when they went out on the land, and when it was time to find their way home the GPS did it for them.

An old man I saw in the clinic in Rankin Inlet told me about this. "When I was a boy we learned what the land looked like, and we knew the *inukshuks* that the people had built on the land, because we were a part of the land and we knew it because if we didn't we would not live. Now these computers that the young people use to find their way — it makes them afraid of the land." (Inukshuks are piles of stacked stones that serve as landmarks in the swirling snow.)

"But people have always gotten lost on the land, even when you were young."

"Yes, many times."

"And these GPSes almost always work."

"But they make you afraid of what you should know."

I thought about that. The old man looked at me impatiently. We were sitting together in the clinic examining room and he wanted some ointment to put on his athlete's foot. He was wondering what he was to going to have to do to get me to just give him the tube.

I received a letter from Don. He had sailed the boat from Tahiti back to Penrhyn, and was very happy. He had become a close friend of a man who lived there, Joe Tangi. Joe's house was on the other side of the lagoon from Omoka, and the *Sea Mouse* was tied up just outside it, with a bowline, to a coconut tree. Don really was looking for a wife. Joe was enthusiastic about this idea and was quite certain that one could be found. The transmission was fixed now, Don wrote. He needed more money. He was very happy. The *Sea Mouse* was tied to a coconut tree. It was February then and the Arctic was corrosively cold.

In the emergency room in Winnipeg where I worked between stints up north, there was a doctor I had gone to medical school with. Ron Maier and I had become close friends, spending our afternoons at the café near our apartments playing chess and, when exams approached, reading textbooks and quizzing each other. It is difficult to know whether that time was really as pleasant as I remember it, but when I shut my eyes I can taste the omelettes they served in that café, and smell the Turkish cigarettes the Russian émigré cab drivers smoked there. As interns we had often been assigned to the same wards together and my memories of that year of sticky-mouthed fatigue are of him as much as they are of deliriousness and caffeine jitters.

When I had left for the army we had drifted apart, from the effects of geography and distraction. It was very fine to find him here again and when I was down from the Arctic we went to bars and played cards with his wife, Colleen. I found myself telling them about the sea and Palmyra and they both leaned forward in those smoky prairie bars and asked me to tell them more. Don was either going to stay for good on Penrhyn or fly home alone, I told them. You guys should come with me, help me bring my boat back.

Soon it was all we talked about. I felt like an imposter, representing myself to my friends as any kind of authority on matters maritime. But we talked about storms and the different strategies that had been employed on the *Sea Mouse* and we talked about the aerodynamics of triangular sails and about cooking at sea and soon we were all excited and imagining that we were already out there. We started drawing up menus and going to gadget shops together. One of us bought a portable chess set. And groovy little sailing gloves with the fingers chopped off, so your hands won't get sore when you pull on the ropes. It was a lot of fun.

One night Ron and Colleen picked me up when I got through at work. It was insanely cold and we decided to go a bar. On the way there, we fantasized aloud about tropical heat and sun-drenched languor. Colleen: "I'm wearing a bathing suit and I'm horizontal, the sun is so bright I have to put a hat over my eyes. I sip an iced tea when I wake up. I can hear the sea surging along."

Ron: "It's night and it's so hot I can only wear shorts, the boat is rocking slowly and there are so many stars out it looks like mica powder has been thrown on wet black paint."

"Yeah." Me, sighing.

We got to the bar and it was packed. We stumbled in and the warm air blasted our faces. We shrugged off our enormous parkas and found a table beside the dartboards. There was a woman playing darts who knew Ron and Colleen. Her name was Jude. Ron and Colleen met other friends of theirs and Jude and I started playing darts. One of us suggested we go across the street to some restaurant to get something to eat. Over the appetizers I told her about the *Sea Mouse* and Don, and my plans to bring the boat home. She seemed interested. Over coffee, I asked her if she wanted to come. She said yes without even swallowing.

CHAPTER THIRTEEN

J UDE, RON, COLLEEN and I quickly fell into a fervour that reminded me of my first preparations for going to sea. We spent most of our time occupied with trivialities: towels, we had to have nice towels, and sun-dried tomatoes. Mustn't forget sunblock and snack food. I tried hard not to think about storms and about waves as high as houses. Flashlights, we needed more flashlights. And sunglasses with ultraviolet coating. We each accumulated dufflebags full of knick-knacks we deemed essential.

Jude and I went to eat supper with her mother who lived in the country with an apiarist. I had never met a beekeeper. It sounded like Jude had a very complicated relationship with her mother. A couple of times when she slept over she called her mother in the morning and I listened in bed to one half of the conversation; it was as if her mother was a jealous lover being mollified. Until I heard about the bees I was frightened of meeting the woman. Her mother had ideas about what Jude should be doing with her life, by her age. Yikes. But *domesticated bees.*

It was late spring when we went to visit her mother and the apiarist. The prairie was gorgeous. As we drove out there we both became drunk with colour. Jude's mother and her lover lived in a house surrounded by poplar and spruce trees. The beehives hadn't been placed in fields yet for the summer. Jude and I walked among them and she explained to me about the subtleties of beehive construction, and about how in the wild the hive spends most of its energy laying eggs and caring for the pupae. In the domesticated beehive, however, there were narrow passages built to keep the bees necessary for egg-laying confined to one small part of the hive. Elsewhere, the workers made honey and sealed it up with beeswax, wondering why there were so damn few pupae around. In the meantime, ours is not to reason why. And the more honey the better. Buzz, buzz, buzz.

Jude showed me the presses and the devices used to extract the honey from the combs. She told me about the taste of buckwheat honey versus clover, sunflower and wildflower.

She talked about the mite disease that is sweeping through North America and she told me about the techniques apiarists use to control the interbreeding between hives. "It's the most interesting thing," she said, "how you can slowly build your hives up until they are healthier and healthier, and you get a sense of their character, their aggressiveness, their determination. They get stronger over time. You help them. It's pretty satisfying."

Her mother and the apiarist fed us and later we talked about books. Her mother had been an English teacher. She was reading Ben Okri's *The Famished Road*. A pileated woodpecker began hammering away at a tree. The apiarist stood up to watch it better. We all crowded around the window. The sun set and Jude and I made our way back into the city. We held hands as she drove.

Jude was twenty-eight and a kindergarten teacher. She described the children she taught in such affectionate terms she was pretty much incoherent. A few months earlier she had broken up with a long-time boyfriend because he had made it clear that he never wanted children. Her brother had married a pediatrician and recently they had had their first baby. They were very happy. Everything just felt so right over at their house, Jude said. It's a necessary step in personal evolution, she said, taking care of little ones. This conversation was at night, in my apartment. She was smoking a cigarette and looking out at the dark.

In another three weeks we would be at sea, but headed home.

The General's Wife

My last year in the army I was posted, to my enormous relief, from the artillery regiment to the National Defence Medical Centre in Ottawa. This business in Ottawa struck me as a kind of idyll, with sicknesses that could be treated and CT scanners and a real laboratory. I drove eastward smiling all the way, listening to "Shiny Happy People" by R.E.M. over and over again. That winter I worked on the internal medicine wards — nephrology, respirology, neurology, gastroenterology: all the "ologies." I began with oncology, the cancer ward.

The cancer patients in that hospital could be broadly divided into those with leukemia and lymphomas, for whom there was generally some hope of cure, and those with solid tumours, for whom there was generally no such optimism. If there was solace to be found, it was in the relative ages of these two groups: young soldiers, stricken-looking and feeling newly mortal had mostly leukemias or lymphomas, while the oat-cell lung cancers and sarcomas and clear-cell carcinomas — these were older soldiers mostly retired. They eroded steadily over the year following their diag-

noses in a succession of reversals leading to rout. An army in col-
lapse has an unmistakable air about it, an old armoured officer
told me. Abandoned field guns and sloughed off uniforms lie in
its trail of disintegrating order and there is no denying what is taking place when you see that. It is painful to look upon, he said,
even when it is the enemy.

I knew no one in Ottawa. My colleagues at the hospital were
pleasant and kind men and women, but they were mostly married
and older than I was. None of them shared my intense antipathy
for the army, or if they did were circumspect enough not to give
voice to it. After the round of welcome parties and introductions,
I emerged with about as many friends as when I'd arrived. I took
to spending my evenings reading in one of two restaurants close
to my apartment. I wrote more letters in my first few weeks in
Ottawa than I have ever written in my life. Friends from back west
began phoning me in concern, and I learned to rein in those letters a bit.

I became friends with a waiter at one of the restaurants, and
he and I ate supper together on Sunday evenings, his night off.
His name was Pierre and he had spent his twenties trying to be
an actor. He had eventually abandoned what he called his self-
delusions, and he spent these suppers making detached and sar-
castic jokes at his own expense. He told me he had never had what
might be called a relationship in his thirty-five years, although he
couldn't count the number of cocks he had sucked in the back seat
of taxis and in public parks. I sat stupidly silent when he told me
that. We were eating cannelloni with ricotta and pesto. He had
spent the afternoon working on it. It was delicious. For dessert
there were *poires belle Hélène*. Magnificent.

The thing about a solid tumour is, if the patient winds up on the
oncology floor, it's because the tumour has spread or metastasized
before surgery could excise it. There may have been happier out-

comes following the detection of these tumours, but we never saw those patients. They went home from the surgical floor and did not return. When *we* met them, it was through the introduction of a chagrined surgeon, who assured them that this just meant having to put up with hospital food for a few more months, and then they'd be back on the links, they'd see. These folks do wonders. I'll be around to see you soon. Take care now.

The general's wife had first undergone excision of a hypernephroma from her kidney. Then, as the metastases appeared, she'd had a lung resection and then a craniotomy for the tumour in her brain. This sort of surgical practice — removing secondary tumours or metastases — is called cherry-picking by skeptical internists. Once the tumour has spread, the seed is in the soil and, as more and more growths appear in the surgically debilitated body, aggressive attempts to remove individual tumours only hasten the patient's demise. The general's wife was passed on to the oncology service by the surgeons with evident reluctance. Her husband was a war hero and seemed at one point or another to have commanded everyone in the Canadian army.

The day we met I stood in her room while the doctor I was replacing said goodbye to her. They admired one another, it seemed clear. As for me, I knew enough of the military to be wary of such a patient. I knew that she would be three times the work of a similarly afflicted major or sergeant, so often would I be giving status reports and tending to the concerns of third cousins and former colleagues of her husband. This irritated me in anticipation.

She knew her medical circumstances thoroughly and gave me an accurate and succinct summary of her operations and the complications of her therapy. It seemed to me that she understood what the end of all this would be. I took notes rapidly, feeling as much like her steno clerk as one of her physicians. After she completed her recitation, no doubt given a score of times, she asked me about myself. I smiled uncomfortably. No, I was not married, my family was back west, and I didn't know if I would remain in the military upon the completion of my obligatory service, I said. Very good, she said, and I understood that I had been dismissed.

The chemotherapy began that day and the service chief reviewed with me her blood work and the therapeutic plan. A full colonel, the service chief had been in the military her entire adult life and took very seriously the importance of this patient. She spoke to me sternly about the necessity of our care being seen to be highly competent and compassionate. I assured her I understood. She said she hoped I did.

In the restaurant that night Pierre was irritable and distracted. I was concerned that I'd somehow offended him. When he sat down at my table I asked what the matter was. Nothing, he assured me, lighting a cigarette briskly. I looked across my novel at him. He asked me about my day. I told him about the general's wife having quizzed me about my personal life. He listened, uninterested. A friend of his was sick, too, he said. We sat there. All of this could just go, any time. I nodded. He didn't want to sound like some first-year philosophy major but, God, what lasts? His voice breaking. Me, shaking my head.

Sorry, he said, patting my hand and rising to greet a party at the door in his usual ebullient manner.

You are too old not to have started a family, the general's wife informed me. I put my stethoscope back in my pocket and looked at her fluid balance sheet. You must drink more, ma'am, I told her. The toxicity of the cyclophosphamide ... Yes, yes, she knew all that.

It's not just a question of duty, she said, it's a matter of your own growth. You will not be complete until you have faced these matters. When you are older, it will be what you are proud of. It is the only thing that sustains you in the end.

I agreed that it was an admirable undertaking. She was not satisfied with that.

Oncology comes from *oncos*, the Greek for crab. Hippocrates envisioned the claws shredding the body from within. It is an apt metaphor. The general's wife declined steadily through the course of that fall and winter. With each return to the hospital a new complication emerged: she had blood clots in her legs and abdomen, more tumours appeared in her brain. By Christmas her family had no more illusions about the effectiveness of our treatment; nevertheless she insisted on continuing it. Resignation was not an option for her, she said.

By February she could hardly speak, and her previously unaccented English became unavailable to her. I struggled to converse with her in my inadequate French. "*Avez-vous douleur, Madame?*" I called into her ear. Her husband would translate for me. "No, she is comfortable, she says."

I took to spending quiet hours during my call nights sitting up with him in her room. She was so weak. The general had commanded a francophone infantry regiment during the Second World War. With peace he had returned to his wife and her family's logging business in the Gaspésie. When the Korean matter broke out, there was a shortage of experienced francophone field commanders and he was sought out and asked to re-enlist. He did so with relief, the logging business having left him bored to the point of paralysis.

His battalion, along with the rest of the UN forces, had advanced rapidly into North Korea after MacArthur's landing at Inchon. There was talk of continuing all the way to the Yalu River, the Chinese frontier. Everyone felt like a hero. All the systems worked, the tactics seemed designed with prescience. There had never been an army like this one. He told me he remembered the mood in the kitchen messes on the advance. He smiled. It had been fine, he said.

When the Chinese intervened with a million men and threw the UN army back on its heels, almost to Seoul, it was the worst thing he ever saw. One day on his right, an entire American brigade was nearly surrounded. His battalion held the only high ground in the area. They could see the Americans being cut apart. Their brigade hospital was blown to pieces. Again and again the infantry fell back and attempted to hold a new line, only to be forced further back. The primary defence lines and then the secondary ones, too, had all been abandoned; everything was being improvised in the panic. Individual companies had no idea what the remainder of the brigade was doing. In the smoke and haze, firefights broke out between UN platoons thinking one another the Chinese. Further to the west an entire division, twenty thousand men, mutinied and dropped their weapons, heading south. The general had his company commanders call in artillery on the attacking Chinese columns below him. The Chinese turned to face this new problem and for four days not a man in his battalion slept.

I sat in that little hospital room, which had grown abruptly smaller, and leaned back in my chair. It seemed like I had heard the same war stories over and over again that winter and it was hard to be interested in one more old man's youthful heroism. He was smart and perceptive; we had spent enough time together that he would have known this. I had seen nothing similar to what he was speaking of, couldn't foresee doing what he had done. I wasn't going to be charging any machine-gun nests, and nobody I knew was going to either. It was another time and not my time. He saw my impatience.

Soldiers think that their organization is eternal, he said. They cling maniacally to their manufactured traditions in order to persuade themselves of the solidity and permanence of the world. They think that if only they can make themselves and their society sufficiently rigid, they'll be able to face this thing that they cannot even imagine until they are in it. And they do believe in this construct of theirs; like penitent monks, they believe. Then they're confronted with the most violently chaotic and disordering phenomenon imaginable and, if it goes badly, in a few hours the determined jaws slacken in fear and tears chase all that narrowed-eye resolve into the mud.

He told me that in the subsequent years of peace, this was what he thought about the most — all the doctrine that the soldiers learned in peacetime, endless training and whole working lifetimes spent preparing for this thing, that however it might turn out, would not resemble their expectations in any meaningful way. Every army, he said, prepares for the last war. All you know for certain is that you will be surprised.

The general had grown concerned about me in his wife's final days. I stayed late most nights then; the workload that month had been insane, even without her. He brought me sandwiches from home and told me that I didn't look well.

When I read her obituary in the newspaper I was sitting in the restaurant. She had been famous in her own right, I learned, for her work with war orphans. Pierre was having a slow night and in the oscillating fortunes of our friendship that winter, we were again familiar. Pierre's friend had grown very ill and he had grieved privately, not showing me much distress. He hadn't complained again of his isolation, at least not explicitly, and there developed a breezy quality to our discourse that had not been present earlier.

On the local news that night I saw the general at the funeral service. Beside him stood his many children and their spouses. The younger men and women stood there blinking away their tears. The old man wept disconsolately. I watched him closely, as he stood hunched over in the late winter snow, propped up by one of his sons, but I am unable to say what endured, for him.

CHAPTER FOURTEEN

Navigation

> *Accurate dead reckoning is difficult on any vessel, but it is especially so when one sails alone, because the boat may sail an erratic course when there is no one at the helm, and very often, temporary course changes, from a windshift, for instance, will go unrecorded [...] Averaging yaws may not suffice, since the boat may swing in one direction and remain there for a longer period than she does in the opposite direction [...]*
>
> *Most offshore sailors use taffrail logs towed astern [to record distance travelled]. These are quite accurate, and they use no electricity, but their rotors are occasionally fouled with weed or bitten off by large fish. An extra rotor or two should be carried, and they are said to be less attractive to fish when painted black.*
>
> RICHARD HENDERSON, *Singlehanded Sailing*

R AROTONGA IS ONE of Darwin's high islands, and it juts out of the sea like Tahiti or Moorea, full of craggy and lush foreboding, streams of mist sweeping down off the mountain to the hot sand shore and beyond, the reef all around. The island seems directly out of a Somerset Maugham story, and the low whitewashed buildings that line the streets speak eloquently and evocatively of its not-very-distant colonial history.

There is a parliament building there now, and a hospital; resorts dot the coast. An Air New Zealand flight lands regularly and alcohol is available freely and without permits. It is to Tahiti what Buffalo is to New York. Provincial, but not in the mind of anyone there.

Don was to meet us with the *Sea Mouse* in the Avatiu harbour. It made more sense to meet there than Penrhyn, we had decided. There were supplies and equipment available on Rarotonga, and flying on from Rarotonga to Penrhyn would have been an expensive trip in a small light aircraft that did not allow much luggage.

Immediately after we checked into our little huts I walked down to the harbour. The *Sea Mouse* wasn't there yet. This was not that surprising. I walked back to the motel. Colleen and Jude were only a little disappointed at the news. "Maybe another day or two," I said, "or three."

We spent that day walking through Avatiu. Even by Manitoban standards it's a small town; we walked from end to end in the course of an unambitious afternoon. It looked like Rick's Café-era Casablanca. The ocean was at all times visible on one side of the main road and, inland, the mountain sloped steeply enough that the big Pacific rollers erupting against the reef were always visible.

We spent the next day snorkelling in the lagoon inside the reef. We ate a picnic on the beach and I studied the horizon for signs of the *Sea Mouse*'s white masts. Jude kept trying to make conversation with me. I found myself preoccupied with the upcoming voyage. Ron and Colleen asked me if I thought the boat was okay. I assured them that it wasn't unusual for the *Sea Mouse* to take longer than expected to make a passage. We all watched the horizon. Pasty-skinned Canadians, we should have watched the time. That night we groaned in crimson agony.

We discovered that the owners of the motel, a retired English nurse and her oil-worker husband had known Mac and Muff Graham, the Palmyra dead, in Aden in 1964, where they had visited in the course of their circumnavigation. Lois, the nurse, lent Jude a copy of *And the Sea Will Tell*.

I had gone on at some length about what I had taken to be the extraordinary beauty of Palmyra. When Jude came upon Bugliosi's portrayal of that atoll as a haunted, sinister place, inhabited only by Hitchcockian seabirds and the spirit of eerie discontent, she wondered aloud just how much I had distorted the sea and the *Sea Mouse* beyond any reasonable person's recognition. It was actually a pretty good question.

There was a thatched-roof bar beside the harbour where the beer was cheap and boat people drank and told stories. One night I left my friends to take a walk. I found myself sitting in the bar reading a book and feeling self-conscious. A Frenchman named Michel approached me. He was singlehanding his way around the world in a tiny, twenty-three-foot catamaran. It was his third trip around and he said it was the best so far.

"You mustn't have much room in there," I said to him.

"More than enough — singlehanding, it is necessary to spend the most part of one's time up top, steering and keeping watch."

"That must get exhausting."

"One time, in a storm, I was unable to leave the wheel, the waves were so large she would have foundered *instantement*, I could not let go of the wheel even to shit or piss and so I did that right in my foul-weather gear, and kept steering."

"You don't say."

"Oh yes, it can be hard, the sea, in a leetle boat."

Michel had raced in one of the round-the-world races, and had rounded Cape Horn when it was flat calm — "such an anticlimax," he put it, waving his cigarette over his head. And he had known Moitessier. "But he was not so grand, in the end, sleeping in the shade and smoking hashish all day." This was not an image I was prepared to absorb.

The next night we all went to the bar and there were many men and one woman there, all very brown and the men extensively tattooed; they had the jauntiness and exuberance of too-large mountain-climbing parties. They were mostly young and appeared very pleased with themselves. Colleen spoke to the woman among them, whose name was Mahine, and learned that they had just that day made landfall on Raro, after sailing a flotilla of traditional Polynesian *vakas* from Tahiti. Mahine joined us at our table.

The *vakas* were built in 1992, as a part of the Pacific Festival of Arts and Culture by the people of Samoa, Tahiti, Hawaii, the Marquesas and New Zealand. These canoes were laid down after the drawings of them made by the early European explorers — Cook, Bougainville and others — and after the dimming memories of these vessels among the elders of the islands. The last *vakas* had been built a half-century previously.

Mahine was a doctor. She was born and had grown up on Easter Island. She had travelled to Santiago to study medicine but then, disenchanted with the Chileans and their rule of her home, she had written the American qualifying exams and had gone to the States to do her family-practice residency; later she had set up practice in Hawaii on the Big Island. It was there that she had learned of the *vaka* expedition. Thrilled with what she saw as a resurgence of pan-Polynesian nationalism, she had volunteered to travel in one of the canoes and to provide medical care to the other mariners. When she learned that Ron and I were physicians too, she was pleased; the three of us spoke self-importantly about saltwater sores, immersion rashes and the nutritional challenges of such trips. At length we paused, and Jude steered the conversation back to the voyage Mahine had just made.

The revival of interest in the old skills was the important thing, Mahine thought. This renaissance began when David Lewis, a well-known singlehanded sailor, had published *We, the Navigators* in 1972. Lewis had spent many months interviewing some of the last of the old men who remembered the traditional techniques of navigation. He travelled to Tonga, the Caroline Islands, Kiribati and Papua New Guinea, and wrote with deep respect for Tevake, Mau Pialug and Hipour, all *ppalu*, or initiated navigators, from islands in Polynesia and Micronesia. His admiration was based on his own appreciation of how subtle the sea can be and how complicated the patterns of the waves and the winds. Anyone who has been alone in a boat, weeks away from land, understands this. The idea that one's way can be found with only one's eyes, patient observation and the knowledge in one's head is both reassuring and profoundly humbling.

The Pacific Islanders had neither a written language nor the magnetic compass, but did have a precise and thoroughgoing understanding of currents and wave trains. They used these, and close observation of seabirds and bioluminescence to guide them, along with the more familiar — to Europeans — celestial tools: the stars, the sun and the moon. The old men who spoke to Lewis put particular emphasis on the pattern of the wave trains. In the latitudes of the Southern Ocean, between the southern tips of South America, Africa and Australia and the coast of Antarctica, there are no land masses to slow the wind. Storms sweep around the earth in these latitudes accelerating steadily and they kick up huge waves that are never stopped. These waves survive thousands of miles to the north as subtle but persistent swells that may be discerned alongside and within the waves created by the more immediate winds of the tropics: the easterly trades and the episodic cyclones that maraud their way through these waters.

This, as far as it goes, is not so surprising — the swell from the Southern Ocean is present and, with patience, observable to the interested eye, even mine. More startling is the idea that in addition to the single deep southern swell, there are up to a dozen other smaller and more subtle swells, deflected and refracted by distant land masses, all of which these navigators monitored simultaneously. Mahine spoke of this and I was spellbound. From *We, the Navigators*, I learned that David Lewis had grown up on Rarotonga, and had swum in the harbour we looked out on.

For swells to remain perceptible after travelling hundreds of miles, they must have their origin in regions of strong and persistent winds, the more important swells originating in "permanent" weather systems such as the Trades. Trade-wind-generated swells tend to be from east, northeast or southeast, depending on latitude and season. The other main source is the Southern Ocean belt of strong westerlies, whence long southerly swells sweep even beyond the equator. Largely seasonal swells originate in the monsoons of the western Pacific and others, more temporary still, are caused by tropical revolving storms.

Waves thrown up by the immediate wind tend to be temporary as well as having breaking crests and other recognisable characteristics. This distinction is well recognised by Pacific Island navigators and its importance was repeatedly stressed to me by Tevake and Teeta, among others. The Papuans Lohia Loa and Frank Rei carefully explained that the swells they used were "not wind waves," but were more permanent.

Swells from relatively distant origins are long in wavelength from crest to crest and move past with a slow, swelling undulation, while the wind waves and swells from nearby sources are shorter and steeper. The former are not readily abolished even by prolonged gales.

The skill required to read the ocean as if it were a municipal road, signed and marked, was far beyond what I could imagine. I remembered the conversation I'd had with the old Inuit man and wondered if his grandsons would find the idea of navigating unaided across the tundra similarly incomprehensible.

This sense of deep intuitive understanding of the place where one lives, I thought, lies at the heart of what is missing in Selkirk, Manitoba. There is no sense of complexity of the land there. It grows wheat. Geese fly over it in the fall and in the spring there are fish in the river. There are those who will go out and put a hook in the river and who will shoot the geese from the reeds, and they, together with the farmers, at least have a glimmer of a sense of where they live. But it is a weak glimmer, with fish-finder sonar machines pointing out the weed beds to the fishermen, and the farmers driving quickly over their dirt, and the hunters (if they were like I was) mostly dreaming of something altogether different.

The old Inuit could find their way across hundreds of miles of blasted tundra just by remembering the rocks. And the old navigators could look at the sea and establish where they were by the shapes of the waves. This sense of the sea was less cerebral than somatic, more like musical genius than mathematics:

> Holding course by swells seems always to be a matter more of feel than sight — which emphasises the value of the art on overcast nights. Tevake told me he would sometimes retire to the hut on his canoe's outrigger platform, where he could lie down and without distraction more readily direct the helmsman onto the proper course by analysing the roll and pitch of the vessel as it corkscrewed over the waves. In distinguishing swells, he stressed, you have to wait patiently until the one you want has a spell of being prominent and discernible. Rafe of Tikopia also spoke about "feeling" the swell, and Gladwin points out that Puluwatans too "steer by the feel of the waves under the canoe, not visually." One might perhaps be tempted to refer to keeping course by the swells as "steering by the seat of one's pants," were it not for the more anatomically specific detail supplied by the veteran island skipper Captain Ward, who writes, "I have heard from several sources, that the most sensitive balance was a man's testicles, and that when at night or when the horizon was obscured, or inside the cabin this was the method used to find the focus of the swells off an island."

Mahine had read Lewis, and quoted him at length by memory. Jude sat there with us and would not lean back in her seat. Mahine grew self-conscious and stopped her lecture abruptly. We should come with her to a party, she said. We could meet some of the other crews of the *vakas*.

The party was at the estate of a family of Rarotongan aristocrats. The two sisters who owned the house welcomed us. They were descended from the hereditary chiefs of Rarotonga, and we were very fortunate to be able to meet them.

Several of the sailors from the *vaka* fleet were being feted with the admiration that in Canada might be visited upon an alcoholic poet who had just won a foreign literary prize. I eavesdropped on these men and found them like adventurers everywhere, absorbed by their own virility and strikingly dull. I wandered among the bookshelves in the main room. There were many old and interesting-looking books about celestial navigation and the traditional social structure of Polynesian society. Maugham was well represented, along with Evelyn Waugh.

Mahine found me and took me through the room, introducing me to the other sailors, the people from the *vakas* and our hosts. Then she took me down to see the lagoon that lapped on the beach that served as a front lawn of this house. We looked at the moon. The ocean shone like mercury. We did not speak. We walked quickly back to the party.

One of the guests was an old Polynesian man who had been a medical officer in the New Zealand army during the Second World War. He told me he had travelled to Canada then, to do research on cold-weather survival. He had been to the Queen Charlotte Islands and had seen the cedar canoes of the Haida. The Haida had resembled his own people, and the appearance of their canoes evoked the inshore vessels used on many of the Pacific Islands he knew. He was familiar with most of the dialects of the Eastern South Pacific and was able to speak fluidly with Mahine, for instance, although the Easter Island dialect had been isolated from the others for fifteen hundred years at least. He had expected that these Northern Pacific peoples would have a language similar to his. He tried for weeks to speak to the Haida people he met there, but without success. "We sounded like machinery to each other," he said.

Everyone called the old man Papa. He asked us to call him that too. He had been instrumental in the building of the Rarotonga *vaka*. He remembered a little from his boyhood, of how the *vakas* had been described, and he had read the journals of Cook and his crew and he had, of course, read David Lewis. It was fine to see the young people resurrecting this ability and this lore, their lore, of the ocean and how to survive and find one's way on it.

For supper, there was spiny lobster in coconut milk and curry, taro and breadfruit, and grilled tuna and mahi mahi. The sisters tended to us as if we were visiting dignitaries. Jude found me and sat down beside me. She asked me if I had met the old man everyone called Papa. I said yes. We ate until we oozed.

The next day I was walking to the harbour when a car stopped beside me on the road. Mahine and one of the sisters were going to visit the island hospital and asked if I wanted to come. I said I would love to, but. "Please," Mahine said.

The hospital was a low white building with open windows and a smell — astonishing in a hospital, to me — of foliage and clean ocean air, not at all heavy with Dettol and isopropyl alcohol. It reminded me of the downscaled military hospital I had worked in in Manitoba — built in the early forties and always too large for any medical need. It did not resemble a modern urban hospital in any way at all. Both that building and this one had painted wooden timbers visible in the rooms and the operating suite, uneven floors and the air of remote and obsolete dignity.

But in the Rarotonga hospital the beds were mostly occupied and the image of wholesale underemployment was absent. There was a library in the hospital, full of surgery texts thirty years old. The Maori surgeon who worked there pointed them out with chagrin: the shape of the human bowel does not change, at least, he said, and laughed loudly.

Mahine and I went on rounds with him. A boy with a dreadful shark bite on his leg had been evacuated from Penrhyn. His family sat in chairs beside him and when the surgeon entered the room, all rose. There was a whole ward of young men who had sustained fractures in falls from coconut trees. Another ward had cases of dengue fever. There were few old people. I asked about this and the surgeon told me that the old people preferred to stay at home.

That night Mahine was in the bar again and she sat with us and told me about her family practice in Hawaii. I told her about my time in Northern Canada: the Inuit resemble the Pacific Islanders more thoroughly than their language difficulties would suggest. After years of nomadism they both now exist in isolated enclaves against a backdrop of flat and often inhospitable monotony — the tundra and taiga in one instance, the cyclone-churned sea in the other.

Today their respective cultures are everywhere in retreat, with their diets of protein and occasional starches so supplanted by Cheez Doodles and frozen pizzas that diabetes in each culture is becoming a pathologic constant. Among the Cree in the sub-Arctic twelve-year-olds are developing adult-onset diabetes and even in small communities there are dialysis machines to stretch out for a few years the lives of those whose kidneys have failed from too-sweet blood. Mahine nodded, and told me that it was the same among the Maori and the Hawaiians. After millennia of eating fish and meat and complicated polysaccharides, the simple sugars of beer and pudding cups were making the Cree and the Polynesians sick. The effect of televisions and bought aluminum boats and outboard engines were less demonstrable, but just as strong and malevolent. In Nauru, she told me, the principal import from Australia was canned beer. Everyone was obese, even the little children. Her people, all across the Pacific, were in terrible trouble.

At some point Jude had risen to use the washroom and had not returned. Mahine asked me if we had excluded her.

"Conversations between doctors can be pretty boring sometimes," I replied. I looked around. Jude wasn't in the bar. Mahine asked me how long Jude and I had known one another. "About three months," I said.

"Are you going to get married?" she asked. I looked away.

"I don't think so," I said.

"She's lovely," Mahine said.

"Yes," I said.

There seemed to be nothing to say that could salvage the mood of the evening so we walked out to the edge of the harbour and looked at the ocean. Mahine asked me when my sailboat was coming. "I don't know," I said. "Soon, I think."

"How long will you stay here after the boat arrives?"

"Probably just long enough to put some food on board and check the rig."

"So a couple of days."

"Yes."

CHAPTER FIFTEEN

I WAS SITTING AT THE kitchen table in the little motel, writing in my journal, when Don knocked on the door. I recognized only the glasses. He was thirty pounds lighter than he had been when we had left Victoria. His hair was short and neat and he was as brown as a coffee bean. He grinned at me through the screen door like his face was about to split.

He had spent six months with the *Sea Mouse* tied to that coconut tree in the Penrhyn lagoon. The house immediately in front of it was owned by his friend Joe Tangi. They had met in Omoka, when Joe had come over to speak at an island council meeting. They became friends in about ten minutes. Better friends than he had been with anyone before.

They had spent the next six months diving for pearls together, and fishing on the reef. They arose every morning at dawn and ate breakfast quickly before launching Joe's skiff. In the course of the day's fishing and diving they were often comfortably silent for hours at a time. In the evenings Don ate supper with Joe's family. Later, out of sight of Riri, Joe's wife, they made bush beer and drank that together. Then Don would row the *Sea Flea* back to the *Sea Mouse* and sleep. In the morning, if Don was hungover and overslept, Joe sent his daughter out to the sailboat to roust him.

They dove in the lagoon to search for pearls. The oyster beds were as deep as one hundred and ten feet. Don had been a commercial diver in British Columbia but, still, when Joe told him they were going to free dive to that depth, he thought Joe was joking. And then Joe jumped in the water.

The technique they used was to tie a line to a lead block. Once the diver was in the water, he would be handed the block, which he would grip tightly, and down he would go. On the bottom he would grope around for some oysters, and then let go of the block and come up. The block would then be pulled up. The descents were many minutes long. Don started at forty to fifty feet, and Joe slowly coaxed him until they were both going to the deepest parts of the lagoon. It took a few months. Most of the men on the atoll did this regularly and had been doing it since they were children. They all looked more like Homer Simpson than Fabio, however, and often giggled. No one strutted. But free diving a hundred and ten feet — it would have been easy to understand if they did.

Don's metamorphosis was to no one more apparent than to himself. "My life has changed," he told me, sitting at the table. His shoulders and abdomen rippled. He spoke much more slowly and quietly and at less length. On the boat with me he had seemed vaguely anxious most of the time. There was none of that now. I found him intimidating.

We walked down to the little bar by the harbour. I hoped to introduce him to Mahine but she was not there that afternoon. I asked him if he thought about his ex-wife any more. "Not very much," he said. "I'm pretty happy now. I don't have many regrets about the events that brought me here."

Which, I thought, was a very gracious view of fate and destiny. I told him that. He asked me about Jude. He had met her at the motel.

"She's lovely," I said.

"She sure is. You should treat her right."

"I know."

In his first few letters to me up in the Arctic, Don had spoken of staying there on Penrhyn, after I left with the *Sea Mouse*, but he hadn't spoken of this again. He had decided to return to Canada, had bought a ticket home and was scheduled to leave from Rarotonga in a few days. I asked him if he had given up on finding a wife on Penrhyn. He said no, but that he had a home too, and missed it.

"They don't need another guy just hanging around there, with nothing to offer."

"You have plenty to offer, Don."

"No, something tangible, I mean. Like refrigeration." Don wanted to have a skill he could bring back to the island. He thought he might attend community college. Or do an apprenticeship in something. Then he would come back, maybe in a year or two, and live there. There were women he could fall in love with, he said. He just needed the right conditions.

Don had sailed the *Sea Mouse* to Rarotonga with Joe Tangi and Joe's nephew. It had taken eleven days. Don shrugged. "I thought we could do it in six, with the time of year and all. Sorry to keep you waiting." I looked out at the *Sea Mouse* riding at a mooring buoy in the harbour. I hadn't seen her in six months and there she was, bobbing up and down, shining green in the tropical sun. Don had spent most of the last month sanding and varnishing and painting, trying to make her look as nice as she could for my return. We rowed out to her and climbed aboard. We walked around the deck and studied the rig and the deck fittings. She seemed in great shape. The only things she needed were what I had in a pack back at the motel: a new genoa sail to replace the one I had destroyed that first week on the North Pacific, and a new alternator and a few new electrical parts.

Then we rowed ashore and I met Joe Tangi. He had been visiting relatives but he had hurried back to the boat to see if the anchor was holding okay. He and Don hugged each other and walked with their arms around one another's shoulders. I felt deeply envious of Don, and what he had learned while I had been back in Canada smiling smoothly at women in bars.

Later, Don told me that the first few days he was in Penrhyn after returning from Tahiti he had spent quite a bit of time with Bobby Peru. In the three months since he had seen him last, Bobby had gotten even more dissolute. He was drinking with the unmarried men most nights and many of the boys had gotten sick from the bush beer they made. Don had sensed that Bobby was wearing out his welcome among the islanders, abandoning his plans for a solo circumnavigation as he drank more and more.

In a moment of clear-sightedness, Bobby had seen the islanders shrinking back from him and had resolved to make things up to them. He told everyone he was going to make a trip to Hawaii and if anyone wanted pots or outboard engines or anything he would get them for them. When he returned a month later his boat was packed with shrink-wrapped treasure from Costco. There was a grand night of delivery and effusive thanks. Then, the next day, he began asking people to pay him for what they'd got. Nobody had really understood that they were supposed to pay. Bobby grew angry and sullen. Don was mortified. The islanders asked Don to help. He didn't know what to say. Bobby became angrier and angrier. Finally, in awful display of pique, he had visited the people who had "gifts" of his, and demanded them back. He rowed his dinghy full of used pots and gear to his boat, piled them in and weighed anchor. Don told this story with his eyes on the ground. Even months later his embarrassment was evident.

We spent the next few days installing the new gear I had brought. The alternator didn't quite fit and so we exchanged it at the auto parts shop. The New Zealanders who worked there were kind and helpful. We bought food at the dry-goods store, and filled the water tanks. Then there was nothing more to be done other than to set sail.

That night before we left, Don, Joe, Jude, Ron, Colleen and I all drank until very early in the morning in the little thatched-roof bar by the water's edge. Don and Ron and I had enjoyed the time we had spent together hanging in awkward positions around the *Sea Mouse*'s engine. It felt like a satisfyingly arduous preparation for the five-thousand-mile trip home. Don seemed wistful. By this point he was as attached to the *Sea Mouse* as I was and I think he was worried about her. He was also very sad at the prospect of leaving Joe. But it is possible to love where one is and be homesick at the same time, he said. He was looking forward to getting home.

Colleen and Ron seemed very excited. They had fallen in love with the *Sea Mouse* and they were anxious to get to sea. They interrogated Don like he was a foreign traveller returned from afar. What was Penrhyn really like? What did folks eat? Only Jude was quiet. I watched her. She looked like she was wondering what she had gotten herself into, and was trying to be a good sport.

Mahine walked into the bar and I introduced her to Don and Joe. She sat down with us. She and Joe spoke in Polynesian and I was surprised that they so readily understood one another, each having learned dialects of a language that had been separated for two thousand years. They talked on and we all drank in that rich and sonorous language. I studied Don; I wished he was coming with us. Don watched Mahine. In his search for a wife I think he had imagined a woman much like her — confident and worldly but part of this place too, conscious of the value of community and ease, and of the limited value of possessions. I watched Mahine and Joe talking. I wondered what her Easter Island/Rapa Nui accent sounded like to him.

I looked over at Jude. She was staring out at the sea.

He who starts on a ride of two or three thousand miles
may experience, at the moment of departure, a variety of
emotions. He may feel excited, sentimental, anxious, care-
free, heroic, roistering, picaresque, introspective, or practi-
cally anything else; but above all he must and will feel like
a fool.

PETER FLEMING *News From Tartary*

We set to sea, bound for Penrhyn, the following afternoon, with Don and Joe watching quietly from the seawall. We untied from the mooring buoy and motored out of the harbour. It was late in the day already and the sun was beginning to set. We motored until we were five miles offshore and then we turned off the engine. Rarotonga sat behind us, lit up in the reddening light of the setting sun, green as a jewel and brighter and even more intense in that oblique light than even Tahiti had been. I looked around at my companions. Here we were, making an eight-hundred-mile passage in the South Pacific. I wondered how much I had forgotten about the sea. I hoped we didn't hit any storms, at least in the first few days.

We hoisted the genoa and then the mizzen sail. A steady gentle wind filled them. The *Sea Mouse* heeled over and began shuddering north. Ron and Colleen and Jude looked back at Rarotonga and the dropping sun. I went forward to hoist the main. I pulled down on the halyard for the first time in six months. The main rose halfway and then stopped suddenly. I pulled again, irritated that it was so much harder than I remembered, that only a few months of desk work should have left my arms and shoulders so much weaker than they had been when I had last been on the boat.

I pulled again and the sail did not move. I pulled hard, jerking the halyard down with all my strength. All that I accomplished was to jam the stuck sail slide in the track so firmly that it would not rise or lower. This was serious. If a squall hit us now, with us unable to douse the main, it could be very bad. I returned to the cockpit. Ron said, "We could have checked that before we left."

The sun dipped below the horizon and the light lit up the ocean in a brief orange glow and then it was dark. Now we couldn't return to harbour. What a swell start.

That night I remembered what it was like to be at sea in a small boat. The four of us sat in the cockpit in that warm air and the stars blazed above us. I watched anxiously for signs of fast-moving clouds beginning to eclipse the stars but the wind remained steady and gentle and the stars shone from horizon to horizon all the night through.

The next morning I considered climbing the mast to free the sail. I should have done that the instant it had jammed, but I hadn't climbed a mast at sea before and over the night I'd had a chance to contemplate just how intimidated I was by the prospect. This didn't lessen my intimidation. I sat there all day looking at the mast and the arc it described as the boat pitched, rolled and yawed lazily in the swell. Then the stars were coming up again and it was too late to climb the mast. We travelled slowly that day, not unusual for the *Sea Mouse*, certainly, but we would have done better if we'd had a mainsail. "This is ludicrous," I told myself that night on watch. The half-hoisted mainsail flapped ineffectually against the mast.

The next morning I finally tied the jib halyard around my harness and climbed the mast, tentatively; Ron tailed the halyard on the winch as I climbed. When I reached the jammed sail slide I gave it a quick yank and the sail fell down the mast. I descended, clinging to the mast now and shutting my eyes. It hadn't been that difficult. I was embarrassed by the production I had made over the matter.

It was odd to watch my companions making their acquaintance with the sea. I wasn't much of a teacher. When any of them asked me about some detail of the boat or some nautical term they had read, I usually shrugged. At first they suspected that I was affecting this ignorance, and accused me of false modesty, but after the time I took to get the mainsail down, the horrifying realization came to them one by one that I was not.

The arcana of the patrician men, collected in the bookshelves that lined the main cabin of the *Sea Mouse*, was not something that adhered to me. As we sat out there on the ocean, crawling on our bellies across the chart, we read aloud to each other and marvelled together at all that knowledge. The stars that may be used for celestial sights, the differences between barques and barquentines and all the beautiful and obscure words: cringles and wooldings and coir and carrick bends; chubascos and boras and catabatic winds; drabblers and whoodings. We read these aloud to one another and took turns guessing at their meanings before consulting *The Oxford Companion to Ships and the Sea* for the answers. The boat ambled northward, to Penrhyn and home. As we grew closer to the equator, the intertropical conversion zone and the squally weather that characterizes it began to take hold.

Our first squalls acted as if they had been intended for our use as training runs. The black clouds appeared in the middle of the afternoon and we all set about lowering the sails and closing the hatches and when the wind hit us we were safely below and drinking tea.

As it turned out, I had one firm certainty about sailing: when the wind blows very hard, you should lower the sails. We did that. Colleen lifted up one of the books and asked about this "reefing the sails" business, should we try that? I shrugged. It seemed just as easy to douse them completely and wait until the wind settled down again.

I was pleased that other sailboats are so rarely seen at sea. Other boats with more knowledgeable sailors would no doubt have been dancing forward under shortened sail during these periodic blows. The *Sea Mouse*, meanwhile, sat on her haunches like an unskilled and exhausted ice-skater, waiting to regain her breath. But then the wind would abate and we would raise the sails and get underway again.

The nervous bewilderment that I had felt leaving land for the first time back in Canada showed now on the faces of Ron, Jude and Colleen. *I* had been with Don, who, although he never gave advice until I asked for it, usually had a solution for any problem. My friends looked at the charts with me and together we plotted our trip home, the eight hundred miles to Penrhyn, another eighteen hundred to Hawaii, and twenty-four hundred more after that.

We moved. The water swirled behind us, and the knotmeter clicked away. The days were long and bright and languorous. We were at sea.

Jude suffered from seasickness terribly, but she smiled gamely even during the worst of it, and stuck her head over the cap rails to blow her last meal at the fish. She used to read in one corner of the cockpit, and, with tremendous dignity, she always covered her book, lest it be spattered by an errant breeze, as she let loose a little paroxysm. We didn't kiss very often, and there is a stage between lovers where a good deal of that needs to be going on. It probably wasn't only the seasickness.

She was smart and had a sense of humour, however. In the week we spent crawling toward Penrhyn she might have gone below three or four times. She had this preposterous-looking yellow sou'wester that she wore and even when I went below to nap out of the sun when I looked out the companionway I could see that little yellow hat bobbing bravely along up in the cockpit.

We took our night watches together and talked about where our paths would lead us, once the *Sea Mouse* was home. I talked about living on the *Sea Mouse* on the coast of British Columbia. She talked about returning to Manitoba. It was sad. Nothing had happened with Mahine, I told her. She'd prefer not to talk about that, she said.

Jude was the first to see the familiar green mould-like streak on the horizon and she was dead right: there it was. Penrhyn Atoll. We were all very excited, and our excitement rose nearly to the point of collective tongue-swallowing when a pod of dolphins appeared and began leaping in great arcs in our bow wave. We identified the western pass that Don and I had spent a night drifting away from, before we motored through, fuelled by lamp oil and prayer.

Once in the lagoon we slowed to orient ourselves. I tried to remember the pattern of the coral heads in the lagoon. As we sat there, a small motorboat came charging toward us. It was Joe. He had brought with him nearly frozen coconuts with deliciously cold coconut milk inside. We had been in the tropical sun for over a week and it was like having your feet rubbed with oil.

We all embraced. He had flown home the day after we had set sail and for the previous four days he had been watching the pass for us. He had begun to grow a little worried. I reminded him how long it had taken him and Don. I patted the side of the *Sea Mouse*. He did too.

He guided us to his side of the lagoon, which was unfamiliar to me. We tied off to his coconut tree. We rowed ashore. We were very happy.

With her nose only slightly wrinkled, Joe's wife, Riri, showed us where her outdoor shower was and how it worked. She had heated some water for us. She and Joe lived in a clean, cool cinder-block house that changed forever how I'd interpret the phrase "cinder-block house." There were no glass windows, but rather portals in the walls that could be closed with wooden shutters. The ocean breeze swept through the house in a steady and cool draft. There was no electricity. The floors were covered in grass mats. The lights were kerosene, like on the *Sea Mouse*. We were to stay here, she told us. Jude protested that we were all very comfortable on the boat. Riri looked at her sympathetically and did not answer. She and Joe were staying in town that week, she said. We had come to that point where hospitality corners you, and there was no choice but to gratefully accept.

Chapter Sixteen

Penrhyn is kept in supplies through the efforts of a woman who has run a succession of collapsing tramp freighters between Rarotonga and the Northern Cook Islands for thirty years. Her current vessel, a decommissioned Japanese tuna boat, had been laid up in the Avatiu harbour for months. Food and fuel was running very low on Penrhyn so Joe had asked me to ship some food on the *Sea Mouse*. After cleaning up, we rowed back to the boat and spent an excited hour stacking provender on the beach. There were bags and bags of onions and rice and canisters of pilot biscuits.

Families to whom Joe owed favours came by and their shares were apportioned off. After the food had been taken away I stood on the beach for a few minutes and fantasized about running a trading operation between these islands myself, in a larger sailboat.

I imagined children swinging through the rigging and faded cotton dungarees. I could smoke cheroots.

Everywhere we went on Penrhyn, we were identified and greeted as Friends of Don, and we were asked how he was doing. He had only left two and a half weeks earlier. We were invited in for tea every fifty feet along the main path in Teitautua, the village where he lived across the lagoon from Omoka. Three hundred people, a post office that was open one day a week, and a nurse/midwife. There was also a store, and a beautiful church.

In the mornings we walked into town and visited people. Ron and I were asked to see some of the old men with gout and we advised them to drink lots of water and take their aspirin. They agreed with us.

In the afternoons we fished on the reef with Joe and it was immediately clear why Don had been so pained to leave this place. The sun was relentlessly bright. Spending afternoons out on Joe's boat fishing and talking slowly — it was everything beautiful about a long sea passage, but you never got there. It just went on and on. And when we came home from fishing, there were many friends to eat supper with. It was quickly night. We listened to Radio New Zealand. We fell asleep in the fragrant tropical night wind.

We went to church and each of us was transfixed by the multi-part harmonies of the congregation, sung in Maori and eerily beautiful. After the service we lined up with the villagers and the deacon of the Teitautua church said hello to us at the door. He asked Ron how long we were staying. Ron said another week or so. The old man looked sombre and nodded. We said we had enjoyed the singing. The deacon struck me as worried. Joe avoided his eyes.

Don had found the role of the church on Penrhyn distasteful. He described the deacon and the elders in the church as petty tyrants who kept a close and critical eye on everyone on the island. The surest path to success in business was through influence in the church. All the government jobs were held by church elders or their family members. There was no contraception available, and evolution was dismissed outright. The church had evolved from a London-based missionary society full of Protestant zeal and paternal condescension. With decolonialization, the Cook Islanders had taken over responsibility for the supply of paternal condescension and had done an admirable job. The aristocratic ladies' ideals lived on. The church controlled who was allowed to buy alcohol, and effected a rigid conformity and adherence to church teachings. Sundays were like mourning. Eccentrics and freethinkers were reviled.

But there were still signs of a lingering spiritual tradition that predated the missionaries. Before we went fishing on the reef we prayed, for success and safety. And before a man would dive, he prayed twice. I asked Joe about this. He explained, "The spirit of the water is very powerful."

"So are there different spirits in the water and above the water?"

"There is only one God," he said.

"So why do we pray more if we're going into the water?"

"There is only one God," he said again.

There was a wooden sloop tied to the stone quay in Omoka. It had been sailed to Penrhyn years earlier from San Francisco, by a man named Steve, who had stumbled ashore after a hundred and ten days and resolved never to spend another *moment* bobbing and drifting. He was like Don a little, and he found what Don had found. It was an earlier time, and maybe there were fewer reservations to overcome. He married a woman and has lived here since. I asked Joe if Steve was well liked, hoping that he had found a kind of peace. But that wasn't Joe's answer: the man treated his wife badly and was not liked at all. He drank too much. People wished he would untie his boat again and go back to San Francisco.

It was now forbidden for Europeans to own land or be citizens of the Cook Islands. No one was willing to confront Steve and so he remained, unliked and unwelcome. This was one of the obstacles that Don had faced — a slowly accumulating suspicion of Europeans. The island council had decided not to expand the airport, not to become a tourist destination. There are no hotels on the island and now camping is forbidden. In order to buy a plane ticket to Penrhyn, you're supposed to explain where you will stay. Like Steve and Don and me, Penrhyn was hiding from strip-mall culture.

This is Heyerdahl, echoing Peter Ericson's longing for association with and ownership of the gentler world, away from our dreadful cities:

> Now it happened that when the Europeans came to the Pacific islands they were quite astonished to find that many of the natives had almost white skins and were bearded. On many of the islands there were whole families conspicuous for their remarkably pale skins, hair varying from reddish to blond, blue-grey eyes, and almost Semitic, hook-nosed faces.

It is a refrain repeated over and over again in the European literature of the South Pacific. *Hey, these people are not so different from us; we can be like this too.* Theories that European contact with and contribution to Polynesian civilization occurred unrecorded by historians are trotted forth with the most transparent wish-fulfillment fantasies as evidence. No one is very much more persuasive than Peter Ericson, the man who sold me the *Sea Mouse*. Anyone who imagined that the emergence of mitochondrial DNA typing would put this debate to rest has never looked at the religious yearning the proponents of these theories display on their faces and in their prose.

Bobby Peru, Heyerdahl and Ericson, all longing to own the nobility of kind people. Steve from San Francisco squats on it, and claims it for himself too. Ericson and Heyerdahl manufacture inherited claims; Bobby tried the old-fashioned way, to buy it with cooking utensils.

The anti-colonialism movement in the South Pacific is forever claiming that the French hold on to *Polynésie Française* for pragmatic purposes, to test their bombs, and to protect their global strategies and interests. They miss the point. The French, crowded into wintry misanthropic and suffocating cities are all seeking, like Moitessier, to save their souls. They'll pay for any number of pots to own just a piece of what they see here.

The hopes of the islanders for future prosperity are pinned on the cultured-pearl industry that has sprung up in French Polynesia and the Southern Cook Island of Manihiki. The pearls of the South Pacific are a glistening black that is in fashion these days and there are now pearl millionaires in these islands that have Sea-Doos and satellite televisions. The Penrhyn islanders grudgingly decided to see if such a venture could succeed here.

They hired a pearl-seeder, a Japanese man with jealously guarded expertise in the business of implanting the little bit of grit — chips of mussel shells, from the Mississippi River, for some reason — in the oyster. If this is done inexpertly, as it always is by anyone who hasn't devoted his life to learning this strange skill, either the grit is spat out, or the oyster dies.

Don told me the Japanese man speaks little English and lives in a small house where he reads pornographic magazines and drinks beer. The villagers do not like him, but no one contests that he is contributing to their community. He is a strange man. Don had seen him only a few times, and I did not see him at all while I was there, although his sad little house was pointed out to me. In the five years he has lived on the atoll, he has abruptly left for home four times. He is profoundly homesick.

It got later and later in the season. The winter storms in the North Pacific begin in October and already it was August and we were still eighteen hundred miles south of Hawaii. Every morning we agreed that we needed to get going.

Finally, we couldn't put off leaving any more. The thought of those autumn storms made me shiver. One day we rose and, each of us looking around to see if anyone else had an excuse not to, began putting our clothes in the sailbags that had become our luggage.

We rowed out to the *Sea Mouse*. Joe untied the line from the coconut tree and we motored slowly to the pass in the reef. Joe accompanied us with his skiff towed astern. He guided me through the pass and then he embraced each of us in turn. Then he leapt into his boat. Ron untied the line and Joe roared away back through the surf. As we watched him grow smaller and smaller, and then disappear, we felt similarly shrunken. I wished he could have come with us. I wished we could have stayed there. Neither was possible, in the world of practicalities. Which is a worse world to live in than Penrhyn Atoll, tied to a coconut tree.

Before I bought the *Sea Mouse*, and before I ever met the old doctor, I had known another old man in the Arctic, an American, "Yankee Bill." There was no consensus on what the events were that brought him up there, but it seemed most likely that there had been a divorce, and a subsequent withdrawal. He was from Boston, and had been some sort of electronics engineer. The locals agreed that it would have been the poorest form to have questioned him directly on events prior to his arrival there. Yankee Bill lived in a cabin he had built ten miles out of town. This was in Churchill, and there is a rail line to that town but no road, and so he shipped up his possessions in boxcars. He heated the place with the bent and shrunken spruce that grew on the treeline.

Yankee Bill was very proud of living off the grid, as he put it, independent of the infrastructure that demeans us all. When I visited him, there were rifles and shotguns on the walls, and a moosehide nailed outside, drying. A couple of American survivalist magazines lay on one of his tables and I flipped through one as he made tea for us. The magazine seemed paranoid to me, obsessed with the idea of the need to defend oneself once order broke down, either in the post-nuclear holocaust or as a consequence of free agency in major league baseball. Yankee Bill put on music, and I remember it was opera — Kiri Te Kanawa, the Maori soprano, singing Verdi. He seemed a gentle and civilized man and it was not clear to me what made him so afraid. We spoke about goose hunting and salmon fishing on the Pacific. There was a woman in town, I had heard, who spent time in his cabin. She was thought to be wild, and the gossips whispered of violent shrieking fights in that cabin in the night.

Self-sufficient isolation as a response to trouble — the fantasy of travel literature is acted out along all the fringes of the world. Withdrawal from community and preservation of wealth in one's own isolation. In America, gated communities are so popular that they employ more security guards than there are public police officers. Everyone craves their own enclave. A magazine called *Islands* celebrates this ideal in explicit form. Another calls itself *Escape*, and is filled with glossy and beautiful photographs of refuge. In airports in Montreal and New York and Saskatoon, commuters flip through them and smile desperately at the idea.

It felt strange to be heading home, when we were just where I had fantasized about being those winter months in the artillery regiment. I suspected that if I had a more substantial character, I would have wanted nothing more than to wander among those islands — Manihiki was just a three-day sail to the west, Samoa, a week further and New Zealand two weeks past that. I was ashamed of wanting to get home so badly. And I was entirely unable to understand *why* I wanted to be home. When I had mused about the other

islands nearby, my friends had said they were willing to sail anywhere and fly home. But I did not think seriously or long at all
about sailing further west. Home I was headed. I felt like a migratory ungulate, headed back to the calving grounds simply because
of the time of year.

For Jude, Ron and Colleen, leaving Penrhyn was deflating as
well. It was the most beautiful place — from here on the water
would only get colder, and the architecture more hideous, and the
ocean more violent until finally we were in North America. The
place I was homesick for.

In the army, it was, inevitably, the soldiers who were the most
raucously delighted to be going on deployment who drooped the
most in the subsequent months. The young men, the ones who
had been married recently, affected delight at getting into the field
with an enthusiasm the older men did not share. And then they
would be lined up outside the field telephones at one in the morning, waiting to phone home. The older men mocked them. In
this, they revealed a feature of aging maleness that dismayed me
far more than any number of degenerative and senescent prostate
disorders I might read about in my heavy books.

It feels appalling when it is upon you, but homesickness finally
betrays an affection for, and an involvement in, our homes that
could never be guessed at from the decisions we make about architecture, for instance. But it doesn't feel redemptive at the time; it
feels like you are weak, weak, weak, and all that talk about wanting to smell foreign air and learn another language of thought and
speech was all so much posturing for your friends. Spouting off in
fern bars about your craving for the exotic.

And once there — the ache in your belly begins to grow and
claw, bad some days, better others, but trending worse with increas-
ing time and distance.

Worse. And better — people do move to other places and make
new homes, and stop missing the original one. But that is replacing one home with another and is not what Chatwin was talking
about, nor is it how homesickness is best approached. When a

traveller is far from home for a long time, after months or years, homesickness becomes as much a part of the topography as the mountains and all the lovely light. Prominent, whether or not it is acknowledged.

Chatwin argued that people are happier as nomads. Without allegiances to home, or possessiveness for it, we are less willing to fight, less willing to destroy other places, less willing to distract ourselves with possessions and neglect our gods. But all of this can be summarized as: without a home, there is no place to love above others. I had been on the road more or less continuously since I left the army two years earlier. I wanted to be home.

The *Sea Mouse* re-entered the doldrums north of Penrhyn and in the light variable winds she ghosted along further north. The rain showers and squalls were still here, but less intensely this time. The boat had twice the crew and it was less possible to be lonely. Jude and I took watches together and slept in the cockpit. She was less seasick now, and it was becoming easier and easier for us to talk.

Ron and Colleen and Jude and I came to feel a free acquaintance, crawling into bedding still warm from another's body after trading watches, making breakfast for each other, guessing one another's thoughts. There were games of chess and cribbage and bridge. It was like it had been with Don, but with more history and less histrionics. With none of us rubbed raw the way Don and I had been coming south, it was easier but less intimate. If intimacy is the word to describe sitting on the boat with another man I had met for the first time only weeks earlier, both of us brooding like skunk-sprayed farm dogs.

After drifting through the doldrums we finally picked up the northeast trades and began beating toward Hawaii in mounting seas and a freshening wind. But our daily averages did not improve much, as we lost all forward momentum each time the bow buried itself in an oncoming wave. One day we were shuddering along under shortened sail and rain gear when Colleen pointed at the horizon and said, "Look, a boat!" Ron and I were preoccupied with adjusting the jib trim and we did not look up, certain after thousands of surveys of the empty sea that we were the only creatures out there. "Look! It's right there!" Ron and I looked up and there it was, another sailboat, a trimaran, dancing before a following wind at four or five times our two knots. I turned on the radio and a woman hailed us.

"Where are you going?" she asked.

"Kaua'i," I said.

"We just left there three days ago, the weather has been great."

"Where are you going?" I asked.

"Tahiti. We're hoping to be there in ten days or so."

"At the rate you're going you will be," I said.

"Well, we don't always do twelve knots," she said.

"Twelve knots," I said. "When did you leave again?"

"Three days ago."

"Bon voyage," I said.

A week later, we bobbed our way past Christmas Island. Halfway there.

At some point in my acquaintance with the *Sea Mouse* I might have figured out that she was a slow boat. Slower even than I would acknowledge. She was heavy and had been a year in tropical waters, and her bottom was thickly barnacled, but I sailed her slowly too, and the wind vane worked poorly. All of this is to say it wasn't astonishing that the *Sea Mouse*'s progress north was slow. It was late in August now, and all three of my friends needed to be back in Canada by September.

We were all sitting in the cockpit, sprawled out in poses of varying dignity, when I said that, if they all had to fly home, I was considering sailing to British Columbia by myself. Jude said don't be ridiculous. Ron said he could understand the appeal. Colleen said she thought it wouldn't come to that.

CHAPTER SEVENTEEN

No man is an Iland, intire of it selfe;
every man is a peece of the Continent, a part of the maine;
if a Clod bee washed away by the Sea,
Europe is the lesse, as well as if a Promontorie were …
any man's death diminishes me, because I am involved in
*   Mankinde …*

JOHN DONNE

FROM HAWAII to Victoria is twenty-three hundred miles by rhumb line, but to avoid the North Pacific High and its attendant horse corpses one must go well north before dog-legging it back east toward the mainland. The route becomes three thousand miles or so, one of the longest uninterrupted passages on the sea. There is some argument about how far north it is necessary to go — some say almost as high as the southernmost Aleutians, others say not as far as that — forty-five or fifty degrees, perhaps. I heard all these arguments while I was docked in Hawaii, trying to talk someone into sailing home with me.

The North Pacific is cold and volatile in the autumn and anyone who knew enough about the sea to consider sailing to Canada knew that much.

I spent a week and a half moored in Kaua'i, asking everyone I met if they knew someone. By this time the *Sea Mouse* and I were both looking a little tired, rust streaks dripping from our topsides, hair unkempt and scattered, vacant stares and pursed lips; I could understand the caution we provoked.

Ron, Colleen and Jude had all gone home. They each had jobs to get back to. We had lingered too long on Penrhyn and once again stretched every estimate of how long the passage would take to Hawaii. They were each tempted to stay behind, and throw caution to the wind. They all asked me if I was sure I would find someone to crew with me. All three asked me this around the others, and again in private. I was positive, I told them. Don't worry about me.

I stewed on the question of whether or not to go alone one night as I lay trying to sleep in a thin sheen of sweat. I wanted so badly to be home. I thought about all the aborted circumnavigations, about Bobby Peru, who, people told me, had been through Kaua'i on his way home a month earlier. He had broken his main boom two hundred miles south of Maui. He had kept to himself, everyone said, and had looked thoughtful. I said that I had known him on Penrhyn. He must have been disappointed to be returning, I ventured. Shoulders were shrugged. You know what it's like when your boat starts to break. You can't get home fast enough.

Steven Jackson was docked beside me. He was a greying and deliberate man in his fifties. A few hours after we had arrived, he'd walked over to the *Sea Mouse* and introduced himself. He'd looked at the peeling paint on the hull and asked us how the trip was. "Fine," I said.

"Where did you go?"

I told him.

He asked my friends and I if we wanted to go for dinner. We all said yes.

Over dinner I asked him what he did for a living, expecting him to tell me about his flourishing legal practice. It turned out that he tested missiles for the US Navy. He didn't elaborate and I didn't press him. We talked about our boats, what we liked and disliked about them, and we told ocean stories. We fell into an easy and comfortable friendship, striking in its immediacy. He made no apology for his expertise in missiles, though he sensed my unease. In his position, I would have dissembled, said something about electronics and the government. I had been a soldier too, but had asked my comrades to call me "doctor" rather than "captain."

After my friends left I told Steven I thought I'd go home alone. We were eating oysters at the time. He stiffened his neck and asked me why I thought that was a good idea. I told him I thought my good luck would carry me through. He asked me to think about it some more. I said I would, not wanting to argue.

> *An old man fishing from a dugout canoe called out to me. "Why are you paddling there, listening with those earphones?"*
>
> *I was listening to Chuck Berry.*
>
> *"Because I am unhappy," I said.*
>
> *"Where is your wife?" he yelled.*
>
> *Then the wind took the rest of our talk away, and it also separated our boats.*

PAUL THEROUX, *The Happy Isles of Oceania*

Before we arrived in Kaua'i a man telephoned my father and told him he was an old friend of mine. He asked my father where I was, where the boat was. My father said, "On the ocean." The man didn't want to leave his name or number. Several days later Catherine's husband telephoned my parents and introduced himself to my mother.

He asked her to help him find his wife and son. He was sure that Catherine and Sam had gone with me on the *Sea Mouse* and were now in the South Pacific. My mother said she knew nothing about the matter, had never met the woman. He thought my mother was hiding something. He expressed that suspicion to her. My mother, who fears conflict like housefire, insisted she was telling the truth.

She relayed this conversation to me as I stood on the dock at a pay phone. Her voice was full of alarm. Catherine's husband wanted me to call him, my mother added. He had given her a number. I wondered if Catherine had gone to Guatemala, where her family maintains a house. Her husband knew this, of course, and I knew nothing else that would be useful to him.

I didn't call him. I was irritated that he had phoned my mother, and I was irritated that he had sought to involve me in his tragedy. As if I hadn't involved myself. As if it weren't altogether more important than my own little problem concerning the autumn North Pacific and fear.

(Much later I would learn that he used his political connections to have the Canadian police follow me for most of the winter following my return. I *must* have spirited his family away. How else could she elude him? I was surprised at his resolve and that things like this actually happened outside of movies. I would wonder then if she had not been wise to hide from him. Both these people were determined and powerful. I wondered how much money and heartache they squandered on their anger at each other. I wondered how long it would take the boy to forgive his parents.)

Exile: wherever Catherine was she knew isolation more complete than anything I might pretend to. Police warrants had been issued for her on three continents. I wondered if she had come across my imagined escapee in Ecuador. Even the women she says hello to when she eats a sandwich in the local café don't know her real name. She is distant and frightened, wary of men and women with urban mannerisms, and she does not ever say anything self-revelatory. The rest of us can only guess what Sam thinks of all this.

She has chosen this. But she would not, again, I thought.

A couple of days later Steven knocked on my boat and took me for a drive around the coast road on the east side of the island, where the breakers erupted against the reef. He told me about accidents he'd seen in the army. I listened. He told me that from what he had seen the really bad decisions were mostly ones made too quickly, and too rigidly. He thought that I'd decided to go alone very early in the course of my attempts to find crew. I said I didn't want to be in the North Pacific in October. If I didn't leave soon I couldn't leave at all. He said that this was exactly the way in which bad decisions are made.

"The point isn't that it would be unreasonable to be out there alone in another month, the point is that it would be unreasonable to be out there alone *right now*." We kept driving.

The next day he brought me his autohelm — a two-thousand-dollar electronic self-steering system. I told him I had a wind vane. He looked at it and said, "If you don't use the autohelm, fine, just mail it back to me unused. But if you do need it, then better you should have it." I shrugged. He told me more about his time in the army. He had been in military intelligence, in Berlin in the sixties. Did well, learned German, married a German woman.

I had met his wife, Christina, a wonderful woman who had been very sick that spring. She had had her surgery and had just started chemotherapy: so far, so good. Boy, they had had some tough times over the years. Long pause. I wondered about the metastasis they had excised, and remembered the general's wife and the cherry-picking she had been subjected to. But things were way better now, Steven said. We were now sitting in the dishevelled cockpit of the *Sea Mouse*. It was early evening and very warm. Things were definitely looking up, said Steven.

Being alone was the oddest aspect about my traveling in
Oceania, because the island people of Oceania were never
alone and could not understand solitude. They always
had families — wives, husbands, children, girlfriends, boy-
friends. To the average person on a reasonable-sized island,
nearly everyone was a relative. Wasn't this extended family
one of the satisfactions of being an islander? Living on an
island meant that you would never be alone.

PAUL THEROUX, *The Happy Isles of Oceania*

I made a pretense of telephoning friends in Canada and offering to
fly them to Kaua'i to sail home with me. I made impossible conditions, though — I said I would have to leave within a week and
they had to decide right away. One by one, my friends said "sorry."
I phoned Jude, who was getting ready to start a new teaching job.
I told her I thought I would go alone. She asked me if I wanted her
to see if she could start a few weeks late. I told her I couldn't be certain how long the trip would take. She said she had waited for years
for a job like her new one. I said that I understood. I have no idea
what I was trying to accomplish, by calling her.

There was a Borders bookstore in Lihue and I walked up to it
to kill an afternoon. I bought a reader's guide to *The Odyssey*, to
help me with the mythology and the rosy-fingered dawns and
flashing eyes. I had been trying to read that damn book for a year.
I bought short stories by Linda Svendsen and Amy Bloom, and so
many novels I had to hire a taxi to take me back down to the boat.
I was nearly ready.

During the last winter I spent with the artillery regiment we
went on a week-long exercise with the local army reserve batteries.
On the last day of the exercise, the mortar platoon of a battalion
of Princess Patricia's Canadian Light Infantry, the howitzers of the
regiment and several batteries from the reserves carried out a combined fire mission. A 105 millimetre high-explosive round landed
in the centre of the mortar platoon. I remember standing over one
man, his thigh shredded like steak tartare, shoving an intravenous

line into his arm. Another man was struck in the abdomen by a shard of twisting steel that penetrated his intestines and just skirted a kidney and his aorta before lodging in his back. In the operating room I retracted on his abdominal wall as the surgeon sewed furiously and seethed at the evident incompetence of "these idiots and their big guns." It wasn't possible to argue.

As we rode in the ambulance to the hospital I asked the medic to give the man with the shattered thigh a shot of morphine. Medics in the Canadian army carry these spring-loaded syringes that, upon being activated, are simply pressed into the flesh. The needle pops out and automatically injects the morphine deep into the muscle. The medic pressed the syringe into the man's arm upside down and watched as the needle shot up instead through his own thumbnail, spraying twenty milligrams of morphine directly into his eyes.

Steven and I were sitting at the table in the main cabin of the *Sea Mouse*. He described the crowded, dishevelled interior as "comfortable." I took this as flattery and it was. The kerosene lantern was lit and we were drinking tea. There was a slow swell in the harbour from a southeastern wind and the lamp rocked back and forth. In the army he had interviewed defectors for a long time, he said. I nodded. That was interesting work. Those men always seemed so frightened during the interviews that he was never certain they were relieved to be free. Change can be as frightening as tyranny.

Then he went back to university, got his degree in electronic engineering. When he got out of the army he went to work for Raytheon, made missile radar in Oregon. Here in Hawaii he worked for the Pacific Missile Testing Range of the navy. In the middle of all this, he and his wife had two kids, a daughter who was in some trouble, and a younger son who was just starting to figure things out, he said.

His wife knocked on the hull then, had wondered if I was still here. When she joined us she said she had been worrying about me. I was just telling Kevin about Debbie, Steven said to Christina. Her eyes tightened. But the lesson in that, he said, was that there's a large element of the uncontrolled in these things. Even if we understood things as well as we sometimes think we do, he said, and even if we're able to figure out the best response to a situation, even then nothing is certain. There are always flukes. Bullets don't always fly straight, circuits fail, weather goes crazy. Hence the danger of rigidity, of prejudging your options.

He and Christina both leaned forward. I leaned back, smiling tightly, embarrassed enough by their concern that I briefly considered just selling the boat. But then they leaned back and I wriggled loose. They changed the subject to their joint discovery of Native American spirituality and I was free. After another slow half-hour they rose and promised to come visit me the next evening, if I was still at the dock. The next morning I woke up and untied the lines and motored out into the swell.

CHAPTER EIGHTEEN

*Partly because he is so near the boundary, so near the
point where the circle closes, Odysseus is the hero who most
often tells stories. The circle began with the majestic and
suffocating obscurity of the world's origins, commanding
silence; it ends with this warrior disguised as a Phoenician
merchant, who some suspected of being a Phoenician merchant disguised as a warrior. Odysseus invited irreverence,
insinuation. Certainly, he inspired less respect than any
other hero ....*

*... But in the centuries after Homer, people would go
on wondering about Odysseus, and question and answer
would pass from mouth to mouth, as if in a long stubble
fire.*

ROBERTO CALASSO,
The Marriage of Cadmus and Harmony

THE SOUTHEASTERLY SWELL hit me the moment I
cleared the breakwater. The boat rose and fell as if on a
mogul run, pitching violently in the steep stiff seas. All
the equipment I had packed away seemed to break loose at once
and the crashing from below was like huge kitchen drawers being
emptied. My spotlight wriggled free of its confines and made a bid
for freedom — a bottle of whiskey too, and soon the scent was as
big a deterrent to going below as the shards of glass. This wasn't

going to be any problem at all, this ocean business. It was just a question of preparation. Everything was prepared just great.

I closed the companionway hatch and smoked cigarettes in the cockpit until I was nauseous. The *Sea Mouse* rumbled as she inched away from the reef, pitching and rolling with vertigo-inducing abandon. I longed for deeper water and for the short choppy waves to ease into long ocean swells. "Got to get away from land before I start smelling pecan pie everywhere," I thought.

And then I was. I was miles off the coast of Kaua'i and the mountain began to sink a little lower. It was astonishing how quickly it shrank.

I felt as if I were riding a bike no hands with my mother watching. Some juvenile gesture of bravado. It felt preposterous and absurd. Extravagantly ill-conceived. Each minute of the lengthening afternoon had me fighting back the temptation to turn the boat around and find a harbour to anchor in. When the land astern began to disappear late in the afternoon I stared after it until my eyes hurt and I was imagining clouds to be mountains.

I turned the engine off and raised the small working jib. The wind was only ten knots and the *Sea Mouse* was laughably under-canvassed, but I was not about to leap into anything here; this was the first time I had done this by myself. In the next hour I sailed about a mile. I studied a floating weed that had been within sight of the *Sea Mouse* for long minutes, and decided to raise some more sail. I hoisted the mizzen. Our rate of progress increased fraction-ally and at least the masts were no longer quite vertical. I sucked it up and hoisted the main. I paused at each reef point and then kept going. The main was all the way up. The *Sea Mouse* was under full sail. She heeled over another ten degrees or so and finally a wake was appreciable beneath the transom.

Night fell and Kaua'i dipped below the horizon. The swell un-dulated its way across the sea in black waves that lifted the *Sea Mouse* gently and then set her down again. There were no lights visible anywhere. I was the only one out there. I began whistling. Then I remembered that whistling is bad luck, an invitation for the wind to freshen ("whistling up a storm") and I stopped. It was very quiet. I twiddled my thumbs.

I tuned the radio to the coast guard weather forecast and I listened to the description of the North Pacific High, the centre of which had left Don and me bobbing on the sea for those long days. The radio listed the barometric pressure, wind speed and swell-height readings from assorted offshore buoys and the outlook for the next seventy-two hours. The voice was tape-recorded, masculine and mechanical. Upon the completion of its short recitation it began again at the beginning and so on, without pause, indefinitely. I made notes and listened again right through to make sure I had gotten everything right. I reached for the volume knob to turn it off and then paused. I left it on.

For the next two days, I listened for the moment when the forecast was revised, and the recitation abruptly left off and recommenced. I listened eagerly for the news of the atmospheric pressure changes south of Midway Atoll and nodded, impressed that they'd remained the same for the entire day. On the third day the signal began to weaken and the voice was interrupted by static and the ghosts of voices that live within it. Soon there was only static to be heard, but I listened to that too, for another day. Finally, embarrassed, I turned the radio off and it was only quiet.

I was three hundred miles north of Kaua'i, twenty-seven degrees north, and had been listening to radio static for most of two days.

I'd had the idea that I would sleep during the day, when the *Sea Mouse* would be visible to freighters. At night, I had declared to myself, I would nap for fifteen minutes at a time, and then rise to scan the horizon. I had even bought an egg timer at the Radio Shack in Kaua'i to go off at fifteen-minute intervals.

I tried this the first night. I was steadfast in my resolve, and I sat at the helm of the *Sea Mouse*, nodding and hitting my forehead against the stainless-steel wheel. Drool dripped on my thighs. The egg timer went off. My arm shot out and hit it. My head slowly reared up and my eyes twitched to either side. No boats. Thunk. "Ow," I would have said, but I was already drooling on myself again.

About the same time the radio signal gave out, I pitched the egg timer into the sea.

> *I sailed with a free wind day after day, marking the position of my ship on the chart with considerable precision; but this was done by intuition, I think, more than by slavish calculations ... If I doubted my reckoning after a long time at sea I verified it by reading the clock aloft made by the Great Architect, and it was right.*
>
> JOSHUA SLOCUM, *Sailing Alone Around the World*

"God looks after fools and alcoholics," my battery commander had been fond of saying, referring to his soldiers' resilience in the face of misdirected high-explosive shells and calamitous love affairs. The weather was gentle with me throughout my battle with the egg timer. The wind remained restrained but co-operative. Handling sails proved no more difficult than with a tired companion. I just did everything slower, and planned things out more. I reefed in the main quickly as the wind grew, and never went to bed with full sail up. I paid closer attention.

My days had no identifiable beginning or end. It was like taking an all-weekend call at a slow hospital. When things needed doing I did them. Then I went back to sleep. I surrendered any sense of schedule because the adjustments to the rig would not be scheduled, and when the rig was trimmed well there was very little to do. I watched the water drift by. I stretched. I napped.

At night, while I was still in the trades and the wind was warm, I slept in the cockpit, stretched out on life preservers, with a blanket over me. Shortly after dawn, it became too bright and warm to remain there and I went below to nap on a sea berth. At some point in the day I would check the GPS and plot my position. Then I would calculate my course and adjust the helm. Every third or fourth day I would run the engine for an hour or two, to keep it lubricated. From time to time I checked the batteries. I ate. I read. I trimmed the sails. I peed in the sea.

A week out I was eating supper — curried noodles and tea — and thought, "This is it, I'm out here completely alone. Nothing awful has happened." I was surprised. The ocean was orange and pink.

I tried hard to remember what I had been after. I had wanted to go out by myself from the beginning; I had wanted to do something hard; I had wanted it to be a little dangerous. I remembered that.

Memories of my old girlfriend seemed remote now, like calculus theorems painfully learned but now barely remembered: true but unimportant. I concentrated on keeping the cabin clean and on pumping the bilge often enough that the engine remained dry.

Aug 29/95
31'45"N 159'W
Making good speed today after an unsettled night. Four sail changes, I think, and of course at daybreak we were sailing at 2 kts, under the jib and mizzen. It's hard to avoid, that scenario at night where the wind comes up for half an hour, you shorten sail, but are reluctant to raise it again when the gust is over, given the hour and the fact that I'm alone and tired. So, mornings are frequently seen with gentle winds puffing at shortened sail. Even when we were four I didn't like hoisting sail at night. It isn't wrong, it's just there. It's why this passage takes a month.

A month. Sheesh. Well, I have plenty to read. And paper to write on. I need to bathe; I'm feeling quite grungy now. And I need to sweep the cabin sole — these specks of paint are driving me nuts. Hmmm ... a week only, so far.

By reading I kept a kind of mental order. It had largely been books that had brought me out there, had made it inevitable that I would be attempting a long singlehanded passage. Chatwin and his damned love of the solitary nomad, which neither of us proved equal to.

I read *Singlehanded Sailing* by Richard Henderson over and over again. This book is partly a history of solo passages, paired with long chapters on the boat designs, sailing techniques and rig arrangements best suited to the singlehander. The ethos of self-sufficiency runs like a religious tenet throughout, which, in singlehanded sailing, is hard to take issue with. Certainly considerate and witty conversation-making would rank a little higher on the list I could have drawn up, out there, walking around the boat and stretching and looking at the sky. Henderson devotes pages to the various techniques of wire-splicing and swaging, effective storm strategies and ruminations on why someone would go to open sea alone. Henderson quotes Francis Stokes, circumnavigator: "Unless your crew is extraordinarily congenial, the experience shared will be diluted, less vivid, and less well remembered. Solitude sharpens awareness of small pleasures otherwise lost." Wonderful, I thought, bring on the small pleasures.

I learned that, despite the ancient history of sailboats and passage-making, it wasn't until late in the last century — coinciding with the flowering of individualism in Western society — that sailors began attempting long-distance singlehanded sailing passages. These tweedy and bearded Americans, Frenchmen and Englishmen immediately captured the Victorian imagination and books began selling by the thousands detailing wild and, at times, improbable adventures.

Alfred Johnson, a handline Grand Banks fisherman, was the first to cross the Atlantic from west to east alone, in a twenty-foot decked-over wooden dory, *Centennial,* in 1876. It took fifty-nine days. He navigated by obtaining position reports from passing ships and was at one point capsized by a breaking wave in a gale. He was attached to his vessel by a long safety line, and it took him twenty minutes to right the boat. His water and food was ruined and he lost his stove, but he was able to get supplies from another passing vessel and he made landfall ten days later.

Johnson's adventure prompted other voyages, which seemed to have been done largely as stunts, or grist for books. By the turn of the century there had been a half-dozen solo Atlantic crossings and easily as many books. There had even been races. About half of such attempts seemed to conclude with the master arriving on shore chagrined on some coal- or timber-carrier that had happened by.

Solo ocean crossings were overshadowed for all time on May 8, 1898, when Joshua Slocum arrived in Boston in his yawl, the *Spray*, sea-weary and battered after a two-and-a-half-year solo circumnavigation by way of the Strait of Magellan and Cape of Good Hope. In *Sailing Alone Around the World*, Slocum is coy about his reasons for putting to sea. He was a sailing captain during the last proudest years of the sailing merchant fleet. He and his wife Virginia had sailed all the great oceans; and all of their four children were born on foreign soil. For most of these voyages, Slocum's family accompanied him in his 220-foot square-rigged three-master, *Northern Light*. In 1884, however, Virginia died suddenly in Buenos Aires. Slocum was never the same. His son Garfield said that after her death his father was "like a ship with a broken rudder." Like Derrick, perhaps, drifting to Hawaii and beyond in search of Christian women.

The following years were dreadful for Slocum; misfortune piled upon misfortune in a downward spiral. There was a mutiny and, in putting it down, he shot two men. On another passage the crew was stricken with smallpox. Finally, and catastrophically, he was shipwrecked on the coast of Brazil and lost his vessel and his reputation as a meticulous ship's master. He had always been acknowledged to be a difficult and obstreperous man, but he was also a safe and careful mariner, and so his bluster had been accepted. But with his last command lost on a sandbar, nobody wanted to know anything else about him.

To return home, Slocum built a thirty-five-foot junk-rigged dory, *Liberdade*. He and his new wife Hettie, and his two sons, made it 5,500 miles in fifty-five days, to South Carolina. The success of this voyage was not matched by the success of the book that described it, however, and perhaps it was this unrealized yearning for recognition that prompted Slocum to circumnavigate the world singlehandedly. But he was an old man by this point already, and in reading his book, I didn't detect that particular thirst in the writing. Maybe after five thousand miles with three other people in a thirty-five-foot boat he simply wanted a bit of privacy.

When he had last been on American soil he had been the master of his own sailing vessel and now he was without a ship or employment; his new wife went to live with her sister, who despised Slocum. He was desperate and unhappy. He decided to go see the world.

He built the *Spray* from the keel up on the model of an abandoned oyster sloop. She cost him $553.62. After departing Boston he initially intended to go eastabout, but was alarmed after being chased by pirates off Morocco. He retreated to the west, crossing the Atlantic for the second time and made for the Strait of Magellan. He headed north along the Chilean coast to the Juan Fernández Islands, where Alexander Selkirk had lived, inspiring Daniel Defoe's *Robinson Crusoe*. Then he turned west. He passed the Marquesas without stopping and finally made landfall in Samoa.

Robert Louis Stevenson, who had been living in Samoa for many years, was recently dead, but Slocum spent time with Fanny, the writer's widow. He writes of her:

> The kindly eyes, that looked me through and through, sparkled when we compared notes of adventure. I marveled at some of her experiences and escapes. She told me that, along with her husband, she had voyaged in all manner of rickety craft among the islands of the Pacific, reflectively adding, "Our tastes were similar."

I can imagine his face on hearing that, and I imagine him remembering again his late wife.

Slocum takes his turn making his observations about the ease of the South Pacific, quoting a village chief:

> "Never mind dollar. The *tapo* has prepared ava; let us drink and rejoice." The tapo is the virgin hostess of the village; in this instance it was Taloa, daughter of the chief. "Our taro is good; let us eat. On the tree there is fruit. Let the day go by; why should we mourn over that? There are millions of days coming. The breadfruit is yellow in the sun, and from the cloth-tree is Taloa's gown. Our house, which is good, cost but the labor of building it, and there is no lock on the door.
>
> While days go thus in these Southern islands, we in the North are struggling for the bare necessities of life.

I read this, as I sailed north, and remembered words to this effect that I had written in my journal upon arriving in Tahiti. But I moved on. And so did Slocum. Neither of us really hesitated.

After Samoa Slocum made for Australia. He passed nine months in those waters, visiting and being feted by the deeply impressed citizenry. The *Spray* was given a new suit of sails by the Royal Navy commodore in attendance at Sydney. Slocum was already a celebrity and he was only halfway around. From Australia he made for South Africa by way of Mauritius in the Indian Ocean. Once round the Cape of Good Hope he made for Boston again, up the South Atlantic to the Caribbean and then home.

His book was an immediate best-seller. *Sailing Alone Around the World* has been taught for most of this century in North American high schools. It stands even today as one of the masterpieces of adventure and maritime writing. That it struck such a chord with the public, and so moved even the dry land-dwellers of the Midwest, was evidence of the societal changes that were underway.

Modernism and the cult of the individual were coming to the fore. Until this century, the celebrated feats had been collective —

armies fought in battles, religions were reformed through mass movements and companies were built. Where the individual was celebrated, it was for leading others. But now it is vastly different. Even the word "corporate" is pejorative. In our literature we celebrate the remote and isolated figure, turning his back and quickly walking away from us. And we imagine that he isn't stealing backward glances the whole time.

Slocum eschews any explicit discussion of what took him out to sea alone, and he certainly does not allow himself to hold forth at any length on the spiritual aspects of the sea that so preoccupy Moitessier, among others. But in his conclusion he does hint at part of its appeal:

> To succeed, however, in anything at all, one should go understandingly about his work and be prepared for every emergency. I see, as I look back over my own small achievement, a kit of not too elaborate carpenters' tools, a tin clock, and some carpet tacks, not a great many, to facilitate the enterprise as already mentioned in the story. But above all to be taken into account were some years of schooling, where I studied with diligence Neptune's laws, and these laws I tried to obey when I sailed overseas; it was worth the while.
>
> And now, without having wearied my friends, I hope, with detailed scientific accounts, theories, or deductions, I will only say that I have endeavored to tell just the story of the adventure itself. This, in my own poor way, having been done, I now moor ship, weatherbitt cables, and leave the sloop *Spray*, for the present, safe in port.

Slocum's affection and reverence for the sea holds no suggestion of conquest. He could not have written a modern adventure narrative. His restrained and self-effacing prose reminded me of Derrick, on the radio, wishing Don and me good luck. There is one striking departure from this sober voice; it occurs after leaving the Azores when he has just dined on white cheese and plums. Beset by abdominal cramping he hallucinated "a tall man at the helm. His rigid hand, grasping the spokes of the wheel, held them as in a vise …. His rig was that of a foreign sailor, and the large red cap he wore was cockbilled over his left ear, and all was set off with shaggy black whiskers. He would have been taken for a pirate in any part of the world. While I gazed upon his threatening aspect I forgot the storm, and wondered if he had come to cut my throat."

It was not a pirate but the pilot of Columbus' *Pinta*, come to save him. He advises Slocum that he did wrong to mix cheese with plums. "White cheese is never safe unless you know whence it comes. *Quien sabe*, it may have been from *leche de Capra* and becoming capricious." Later that night Slocum hears the pilot singing:

High are the waves, fierce, gleaming,
> High is the tempest roar!
High the sea-bird screaming!
> High the Azore!

The old boy was two months out at this point and, apparently, still getting used to the solitude.

But with this bit of whimsy, his skill as a storyteller is clear; his humour runs through the book and keeps it from becoming the sort of self-important exercise in breast-beating that it could easily have turned into. *Would* have turned into, had it been written a hundred years later, the proof being nearly every subsequent single-handed circumnavigator's book. The Marlboro Man does not mock himself. The minute he does, he becomes something other than a caricature dreamt up in an advertising agency.

Testimony to the difficulty of Slocum's feat of seamanship, a solo circumnavigation was not duplicated until over a quarter of a century later, in 1925, by Walter Pigeon, another American, aboard the yawl *Islander*. There were another eight solo circumnavigations in the following thirty years. By the end of this century, there have been many hundreds. Westabout, eastabout, via Cape Horn or Panama, in every combination, in the smallest boat, the largest boat — and always, it seems, a book to follow.

In 1968, Moitessier and Robin Knox-Johnston both completed non-stop solo circumnavigations and laid to rest the last of the meaningful feats. If any of them were meaningful for anyone other than the sailor. Someone has yet to circumnavigate in a porcelain bathtub, for instance. It isn't just ocean sailing that has become the arena of conquest and ego, of course — the same period has seen Everest littered with bodies hanging from ropes.

After about twenty days at sea I slowly began to fall to pieces, although I did not hallucinate any multilingually punning Spanish pirates. I began thinking aloud. Conversation, the old doctor in the Arctic had told me, is held by anthropologists as the naked ape's substitute for lice-picking. My coat became clotted and stiff. I had difficulty forming thoughts more sophisticated than the urge for physical release of whichever variety was the most pressing. My attention span had shrunk until I would read the same page of a novel repeatedly, losing my way and having to start over. I read and reread passages from the *Odyssey* at random. They didn't mean much to me. I spoke them aloud, just to hear a voice say something that hadn't arisen out of my own head.

It wasn't at all clear to me that I was unhappy out there. I sat in the sun and stared at the water and watched the sails drawing the *Sea Mouse* along and thought over and over again of how enormous the sea was and how far I was from land and humanity. It remained beautiful to me. But less important for being alone.

I stopped brushing my teeth and I stopped worrying very much about freighters at night. The boat below became a morass of clothing and books. I slept when I became tired and only rose when I heard something banging. I awakened several times to see the sterns of tankers miles distant, steaming away. I have no idea how close any of them came. I remember looking at them and thinking, "This should be upsetting me."

Into this state of passivity and diminished will intruded memories previously held at bay: my performance in an alley before sailing, head bowed, one hand over my mouth to avoid drawing the attention of passers-by. A dozen awful telephone conversations over the course of that love affair. I regarded them detachedly, poked here and there, searching for sensation. I flipped through *The Durrell–Miller Letters*. It occurred to me then that betrayal is not owned by anyone, least of all the betrayed, and is as common as desire. (Commoner still, for the lives of those two men.) It stopped seeming strange. We fall in love, we fall out of love, we behave well, we behave badly. Coils of fouled nylon fishnet floated past me, the skeletons of long-dead fish enmeshed within.

Competing with Moitessier and Knox-Johnston in the round-the-world race of 1968 was an unknown Englishman named Donald Crowhurst. I had bought Tomalin and Hall's *The Strange Last Voyage of Donald Crowhurst* in Lihue. I had not heard his story before; on reading it, I was mystified that I had not come across it sooner.

Crowhurst was an intelligent and gifted engineer who invented a radio navigation device for mariners in the mid-sixties. The company he formed to market the device was never profitable and Crowhurst was often on the verge of insolvency. When the solo non-stop circumnavigation race was announced, with a cash prize of five thousand pounds, Crowhurst rose to the challenge immediately. His motive was as much a thirst for fame as it was for money, and in his dealings with the sponsors and suppliers, he emanated the kind of haughty confidence that one associates with those destined for success.

He set to sea in a hastily built trimaran. Moitessier and Knox-Johnston were already in the Indian Ocean, and charging ahead. There were prizes for elapsed time and for first home. Crowhurst thought he might yet win for shortest elapsed time. He was wildly confident about the trimaran design — as yet unproven in open-ocean racing. He expected to average two hundred miles a day — double what keelboats could do.

His boat was a disappointment from the start. She was nearly as slow as the *Sea Mouse*. It became clear to him by the time he reached the South Atlantic, all his grandiloquence notwithstanding, that he was going to lose the race. Worse, he was going to limp in months after everyone else, like a first-time marathoner caught up in a frenzy of lifestyle reform. And after all that bluster.

He hatched a plan. He remained in the Atlantic and began sailing in circles, alone, as far as he could get from the shipping lanes. He sent in radio messages describing ever more rapid progress across the Indian Ocean. His plan was to wait until the rest of the competitors were in the North Atlantic, racing for home. Then he would appear among them, and finish among the fastest, second or third perhaps, to avoid the especially close scrutiny the winner could expect of his logbooks. He would not win the prize money, but his navigational devices would be publicized. He would not be humiliated. No one would call him a quitter.

He spent months keeping just the same lackadaisical and nearly aimless pace that the *Sea Mouse* maintained during her best efforts. Finally, his competitors were in the Atlantic again and making for home. Crowhurst tried to position himself in the middle of them. Then, without warning, Moitessier quit, to "save his soul." Knox-Johnston made it home to claim the prize for the first boat to ever complete a non-stop solo circumnavigation, and Crowhurst was in line to win the prize for the shortest elapsed time, and the unwelcome inspection of his logbooks. He slowed his pace. There was another trimaran in the race, *Victress*, sailed by a man named Nigel Tetley, who pressed on sail to "catch" Crowhurst. In the middle of this effort Tetley's boat tore apart under the strain of too much sail and Tetley was rescued only after his vessel foundered and sank. Crowhurst was left the only possible winner, his deception certain to be found out. Coupled with the months alone at sea, this shattered his mind. He left an explicit record of this eclipse in his logbooks, which are extensively quoted in Tomalin and Hall's book. I read these alone at sea myself, a thousand miles from shore.

> Man is a lever whose ultimate length and strength he must determine for himself. His disposition and talent decide where the fulcrum will lie.
>
> The pure mathematician places the fulcrum near the effort; his exercises are much more mental than physical and can carry the "load" — his own ideas — taking perhaps nothing but his own and kindred minds along the route. The shattering revelation that $E=mc^2$ is one supreme example of this activity.
>
> The extrovert, say a politician, places his fulcrum nearer the load, for his function is to move the whole politico-economic system of his country — perhaps of the world. Both types of activity shape the course of man's history. The first shattering application of the idea that $E=mc2$ is a good example of this — I refer to the bombing of Hiroshima.

By now Crowhurst was only drifting, and writing furiously. He wrote twenty-five thousand words similar to the passage above in one stretch. He cut all his hair off. He read more Einstein. He elaborated a theory of morality he claimed to be based in Einsteinian physics.

> Free will — the obligations to morality, each man is providing the system with impulses and he should think hard about the nature of them — THIS IS THE SOLE MORAL OBLIGATION THAT the individual OWES TO THE PROGRESS OF THE SYSTEM.
>
> I consider this statement with some trepidation as I think about the conclusions I am drawing so rapidly out of the system, but am at ease about the outcome because the impulse is in the required form — thought.
>
> ... Free Will — the very centre of the theological mystery resolves itself to this childishly simple issue. Will man accept, of his own free will, the stipulation that when he has learnt to manipulate

the space-time continuum he will possess the attributes of God? The choice is simply this. Do we go on clinging to the idea that "God made us," or realise that it lies within our power to make GOD? The system is SHRIEKING OUT THIS MESSAGE AT THE TOP OF ITS VOICE why does no one listen I am listening anyway

Into this preoccupation Crowhurst allowed the telegraph operator to intrude long enough to inform him of the victory celebrations being planned. He radioed back that his wife and children were not to meet him on his arrival. This was the first sign that something was seriously amiss. In his logbook cum treatise he wrote:

> The more things got upside down, the better they fitted. The truth was that there was no good or evil, only truth. Those who know the truth could select one or other of two equally satisfactory sets of rules. Complete freedom of choice beyond the reach of any discipline is the meaning of free will.

By now his navigational calculations were wildly distorted and he had an intimation of his mental disorder. Under one blunder on the first of July, he wrote MAX POSS ERROR. His writing became steadily more incoherent throughout the day. He records an episode he calls "the game," a series of notations made in the log, timed against his frustratingly inaccurate chronometer. The last passage reads:

> It has been a good game that
> must be ended at the
> I will play this game when
> I choose I will resign the
> Game 11 20 40 There is
> No reason for harmful

Then, apparently at twenty minutes and forty seconds after eleven, he stepped off his boat. The trimaran was found drifting ten days later. Moitessier and Knox-Johnston were dumbstruck. And then the logbooks were deciphered and the bizarre tale emerged.

As I read this book I fought back tears most of the time. I sympathized with Crowhurst as a fellow liar. He had imagined himself brave and stalwart, out there on that sea. He represented himself as stoically and cheerfully charging out across the ocean, happy in his own company. He embraced the lie presented by Slocum and Hillary and all the grand explorers — that endurance and isolation ennoble.

I remembered the shame of being caught in lies in public school: the homework not, in fact, done. Oh my God, what hell. All Crowhurst wanted was to see his wife and children, and he was too ashamed to face them. They would have forgiven him. All he had to do was come home.

Other memories floated past in the bright and shining sky. I was returning home with no obvious resolution to the problems that had sent me out to sea. But as I sailed further and further out into the middle of the autumn North Pacific, the desire to get home grew to an obsession. I calculated my progress three times a day and adjusted my estimations of how much longer I would be out there. I remembered the relief Don and I had felt that first morning out of sight of land, after clearing Cape Flattery. I could not imagine, could not recall that yearning for distance. How could I have been thinking like that? I looked at my little crosses on the chart, and I wondered why distance would be sought. I had books that explained the *Odyssey* for me. I wished I remembered Greek mythology better. I wished I remembered the sound of my father's voice better.

August 31, 1994
136' 20"N, 156'W

Beautiful late afternoon; the wind has switched around, now coming out of the ESE to SSE, at about 12 kts. I've got the genoa out on the reaching pole and am drifting along at about 3 kts — I guess the wind is more like 7-8 kts. But anyway, this is just gorgeous: the Sea Mouse is hardly heeling, everything is dry. Man. So this is what downwind sailing is all about. Lets have more of it! ...

... I find my thoughts drifting around like smoke in a still room, chewing on one memory and then another, a couple of gnaws here, a gnaw there (ouch) and then onto another. No theme, no important insights, just window shopping on the past. I've never gone as long as this without speaking to someone before — isn't that odd — just then a passing freighter — Russian perhaps — raised me on the radio.

The freighter's captain was a jovial man who addressed me with moving pleasure: "Hello, Leetle Boat!"

Me (stiff with formality, wanting badly to sound like a Competent Mariner): Unknown Russian Freighter, this is the Canadian sailing vessel *Sea Mouse*, go ahead.

Him: Leetle Boat, where are you going, where are you coming from?

Me: Unknown Russian Freighter, I am bound for Victoria, British Columbia, en route from Lihue, Kaua'i.

Him: And how many people on that leetle boat?

Me: Unknown Russian Freighter, there is a crew of one.

Him: One person on that boat!? For how long have you been at sea?

Me: Unknown Russian Freighter, I am eight days at sea.

Him: Eight days!? By yourself on that leetle boat!? Come alongside and I'll throw you some vodka, some soup and some pornographic magazines!

Me: Unknown Russian Freighter, thank you for the offer but that will be unnecessary. Provisions are adequate.

And after he continued over the horizon and disappeared, I sat there shaking my head at the strangeness of our conversation. I picked up my pen.

> … *I think that seeing him might prove fortuitous inasmuch as he makes it quite evident that there is shipping here and that I do need to be looking about, at night. God knows how many [freighters] have ghosted past me while I've been sleeping in the past week. Mind you, with weather this nice, it will be easier to stay up here [above deck].*
>
> *Anyway, looking back to the matter of this aimless, meandering interior monologue. I don't think that it is determined or focused enough to really discern anything, but there might be insight available from what it chooses to mull over. My friends, […] my parents, most notably. These, more than anything else …*

This was precisely what I'd longed for, those winter nights in the little army house. The days were bright and beautiful, the water streamed under the boat and the sails swelled out in a broad reach. I looked at the sea and saw the grey haze on the horizon. It was that haze that I stared at. A thousand miles ahead was the end of the ocean. The grey on the edge of the water was where I was going and what I thought about. I was aware even as I was doing it that it was a mistake to disregard the accessible beauty in favour of the distant and unseen, assuming it to be lovelier than the immediate. But the logic of escape is premised on this error.

I had a presentiment that the "travelling" phase of my life might be passing. I felt, before the malaise of settlement crept over me, that I should reopen those notebooks. I should set down on paper a résumé of the ideas, quotations and encounters which had amused and obsessed me; and which I hoped would shed light on what is, for me, the question of questions: the nature of human restlessness.

Pascal, in one of his gloomier *pensées*, gave it as his opinion that all our miseries stemmed from a single cause: our inability to remain quietly in a room.

Why, he asked, must a man with sufficient to live on feel drawn to divert himself on long sea voyages? To dwell in another town? To go off in search of a peppercorn? Or go off to war and break skulls?

BRUCE CHATWIN, *The Songlines*

Here, Chatwin himself seems to be suggesting that itinerancy is destructive. Later in the same book, paraphrasing Pascal, he writes: "One thing alone could alleviate our despair, and that was "distraction" (*divertissement*): yet this was the worst of our misfortunes, for in distraction we were prevented from thinking about ourselves and were gradually brought to ruin."

I came upon that passage and was astonished that I had not noticed it before, at least could not remember reading it. I read ahead quickly, but the suggestion was not pursued. The remainder of *Songlines* is largely devoted to extracts from Herodotus and the Bible and dozens of other sources that discuss the compelling and irresistible forces that move people to movement — the evidence of Chatwin's erudition is apparent and the quotations are beautiful. But his thesis progresses no further. We are moved to move, he states. And it is true. But incompletely true.

Life rafts have killed hundreds of sailors by offering a false solution to problems on the boat. In a storm in 1979 a fleet of sailboats in the Fastnet Race was hammered off the coast of England by Force eleven and twelve winds and twenty-eight-foot seas. Of the twenty-four boats that were abandoned during the worst of the storm, nineteen were subsequently recovered afloat. Seven of the sailors from these abandoned boats died in the sea. If they had remained on their boats, and worked to preserve them, they would have preserved themselves. It is not surprising that sailors in battered boats start looking toward the life rafts. But it is often a fatal temptation.

I wondered what Chatwin might have written if his illness had proceeded more slowly. The care and support he received from his wife and his lovers and friends were only available to him for having spent time with them, for having stayed still long enough to know and love these people, for them to love him in return. I wondered if protease inhibitors had come along just a few years earlier, would he have been able to sustain his passion for the idea of the solitary nomad.

His friend Theroux wrote *The Happy Isles of Oceania* after Chatwin's death. In this book, which I read on this passage home, is none of Chatwin's romantic and ecstatic vision of the road. Theroux is and has always been an altogether less romantic and ecstatic writer than Chatwin — he depicts himself as a gnarled, furred and baying-at-the-moon misanthrope. But in the narrative of his paddles through the slow and troubled lagoons of the South Pacific, there is no argument made for the superiority of movement itself. Theroux's focus remains on the place. And we can't forget, are never allowed to forget, that he went there as his wife was deciding to part from him. Theroux is moved to move, too, but he does not see his salvation as lying there. He respects the erosive quality of solitude.

There was no concept of solitariness among the Pacific islanders I traveled among that did not also imply misery or mental decline. Book-reading as a recreation was not indulged in much on these islands either — for that same reason, because you did it alone. Illiteracy had nothing to do with it, and there were plenty of schools. They knew from experience that a person who cut himself off, who was frequently seen alone — reading books, away from the hut, walking on the beach, on his own — was sunk in deep *misu*, and was contemplating either murder or suicide, probably both.

When Père Fournier had sought to isolate himself with his dogs and his rifle forty years previously, the Inuit, too, would not let him alone. He came to understand the true nature of isolation out there, I think. He learned it from people who live in the topography of loneliness. He has subsequently chosen to remain only with those people, and will not leave as long as he is able to stay there. The Inuit families who pitched camp beside him wouldn't leave, because they did not resent the close breath of others; they understood that the only buttress against the fearsome and shrieking wind lies in humanity huddling together to keep warm.

Which is the importance of the companionship of books and which becomes the redemption of travellers and their compulsion to tell tales. Their stories, when they are meaningful, are not about the road, or nomadism, and certainly not about the solitary traveller. They are about home, and the travellers' relationship with it. And however troubled those homes may be, being awake at night, alone and cold, severed from others, does not have a patch on home.

I knew now that I had put a world behind me, and that I was opening out another world ahead. I had passed the haunts of savages. Great piles of granite mountains of bleak and lifeless aspect were now astern; on some of them not even a speck of moss had ever grown. There was an unfinished newness all about the land. On the hill back of Port Tamar a small beacon had been thrown up, showing that some man had been there. But how could one tell but that he had died of loneliness and grief? In a bleak land is not the place to enjoy solitude.

JOSHUA SLOCUM, *Sailing Alone Around the World*

By this standard, Chatwin's work is not meaningful. As lush and stirring and precisely crafted as his words are, in the end his

books are cynical — vastly more cynical than the superficially misanthropic Theroux.

Chatwin's deeper misanthropy springs from the reek of our
dreadful cities and the puerility of our tastes. Chatwin's assump-
tion was that our city culture could not be salvaged, that living
together is inescapably oppressive. In letting cities remain as awful
as they are, city-dwellers seem to have collectively concluded the
same thing. In either instance, the conclusion is cynical.

Chatwin had "the eye" for a precise aesthetic, perhaps, but it
may have been exactly that understanding of this sensibility —
which values pictures so much more than communities — that
doomed it. In his writing we learn all about ancient marble frag-
ments and tapestries. We would have to guess that he had a wife
who stayed by him every minute as he withered like a cut stem.

Eleven hundred miles off Vancouver Island, the skies grew abruptly
darker and the air colder. The wind shifted around to the southeast and began to build. I shortened sail quickly, dousing the
genoa and putting up the working jib and then dousing the main.
The wind built further and soon I was flying only my stiff little
storm jib; even so, the Sea Mouse was surging along at six knots.

Because there was no moment that announced itself as the
transition from windy to dangerous, I did not grow frightened
until long after I ought to have.

By five that afternoon I was steering manually, the seas having
defeated the electronic autohelm, and the sensation was just wild:
the stern rising as the sea passed beneath and then falling as the
wave crested, the bow rearing up like a frightened Spanish horse,
the boat slowing and almost sliding backwards down the wave.
Me, swinging the wheel madly to get the boat perpendicular to
the next wave approaching from astern. I listened to the weather
on the short-wave and marked out the margins of the gale. It
stretched six hundred miles north and south, with the centre, the

worst of it, passing to the north. In the blackness the rain drove into me like insects on a windshield, exploding against my back. I stayed up there until very early in the morning, shivering and singing to keep myself awake. The storm was still building. The wind screeched like a rabbit in the jaws of a trap. To contain my fright I sang "Swingin' on a Star" and kept forgetting the words. When the wind blows that hard you can't even hear yourself; the distinction between interior monologue and speech becomes moot.

I doused the storm jib. As the boat swung precariously in the still-building seas I hoisted a reefed mizzen sail and sheeted in tightly. With only the small aft sail aloft, the boat weather-vaned around further into the wind and the heavy seas struck us bow first. In the dark I saw breaking seas on either side of me and as these roared too close, I closed my eyes. I went below.

In the dark down there, cold now, the last of the tropical weather a week distant, I lay in my wet sweater and foul-weather gear, steeling myself to go up top again. I wondered whether any-one back home knew of this storm. I tuned into Radio Canada International: the stock market was doing well, the Booker Prize nominees had been announced. The weather in the east was bright and warm, some rain was expected in the west, the coastal areas could expect moderate winds.

"Moderate winds." This front would weaken, I supposed, as it drew closer to shore. Vancouverites would curse as they awoke and looked at the sky, sighing wearily as they reached for their umbrel-las. No one knew of this gale out here then. On the weather map in *The Globe and Mail*, perhaps my father would notice the tightly concentric rings off the West Coast and wonder. No one else would even guess.

Choosing to go off alone onto the heath, and then despairing because nobody knew how you were doing — the absurdity of this was clear even in the storm. The opposite of the calculus theorems: incongruent and unjustified, but all the more insistently important nonetheless.

The memories that do not fit at all well into the patterns of our day are the richest sources of insight. This time alone on a little boat at sea in the middle of a wild storm and longing for company is like nothing else in my experience. I have leaned back from others, resenting their close breath upon me, imagining that the most important virtues are self-reliance and independence, fantasizing about post-apocalyptic survivalism (myself the only survivor). Into this resentful misanthropy intruded a frank and uncovered loneliness. This is why people venture out alone on mountains and little boats and across deserts — not because they can, but because they *can't*. And the reason why they can't is that men and women need each other. We make one another better.

It is true that we are ingenious and resourceful creatures and we can survive without espresso and *poires belle Hélène*, but we cannot last without companions. In cities we live badly with one another, and blame others — the pressure of their presence — for the vileness of our days. But the fault does not lie there.

The next morning it was vastly worse. The storm had blown hard all night and the seas were only higher. For long minutes I would think that the wind was abating, and I grew optimistic that the worst had passed. Then, with a howl of pure malevolent force, the wind would reach for a new crescendo, louder even than anything I had heard before. The tendency to turn the weather into a fickle psychopath is irrational, and to the extent that the habit prompts frustration and self-aggrieved resentment in ourselves, it is dangerous. But my God, alone on a small boat, listening to wind like that, there is nothing so full of what sounds like unstoppered human rage, loneliness and malignancy. When I first woke again and heard it that morning, I cried with disappointment. I had become used to the squalls and fronts that were only ever truly bad for a day, with a day before and after of unpleasantness, but this,

this was more fierce than the first day had been by a wide margin. And getting worse. I lay below on the cabin sole in my foul-weather gear, wrapped in a blanket. The boat was lying hove-to into the wind and from the violent pitching I was too frightened to even look at the sea.

The peak wave height in a storm is partly a function of wind strength, but even more important is the duration of the wind. It had been blowing now at Force eight and nine for thirty-six hours and the waves were mountainously high. When the *Sea Mouse* was in the trough of a swell it felt like I was riding on a sugar cube in the bottom of a teacup. The sails went slack in the lee of the sea itself. The tops of waves blew right off, and when I went up top the spindrift and foam hit my face with the force of a caning.

I wedged myself into one of the sea berths and held on. The whole day and night.

The next morning it was clear the wind had lessened. The *Sea Mouse* was still shaking with fright at the strongest gusts, but it was not as bad as it had been. If, when I had first gone offshore in the *Sea Mouse*, I had heard wind like this, I would have been nauseous with fear. But now I viewed it as quietening. I heard gear creaking on the deck in a way I had not heard before. I knew things were broken. But there wasn't any water on the cabin sole, and I was sure I would have heard the mast going over.

When I went up top the sky was grey and cold. The seas, lagging behind the changes in the wind, were still huge. But when the spray hit my face it was not as slashingly painful as before.

Most of my spare water jugs, which had been tied to the life rails, were gone. The whisker pole on the main mast had been twisted away from the track on which it was mounted and now lay obliquely across the deck. Shards of wood were scattered across the foredeck. The dinghy was askew, but we were all still afloat.

I began cleaning up. The wind settled to a steady fifteen knots. I hoisted the working jib. The *Sea Mouse* began making her way to shore again. It was a relief to be moving. I was still badly fright-

ened and my arms felt rubbery and weak. I hoped that things would
be a little easier for the next day or two.

The wind eased further and further until I was again nearly
becalmed. My boat looked like it had been turned upside down
and dropped but to look now at the placid sea you would never
guess it capable of such histrionics. I wanted to be home so badly.
I started the engine and began motoring, even though I was hundreds of miles offshore. It was not possible to just sit there.

September 10, 1995

*Slow night — the wind swung around to the north, and
dropped off to 10 kts or so, made virtually no headway. This
a.m. I started motoring, promptly blew the v-belt. I have 1
spare, bad — but now things go well. I just checked the GPS —
903 miles to Victoria. Ay, yi, yi. Reading* The Odyssey *and
worrying about the engine — the stuffing box, the transmission,
the injectors, etc., etc., etc. So far so good, though. I can't wait to
make landfall. Nine, ten days. It's okay. I'm not dying here. It's
warm today, there's some sun, it isn't raining. I'm not dying. I
am sick of pasta, though. But I'm not dying.*

*Later — sunset. The water is glassy calm. My God, it is
beautiful like this. Not much sailing to be done, of course, but
still, mighty beautiful. The engine goes just fine. The stuffing
box remains tight-looking — I've pumped the bilge a couple of
times though. That new bilge pump was a good idea.*

*The wind situation is nuts. Gale or calm. Christ. Oh well.
Only eight hundred and change to go. When we're at five hundred, then we'll be close.*

*Pleasant, languorous evening. Engine works well. Beautiful
sunset. Doing little, long-deferred jobs, gives me a feeling of
progress and stability. I'm pretty happy, becalmed or no. It's just
those dang gales I don't much like. If you could just eliminate
those from the equation, all this would be magnificent. It still
is, I mean, but — singlehanding in a storm is just tense, is all.*

The right boat might be different, or at least less tense. Roller-reefing on the main, all lines [led] aft, a legitimately reefable headsail — these would make it easier. But for now, this is okay. My little Sea Mouse.

Then the spare v–belt fell apart. I checked the engine again. I realized that the alternator mount had become loose and both the v–belts that had failed had been rubbing against the engine block. It took about five minutes to fix it. I didn't have another spare. I hit my head on the floor. What a moron.

The next day we sat there bobbing. I worried about trying to get into a harbour with no engine, or making my way up the Juan de Fuca Strait against the tidal current with no engine. It would have been another thing if there was crew and we could take turns watching out for shipping. But I couldn't be asleep in the middle of the strait or even its approaches.

I tried sewing together ⅜-inch line in loops, to fit the pulleys on the engine. I tried many different techniques. Eventually I found that, with refinements, I could get them to last about fifteen minutes. Maybe that would be enough for docking, I thought. But in the meantime, we could not make progress. This was disappointing. We bobbed.

This is hard, here. I'm finding this hard.

Later. I'm writing this by flashlight. The engine will run for at least a few minutes with the current rope/v–belt. I've started her up and there is actually not even all that much chatter and squeal. The origin of all this, the broken bolt on the alternator mount — which led to the angled v–belt and hence their early demise — is fixed. Nothing like shutting the barn door after the horse is gone. But this is not so bad. The engine will probably be fine for docking at least. Now I just have to sail to Victoria — or Port Renfrew, or Neah Bay, or Gray's Harbour — whichever place I end up at. Victoria, preferably.

This is still hard — but not awful.

I spent the following five days cursing my stupidity at not having brought more v–belts with me, not having checked why the first belt failed before replacing it, and so on. Then one night, while writing a letter to a friend, a thought struck me like I was a schizophrenic being whispered to by angels: *You bought another v–belt in Hawaii and tossed it forward, under the electrical supplies.*

I ran forward and dug out the fo'c'sle. I remember doing a little dance with the belt in one hand, hooting with pleasure. Then the boat lurched and I fell on my rear. Within minutes the engine was running again.

September 19/95
I found a v–belt! In the for'd locker! The engine has been running now for twenty-four hours with nary a hiccup. I am now 248 miles from the mouth of the J de F. Excellent.

As I approached Cape Flattery, I realized that my fuel was running low and that the prudent thing would be to sail as close as I could, so that I would be able to motor in to shore. I told myself this aloud, over and over, but I was unable to turn the engine off. The sea remained glassy.

September 21, 1995
76.5 miles to the mouth [of the Juan de Fuca strait]. Exhausted. Motorsailing at 4 to 5 kts, a little east of where I want to be, but not much. Looking to make the mouth of the Fuca a few hours after dawn. Will probably have plenty of fuel left after all. Say a five-gallon reserve. I put in about seventeen gallons today, albeit of highly crud-laden fuel but that should do me for a day and a half anyway. Which, together with my reserve could well get me into Victoria. It would be nice to make Victoria tomorrow. Oh man, it would be nice. But, either Victoria or Port Renfrew. Either way, landfall tomorrow. Let's hope it's not Flattery Rocks, or something crazy like that. Man, I am tired. What I need is a shower (desperately) and a shave, and ten

hours of uninterrupted sleep. Wouldn't that be nice? Won't that be nice? Pick up my mail, maybe not till Monday, buy some clothes, find a café someplace. Make some phone calls. Heaven.

I checked the fuel tank and could see the last few gallons sloshing around the bottom. I turned off the engine and hoisted every sail I owned.

Fifty miles before the continental shelf, the water slowly began to change colour, from a cobalt blue into a muddier and muddier green. For three days I watched the water lighten and grow more opaque. The wind barely moved me along, the *Sea Mouse*'s wake shrinking until it hardly disturbed the surface at all. We bobbed out there all but immobile and when Mount Olympus finally poked her head above the horizon, I just stared.

When I judged myself within range of the fuel I had saved, I started up the engine. The nearest Canadian port was Bamfield, on the west coast of Vancouver Island. The engine sputtered to a stop fifteen miles offshore. The wind blew only out of the east, and I watched, horrified, as the *Sea Mouse* began to back up and drift toward Hawaii. I called the harbourmaster and asked him if he could have someone come out in a boat with some diesel fuel.

Shortly before sunset the local coast guard rescue service roared out of Barkley Sound in search of the lone mariner in distress: "Coast guard, this is the *Sea Mouse*: I am not in distress."

Coast Guard Headquarters: Uh, could you verify that last statement, *Sea Mouse*.

Sea Mouse: Uh, yeah, I don't have any problems that five gallons of diesel fuel wouldn't solve.

Bamfield Detachment: We are en route with diesel fuel for that ship in distress, Coast Guard Headquarters.

Sea Mouse: I am not in distress.

Bamfield Detachment: Roger that. Diesel fuel en route.

The orange rescue vessel roared around until it finally identified the rust-streaked *Sea Mouse*. Then Jim and Don and Albert pulled up and Jim jumped aboard with a jerry can. These were the first people I'd seen in over a month. They were fishermen volunteers who staffed the coast guard station and liked roaring around in the big orange boat. They were friendly and not at all condescending about my fuel misjudgment and they saved my sorry butt. Together the *Sea Mouse* and the big orange boat rumbled into the Bamfield harbour that night and, oh my Christ.

I stepped up onto the dock and tied some loose dock lines. I stood there staring at the trees and swaying on the bafflingly stationary concrete dock. Again I thought, "I will remember this situation, but this feeling will never be retrievable. I will think, of course I was going to make it, I had a good boat. It was just a matter of time." Someone touched me on the shoulder and told me if I hurried I could make it to the bar before the grill closed.

At the pub I knew no one, but sat there and ate a cheeseburger with such joy as has never before been prompted by fried food. I drank a bottle of cold beer and had to hold on to the table to keep from falling to the floor. I lolled my eyes around like a Hereford with a belly full of bloat grass. I smelled awful, I realized, and my beard was atrocious-looking. The waitress kept coming up to me and asking if I needed another beer. The fishermen sat a long way from me. I believe this is the only time in my life that I have ever been the Dangerous Man in a bar. My sweater was stiff with perspiration, and my trousers crinkled when I moved.

But I became a part of that crowd that night, even if cordoned off by my aroma. On the wall were pictures of maritime disasters from years past. A barquentine stood awash on the rocks, spilling lumber into the surf. I looked at that and was glad that I hadn't hit that rock. I was pretty glad, in general. Glad, and malodorous.

I walked to the one motel in town. I woke up the proprietor and asked him if I could rent a shower. He said sure, five dollars. I reached for my wallet. He rubbed his eyes and asked me where I was coming from. I told him I had just crossed from Hawaii in a sailboat by myself.

He straightened up. "How long did it take you?"

"Thirty-one days."

"Good for you," he said.

"It was a crazy thing to do."

"You'll remember this for years."

"It already doesn't make sense to me, I'm forgetting it right now."

"You just need some sleep."

"I guess so."

"Shower's on the house," he said, nodding, and turned to go back to sleep.

I stood under that shower for an hour. I soaped up and rinsed off again and again and again. For the remainder of my life I think that when difficulties seem interminable, I will think about that shower. In the Indo-European languages, fresh water is usually "sweet water" and the idea is right — it is vastly more than fresh. I cut off my beard with scissors, and then scraped off the thick sun-bleached and salt-stained stubble methodically, until my entire face was gleaming pink and felt like I had just had an acid peel.

Then I walked back to the boat. The tide was ebbing and the tidal current flowed quickly out the channel. The *Sea Mouse* bobbed alongside the dock quietly. There was no one around; the whole town was drinking in the pub. I sat down in the cockpit and wished I knew someone who lived nearby.

I blinked and breathed slowly in and out. This would retreat into memory as soon as all this came to seem normal again. I looked at the dock and marvelled at it, that there existed a thing such as it, that you could tie your boat to it and not move. What a wonderful idea. What a thing to think. I shook my head and the wonder receded a little, ebbing from me, slinking back down the beach, leaving behind the drying mud. Along the shore the high-tide mark ran as if delineated by a spirit level. The grass abruptly stopped, edged right against the impermanent shore.

I retied the dock lines and went below. I changed my clothes and went up top again. It was one of those very clear nights that come in autumn and the stars shone almost as brightly as they had at sea. Overhead a satellite tracked slowly across Orion. I stared at it until it went away and then I looked at the familiar, unmoving stars. The water glistened like cool molten metal.

ACKNOWLEDGEMENTS

Neither the trip this book describes, nor the education I received for being on it, would have been possible without Don Lang. He is a kind and gentle man, and would be happy to be your skipper/teacher/first mate and go anywhere warm you might take him. He'll never raise his voice, except to be heard over the wind. Write to him at P.O. Box 903, Station A, Nanaimo, British Columbia, v6v 1E1. Feed him well, and consider what he says. He's a pretty smart guy.

I've changed names and some identifying details of other travellers I met on this journey at sea and through doctoring; I thank them for sharing their experiences.

Andreas Schroeder gave me insightful advice and encouragement on the early drafts of this book. He is to the book what Don was to the trip.

Linda Svendsen, Christy Ann Conlin, Dale Thomas, Butch Connelly, Joe Tangi, Bruce Martin, George and Anita Lang, Maria Fernandez, Sue Lightford, Kevin Oneschuk, Noel and Martha Keeley, Jude Fraser, Ker Wells, Megan Saunders, Ron Maier and Colleen Cariou, Charles Myers, Arnold Shoichet, Andy Edelson, Karen Berg and everyone at Moby's dock and bar have all been very kind to me since this trip started and I owe each of these people a great deal. I would also like to thank my twin brother Tom Patterson, my other brother Michael, and my mother and father, Margaret and Roger Patterson.

Finally, I am incredibly grateful to my agent Jan Whitford at Westwood Creative Artists and to my editor Anne Collins at Random House Canada.

PERMISSIONS

Every effort has been made to contact copyright holders; in the event of an inadvertent omission or error, please notify the publisher.

Calasso, Roberto, *The Marriage of Cadmus and Harmony*. Copyright © 1993 Alfred A. Knopf, Inc. Reprinted by permission of Alfred A. Knopf, Inc.

Cherry-Garrard, Apsley, *The Worst Journey in the World*. Copyright © Angela Mathias 1922, 1965. Reprinted by permission of Picador, an imprint of Macmillan General Books Ltd.

DeBlieu, Jan, *Wind: How the Flow of Air Has Shaped Life, Myth, and the Land*. Copyright © 1998 by Jan DeBlieu. Reprinted by permission of Houghton Mifflin Company. All rights reserved.

Durrell, Lawrence, *Bitter Lemons*. Copyright © Lawrence Durrell, 1957. Reprinted by permission of Faber & Faber Ltd.

Durrell, Lawrence, *Justine*. Copyright © Lawrence Durrell, 1957. Reprinted by permission of Faber & Faber Ltd.

Fleming, Peter, *News from Tartary*. Copyright © Peter Fleming 1936. Reprinted by permission of Jonathan Cape, an imprint of Random House UK Limited.

Gallant, Mavis, "The Other Paris." *From the Fifteenth District*. Copyright © Mavis Gallant 1979. Reprinted by permission of Macmillan Canada, an imprint of CDG Books Canada Inc.

Henderson, Richard, *Singlehanded Sailing*. Copyright © 1988 International Marine. Reprinted by permission of International Marine, a division of The McGraw-Hill Companies.

Lewis, David, *We, the Navigators*. Copyright © 1972 David Lewis. Reprinted by permission of the University of Hawaii Press.

Moitessier, Bernard, *Tamata and the Alliance*. Copyright © 1993 by Arthaud. Translation copyright © 1995 William Rodarmor. Reprinted by permission of Sheridan House Inc.

Moitessier, Bernard, *The Long Way*. Copyright © 1971 B Arthaud. Translation copyright © 1973 William Rodarmor. Reprinted by permission of Sheridan House Inc.

Newby, Eric, *A Short Walk in the Hindu Kush*. Copyright © Eric Newby 1958. Reprinted by permission of HarperCollins Publishers Ltd.

Raban, Jonathan, *Coasting: A Private Voyage*. First published in Great Britain in 1986 by Harvill. Copyright © Jonathan Raban 1986. Reprinted by permission of The Harvill Press.

Rushdie, Salman, *Imaginary Homelands*. Copyright © Salman Rushdie, 1981, 1982, 1983, 1984, 1985, 1986, 1987, 1988, 1989, 1990, 1991. Reprinted by permission of Penguin Books Ltd.

Saint-Exupéry, Antoine, *Wind, Sand and Stars*. Translation and introduction copyright © William Rees, 1995. Reprinted by permission of Penguin Books Ltd.

Somerset Maugham, W., *The Moon and Sixpence*. Reprinted by permission of William Heinemann, a division of Random House U.K.

Theroux, Paul, *The Happy Isles of Oceania*. Copyright © 1992 by Cape Cod Scriveners Company. Reprinted by permission of The Wylie Agency.

Thesiger, Wilfred, *Desert, Marsh and Mountain*. Copyright © Wilfred Thesiger 1979. Reprinted by permission of Curtis Brown.